One More Breath

The Memoir of a Whitewater Kayaker

By

Martin Murphy

Rukia Publishing US
Email: rukiapublishingus@gmail.com
Web: www.rukiapublishing.com
Twitter: @rukiapublishing

Rukia Publishing US is an imprint of Rukia Publishing

ISBN: 9780578711867

Dedication

For Mom and Dad

For my Dad, who has always been a great inspiration to me—he gave me an unwavering work ethic, the need for adventure, and the fortitude to seek it without permission.

For my Mom, whose support and love has carried me through turbulent times. She is my light at the end of the tunnel, always reminding me to remain positive and happy by her own shining example.

"All streams flow to the sea because it is lower than they are. Humility gives it its power."

Lao-tzu

Tao Te Ching

Prologue

It sometimes seems like my life has been framed with the vignette of old spruce hanging over the river with a snow-capped mountain in the distance behind me. In my mind, I am still using all of my strength and all of my skill; my lungs are pushing me as my shoulders pull. I am a monster fighting to become the seamless and smooth on a ripple in the earth. A fault line, a creek that offers me the best that I have to give. The choice is mine, my lungs have filled with fresh cool spruce soaked air as my hands have gripped the paddle.

Into the river that never leaves me, I'm drawn by the raw power, rage without anger. Benevolent yet stifling, there is an art that exists here, a pendulum that must be timed to a moment of a breath.

The risk is simply breathing, it's between those breaths that I really live. The decisions I make between paddle strokes, striving to match the vision in my mind. We are always at the edge of something, always afraid to breathe, but we do, and we must. When the light becomes soft, and the quiet smoke becomes wedges that defy gravity I realize somehow, I am a part of it, or moreover, it's a part of me.

This life on the river… I just need one more breath.

Marty

1

Right Place

Most of my life has consisted of being in the right place at the right time. I am one of the luckiest people I have ever known. But it didn't start out that way.

I was born with amblyopia which, simply said, is a lazy eye. I was made to wear a patch over my good eye for two years to strengthen my weaker one. It was in the fourth grade when the words (normal kid) no longer applied to me. It was pointed out to my parents that I was having some difficulty learning, and the school would like to do some testing. While I had a well above average IQ, my ability to learn and comprehend was well below average. I was writing my letters and numbers backwards. Those tests would change my life forever; forever exiled to the place I called the box.

The box was a small classroom with the shades drawn tight for less distraction; occupied by kids that I had only known as trouble makers. As I timidly walked into the tutoring room, I could feel the eyes of the distain look upon me as every kid in the room turned their head. How did I get here I thought, what had I done wrong? I melted into the chair where I would sit every day for the next three years. Though I still went to regular classes, I would be required to go to the box when difficult subjects were presented to me, only to return to class and have no idea what the teacher was talking about. She certainly was not going to wait for me to start a new subject. I was being looked at as if I were a second-class citizen. I was always frustrated, always mad, and always wrong with the red marks all over my papers to prove it.

My parents couldn't help me and I couldn't help myself; I became tattered and broken. I would stomp through the halls with fists clenched, shaking with adrenaline, and gritting my teeth every time I walked through the door into the box. An hour before school started and an hour after school ended, I was a hostage of the box. With all of the flash cards and cute tricks the teachers had put together to help me nothing seemed to take hold. I would be sent home with homework that would take a normal person two hours to do. For me, it took four to five hours. In grade school my average work day was thirteen hours, which is more hours than most people work in a normal job. I was once asked by a school councilor what I thought I should do to become a better student. As if working thirteen hours a day was not enough. I am in the fourth grade and the only thing that I am good at, is rage!

By the sixth grade I still could not read or write, nor did I have any math comprehension. I was also diagnosed with scoliosis, a curvature of the spine. I was told by the experts in the field of orthopedics that a back brace would keep my spine from continuing to misalign. I wore the back brace twenty-three hours a day. It went from my hips to my neck, had a ring that went around my right shoulder that pushed my spine to the left, and pads on my left ribcage that pushed my spine to the right. I cut wood most weekends with my back brace on. With each lift and fall of the eight-pound splitting maul, the brace grated against my skin until my shirts were bloodstained. I built up calluses and my core strength until my back was tough enough to take the strain. For seven years I wore the cumbersome intrusive brace that ruined my clothes, made leather out of my skin, and caused me pain on a daily basis. The first week of having the brace on, I fell during gym class and broke my arm, which required twenty-seven stitches and three pins through carpal tunnel surgery to fix. I spent more than a month in a cast that went past my elbow. That useless arm hung in front of my back brace making it impossible to sleep or concentrate.

There I was, as an elementary school kid in a back brace, with a broken arm, wearing bifocals, unable to read or write. Needless to say, I failed a year of school somewhere around the fifth grade. In the six grade I had a moment that I will never forget, a pretty girl in my same grade asked me out. I thought about it for a moment and told her no. Being raised in a traditional family I knew that girlfriends eventually lead to marriage and marriage lead to kids. In that moment I knew I never wanted kids, I never wanted

8

someone to go through what I had gone through. I never wanted anyone to be like me.

School eventually became better due to one thing really, I stopped caring. I stopped taking notes trying to make the grade. I knew that all of this meant nothing, this was just time I had to do. I graduated high school one year late. The back brace had done little to thwart the movement of my spine. Four days after I graduated from high school an operation was performed on my back. With my parents in the room, I was told two hours before the operation that there was a chance I would never walk again. A quick glance at my Mom finds her with her hand over her mouth looking down at the floor as if she is going to puke. My Dad is counting ceiling tiles. The doctor is looking at me for some big emotional reaction. I simply sat stoic and nodded my head yes. During the six-hour operation I had twenty-seven and a half inches of Harrington Rods surgically implanted in my spine. My twelve thoracic vertebras were now permanently fused together.

A year later finds me better than I was before, I am strong. No more back brace, no more body cast, I'm working out and life is easy, too easy. My work ethic is fully intact but I need a challenge, people are boring and soft. As you can imagine, I became jaded in life. What might be discomfort to me, would be searing pain to most others. What I might call a setback in life, many would call a life-altering event. People believe that some things are unreasonable, and I believe that, if you aren't going to lose a limb, you will probably be okay. I became unaffected by things most people felt were important. I was not one preoccupied and overcome by trivial bullshit. I have broken away, no longer the timid little kid being held hostage. Hardship is a gift, pain is a gift, my strife propels me forward with discipline and unabashed courage. Because it can't be worse then it was when I was a kid; can it?

2

Two Kinds of People

As an adult, it never occurred to me that people didn't live the way I did until I stepped out of the whitewater world and into the world that normal people live in. Someone would ask me what I did over the weekend and, after I told them, they would stand in disbelief, mouth gaped open, wrinkled forehead, and without the ability to reply. Nothing they could say about their own weekend could compare. I did not mean to upstage anyone; I was simply sharing the great experience I had. That experience just happened to be me finding myself upside-down above a forty-foot waterfall, knowing that if I did not roll up I would careen over the falls, end up pinned at the bottom of the river, with thousands of pounds of water pounding on my head. It took a high-water rescue team three days to get the last guy out. I rolled up by pushing my paddle to the surface of the water, and then pulled it down across my chest with a quick jerk as I snapped my hips keeping my head low righting the boat and myself back to the surface in order to make the line. To me it had been a normal Saturday.

To me there are two kinds of adventurous people. There are tourists, and there are people that make adventure their lifestyle. For me it was not a choice, adventure simply became my lifestyle. Being involved on this level is an exercise in control. The average person doesn't actually sit down and think about fear. The truth is that you are not born with fear, you learn it. Fear is taught to you by doting parents and by a society that is constantly telling you what not to do. It's the 'what not to do' that never suited me. I was tired of being held back because of what other people were afraid of. I'm not afraid of falling, I'm not afraid of drowning, and I'm not afraid of being broken. I'm not afraid of anything! I have a healthy respect for that which can kill me, but I am not stifled by it. Fear solely exists within the mind.

3

Canisteo River

I would never say I was a great whitewater kayaker. For the number of hours that I spent on a river, I should have been better.

The first time I ever sat in a kayak was when my dad and I decided to go on a last-minute canoeing trip with his friend Bill. I had spent a lot of time in canoes, and felt comfortable on a slow-moving river. A few years before, my dad and I had canoed seventy-five miles on the Oswegatchie River in the Adirondacks with our Boy Scout Troop. So, it was a completely new experience when my dad's friend Bill entered the quick moving waters of the Canisteo in a kayak during our trip. Bill brought his kayak and offered to take us to a spot that would be a good place to put our canoe into the water. As we unloaded our canoe, Bill unstrapped his kayak from the top of his car. I remember thinking that it was very small compared to our canoe. We put the boats on the bank and slid into the water.

He shot out onto the water ahead of us and cut through it effortlessly. He sat up straight in the cockpit on a small seat made out of fiberglass, with dimples in it for your ass cheeks. It did not look comfortable. But the thing that caught my attention was, he was able to shoot ahead of us leaving only a small wake on the water with just a little effort of the double-bladed paddle. He would lean and the whole boat leaned with him, going over on his side but not flipping over, then doing the same on the other side. He used his paddle in the water in ways that I had never seen before.

When he asked me if I wanted to try it, I smiled, excited for the experience. We found a piece of land along the river and traded places. He gave me a quick rundown of the boat and how to operate it. I learned that the foot pegs are adjustable with the use of the balls of your feet, that thigh braces keep your knees in the boat, and that the back band combined with the pressure of your feet on the foot

12

pegs keep you in the boat. The more of your body that is in contact with the boat, the more control you have over the boat. The paddle has a 30-degree offset and there is a bump on the paddle shaft that tells you where your hands should be placed and how you should be holding the paddle. The blade should be straight up and down if your hands are straight in front of you. Your dominant hand is your control hand and your other hand should be a little loose on the paddle so it can turn. The blade should enter the water with no splash and be almost straight up pull it to you.

It sounded easy, but an hour later I still could not make the damn thing go straight. My legs were going numb and my feet were on fire. I could not understand the concept of using the paddle to brace off the water. My hands had a death grip on the paddle and my fingers were turning white. If I leaned in any direction, I felt like I would flip over. After the day was over, I knew that I had no idea what I was doing. What I did know was that I never wanted to stop trying to paddle that boat.

Immediately after returning from the trip, I went to the Eastern Mountain Sports (EMS) store and bought a book on how to kayak. It was adorned with photos of guys running waterfalls and big rapids. The book taught me the basics of kayaking, and the importance of learning the basics. Forward stroke, backward stroke and the all-important sweep stroke to help you turn the boat and keep control, when going down a river. The book talked about different types of rivers, how to spot holes and eddies, and how to get in and out of the main flow of the river. The eddies were water that went up stream slower than the water going downstream, caused by something in the water that made it change direction. I studied that book until the pages wore thin.

Bill told me that any time I wanted to borrow his kayak to just come over and take it, along with the paddle and specialized life jacket. After reviewing the book for a few weeks, I decided to take Bill's offer. I called Bill just to make sure it was still ok to borrow his kayak. The book said I would need a helmet, and Bill did not have one for me to borrow. So, I found an old red motorcycle helmet that someone used as a kid. It was tight, but it would work. I found a hydraulic in the local creek, better known as a hole, and went to

13

check on it every time it rained. It didn't look like much, just a white line of water that seemed to be rolling over into itself. It made a lot more noise than the rest of the river. It seemed to be pulsing with recirculating water running back into it from the sides of the hole, called eddies. The hole was higher than the rest of the water in the river, like it was being pushed up from below. Apparently, if I was going to have fun in this kayak, I was going to have to learn how to get in and out of one of these holes. It rained hard one week, and I talked a friend of mine, Ed, into going to the river with me. Ed stood at the river's edge with a rope and a promise to him that if anything happened, I would leave the kayak and start to swim. He would then throw the rope to me and pull my ass out of the river before I was swept away. He couldn't say no! I really only had one problem; I knew the rope would not float.

In the book they had talked about the importance of a throw rope, a specialized rope that was stuffed into a bag and when thrown it unfurled itself in a straight line, it also floated! Only, I just had a normal rope that wasn't in a bag and I knew it wouldn't float. There was no way I would be able to see the thing in the muddy water. I needed to make the rope float, I started looking around the house. I ended up greasy after rummaging through some stuff and had to wash my hands. I used the last of the soft soap and in that moment, it came to me, that this container would float. I washed it out, took a strong string, and somehow tied it to the end of the rope. I provided the rope with the soap container attached to the end to my friend and said "I think it will work!"

I had taken that kayak out several times in moving water, but never in fast-moving water. I now understood the basics of leaning, and getting in and out of the eddies. I had practiced with the spray skirt, and at the time, I thought I had a good handle on what I should do.

Ed and I headed to the local creek. It was running high and the muddy water flew by as waves and lines of bubbles appeared out of nowhere in the center of the small creek. The water undulated and was amazingly loud. The hole that I had studied was now much bigger. I placed that old blue and white kayak on the muddy weed covered bank and got dressed: life jacket, motorcycle helmet, spray skirt, old sneakers, and paddle. Ed suddenly had a moment of clarity. I worked with him at the local gas station; I had also gone to school with him. He knew about my back issues when I was a kid.

He quickly asked me "how's your back? Are you sure you should be doing this?"

"No problem" I stated. "That has been all cleared up." I did not tell him that two years ago I was lying in a hospital bed wondering if my legs were going to work again. But they seem fine now so I was ok with the risk.

I jumped into the boat like I had something to prove and settled myself into the uncomfortable seat. I pushed against the foot pegs, pushing myself back into the back band, and pulled my legs up into the thigh braces. I stretched the spray skirt and snapped it over the cockpit rim. I threw a glance at Ed who stood wide-eyed with his arms flared, while holding the rope with a soap container dangling from the end of it. I gave him a nod and turned my attention to the water.

I threw my weight forward and inched toward the water. I pushed with my paddle until the front of the boat was half in the water. Finally, I was free from land and floating on my own in the eddy next to shore. My heart was pounding as the weeds and brush from the shore stuck in my face. I pushed off the river's edge as I faced upstream and set myself adrift into the rushing muddy waters. I set my ferry angle like the book told me to and I paddled, trying to keep the boat from turning. I shot across the creek amazingly fast getting to the other side in the blink of an eye. I hit the big eddy on the other side and almost flipped, but the water was shallow so I pushed off the bottom with my paddle for a quick save.

The eddy I was in was drawing me upriver to the raging hole. *This is good*, I thought. I started back paddling to slow myself down. I used all of my strength and threw my weight backward, occasionally hitting my paddle on the bottom of the creek. Almost in line with the hole, I pointed my boat directly at it, ready to slay the beast. With a burst of speed, I thrust myself forward with the paddle, paddling at full speed into the maelstrom. *Lean downstream*

15

when you're in, my voice screamed at me over the roar of the river. I dropped into the seam where the brown bubbles met the smooth face of the water. I flipped as if I were being flung out of a slingshot. As soon as my head broke the water's surface, my helmet slammed into a rock shelf. I was underwater, being flung around with no control of my arms in complete darkness. The noise was deafening and my eyes were wide, collecting silt. I had a death grip on the paddle as the kayak bucked, twisted, and turned. My body was screaming as the motion of the water nearly twisted my torso in half. I spun around below the water's edge with the cold water infiltrating my helmet.

Suddenly I felt a huge jerk as the boat exploded off my body. The boat cockpit raked my knees and shins, peeling off the first layer of skin. I hung onto the paddle with one hand and boat with the other. I looked the direction I thought was up and pushed my feet down, touched the bottom of the river and launched myself toward the surface. I broke the surface of the creek and gasped for breath. Panicked, I realized I was about ten yards from the hole I went into only a moment ago. I looked to shore as the rope hit the water and disappears into the muddy depths. The soap container floated, held by the fragile string that was my only salvation. I reached for it and grasped the rope. I yelled to my friend, "got it!" and he proceeded to pull me in. The cold water shocked my body. I ungracefully grappled my way up the edge of the river, up the muddy weed covered bank, gasping for breath, shaking and sore.

Ed looked concerned. "Are you okay," he asked. "You flipped really fast and I heard something hit the bottom of the river." I felt the side of my helmet to find a divot where the collision had taken place. Water ran out of my helmet down my face as I yanked the helmet off to feel my head. Besides my scraped shins and my sore neck, I was fine. I was ready to try again.

Over and over again, I went into that hole. I flipped and hit my elbow, so I learned to tuck my head to the deck of the boat. I became faster than the water, keeping my elbows high and tucked. Each time I flipped, I swam. With each swim I became less and less panicked. Darkness and cold soon had little effect on me and the violent underwater episodes started leaving a smile on my face rather than

16

fear in my heart. I had been in a lot of pain as a kid, so the discomfort I was feeling now was almost pleasurable compared to the pain of the past. What used to seem like an eternity underwater now felt like ten or fifteen seconds. I could have kept practicing all day but I was forced to stop after Ed refused to continue. The whole experience made him far more nervous and uncomfortable than it made me. *He's just not the adventurous type* I thought, no one seems to be very adventures anymore.

I went back to that spot several times during high water, unfortunately I could never find anyone to go with me. Even with the promise of getting the opportunity of pulling me from the river. Being stuck in the hole, I found out, was much better than swimming. But until I knew how to release myself from the hole, I usually ended up swimming anyway. I would get into the hole and get stuck swirling around in the water until I was exhausted. This taught me how to use my paddle on top of the water to keep me from flipping over. The book called this a brace. Eventually, I was working my way back and forth across the river with ferry angles, by setting the front of my boat at about a forty-five-degree angle to the oncoming currant, the currant helps push me across the river with little effort on my part. I was now getting in and out of eddies with confidence.

Eventually, I found a kayaking class in SUNY Geneseo College pool that was put on by a local guy named Red, so I signed up. It turned out that he knew my dad and Bill. In fact, the boat that I was practicing in had once been Red's. He was using the new modern plastic boats that would not break, the way fiberglass did, when they hit a rock. During the class, I learned to Eskimo roll in a half hour. Because I had paddled so much on my own, I had learned to brace on both sides. An Eskimo roll is nothing more than a moving brace. I was already ahead of the novices in class. Red introduced me to his brother, who was selling all of his kayaking gear. I bought the lot: the plastic T Canyon kayak, a paddle, a helmet, airbags and spray skirt all for $200. I was set.

When I finally talked Red into taking me down the river, he brought his son, Little Red, along. They strolled down the mile trail in Letchworth to the river with their boats on their shoulders without

17

issue. I on the other hand struggled, due to not being in shape nor having athletic ability.

We slipped into the silty Genesee River and worked our way upstream along the wall. At a certain point in the river, you could not go upstream anymore because the current simply would not allow it. At that point, both Red and Little Red did a hard ferry angle and shot all the way across the river. They both kept an eye on me as I struggled my way across. Although I did not keep a perfect angle on the biggest river, I had been on to date, I did make it across without flipping. Red looked at me with approval and nodded his head. "Try to keep your angle." he said, "it makes it easier. You don't have to work so hard." I was a sponge for knowledge in a river of silty water.

He had me practice getting in and out of the easier eddies on the slow-moving side of the river. At the same time, Little Red was in the fast water next to the cliff that descended into the river. Looking at the water, I could see defined lines where the river changed speed or direction. With Red's constant input, I was now paying attention and learning when to lean downstream. Downriver and downstream, I quickly learned, are two completely different things. We moved further out into the middle of the river where the faster water flowed. With my heart pounding and my breath shallow I drove myself into the column of fast-moving water and leaned downstream. I was heading toward a wave train. The faster-moving water put much more pressure on my paddle, so it was almost easier to paddle in fast-moving water than it was in the slow-moving water. Here, the waves were two to three feet high, so I paddled for all that I am worth in order to break through them. As I do, the water breaks over my bow and splashes over my face. The water was cold and uninviting, and my hands were cold. The bitter water was now trickling down my back and pooling in the seat around my ass. I paddle my way to the side of the river that I came from and then worked my way back up the river to do it again. These waves felt huge. I felt like I was airborne. At the end of each wave train, I emerge with a huge smile on my face. It was the first time I genuinely smiled in years.

Eventually, we moved downstream to a rapid known as Red Ball, named for the power lines that extend over the expanse of the canyon above. Red surfs the waves, shooting in and out of eddies. He has taken his eagle eye off me and I feel less scrutinized. The guys paddled circles around me and I followed behind them like a younger stepbrother that no one wanted around. But the exercise seemed futile. I was exhausted. I was starting to slice my paddle through the river, getting no purchase because I was not turning my wrist enough as my paddle dives into the silty water. Red could see that I was tired and we took a break on the stony beach. He pulled me and my kayak up onto dry land and kneeled down beside me and asked, "Have you been paddling alone all this time?"

My eyes widened and what little adrenaline I had left in my body pushed my heart up into my throat as I said, "yeah." I expected an expansive lecture on how I should never sit in a kayak again; how I was putting people in danger even being near the river. Instead he said, "Wow, you are doing great!" I was taken back, but his words gave me a new found enthusiasm.

I got to surf a wave just above the take out that is easy to get to. I go back to it several times; it feels like sliding down a hill on ice. You are a little out of control, a little bouncy, and you feel like you are going a hundred miles an hour. It's nerve-wracking, exhilarating and all-encompassing. Side surfing in the creek was much harder, more like an exercise in survival. This is an art! Especially the way Red and his son did it, sliding back and forth effortlessly on the face of the wave.

We started back toward the parking lot. Red and his son simply put their kayaks on their shoulders and walked as if they were weightless. My kayak was big and bulky and was killing my shoulder as I gasped for breath. But I did not want to drag it. They could carry their kayaks, so I could too. When I looked up the hill, they were forty yards ahead. When I looked again, they were sixty yards ahead. The next time I looked up, they were gone. When I met them in the parking lot, Red had a big smile on his face.

4

Black River

Though I was gaining experience on other creeks, rivers, and deep waters, I always went back to my little creek. Eventually, I started to meet other kayakers. I met a guy named Bow who was about the same level as me in the kayaking realm. Bow also knew Red, so we were able to run rivers together. We were getting better all the time. One day, Red came up with the idea of going to the Black River in Watertown. He mentioned the idea after he thought Bow and I were ready. I had heard a lot about the Black River, it was ominous. The Black River was big, fast, and dangerous. But most of all, it was sharp. The rocks were like razorblades. Most people who get cut on the Black River never go back. You absolutely needed to make your lines. Running the Black River sets you apart from other people. If you had run the Black River in Watertown, you could truly call yourself a kayaker.

As we drove over the bridge on I-81, I saw the huge expanse of Black River. I saw wide holes with water spitting up ten feet into the air. The waves were the biggest I had ever seen, and the water seemed to have a smooth black face that pulsed and rippled without reason before exploding into a torrent of white. When we parked and unloaded, I saw some other kayakers there at the river. They weren't like us., they were hard. They had detail in their face and their arms looked like they were carved from stone. Bow did not notice them and Red did not care. I was in a different kayak now, a Pirouette S made by Peception. It was much smaller, thinner, and faster than my T canyon. I hoped it was big enough to keep me out of trouble. We walked down the long stairway and set our boats at the edge of the water. We sat in our boats, flipped our spray skirts on, and pushed ourselves into the steal Blackwater River. We were in a pool above the first drop where the water was moving very slow. Red turned his boat toward Bow and myself. He put his left hand over his right hand, holding onto the center of the paddle. "We are running a class five today, so you guys are on your own." With that, he turned his boat, lunged forward, and with a few paddle strokes he disappeared over the first drop of the river. I looked at Bow and he looked at me. "Do you think he is serious?" Bow asked. I sat with a frown on my face looking down at my spray skirt, making sure my tab was on the outside where I could get to it if I needed to. "I kind of think he is," I said.

We did not know what he meant, but we did not have time to think about it. We worked our way to the drop. The line was evident; don't go under the great big mother fucking wall that the water is rushing under, don't go into the hole on the right, and don't hit the rock that is creating the hole. Our mission was to get to the eddy that Red was in on the river right below the mess. So that being our only option, that is exactly what we did. Clubhouse turn at the end of the first drop, there was a ninety-degree rock wall jutting out our path. It ascended thirty feet straight up in to the air from the bottom of the river. jutting out into the river. On the back edge of that wall was a ten-foot diameter whirlpool, a spinning vortex. Even the eddy we were in was heaving up and down two or three feet. Just sitting still I felt like I was being handled, I had little to no control. Red peeled out first and continued down river, followed by Bow, and then myself; into a big wave train next to another wall. At the bottom of the wall there were crazy eddies spinning and collapsing onto themselves. The river took on a significant downward angle. I paddled with a power that I had never had before, trying to stay in the waves where I was safest. My mind coached me in blips, *stay in the wave train, don't go near the wall, look where you are going,* until I cleared the wall. I relaxed my shoulders, took a deep breath, and looked over at Bow. He looked shell-shocked and unsteady.

I had kayaked with Bow for a little more than a year before that point, I knew that Bow always had timing issues in a kayak. If you were in front of him and you slowed down or wanted to try and catch a wave or hole, he would run into you. He was impossible to run a small creek with. He was always too close to you or would pull out in front of you when you wanted to pull in behind him in the eddy. This would make you do something you did not want to

21

do, like miss the eddy. I put up with him and gave him a wide berth on a river. At this point, I always let Bow go in front of me on the river so that I could make any corrections I needed to make in order to not get tangled up with him. On a river as powerful as Black Rive that was important.

We worked our way down to the next rapid and had a great time. Red turned downstream and paddled on and we followed behind him. Eventually the big highway bridge came into view and my heart leapt into my throat. We were coming up to the rapid I saw from the bridge. Three white lines extended almost all the way across the river with exploding waves and holes all over the place. It looked like absolute chaos.

About fifty yards after the bridge, Red beached himself onto the left side shore of the river. We pulled our gear onto the shore and left it behind as we went to a look at the next rapid. As we walked, Red pointed out all the fossils in the rock. I realized the river had been there since before the time of man. Most of the dams had been washed out, and there were people that had worked on this river their entire lives. I suddenly felt insignificant yet alive. I could feel the river pulse like an electric current through my feet as we walked. I could feel decades passing quietly with every step; time here meant so little.

Yet, my future was growing louder and louder! We stepped into the light, which was kissed by the mist of a raging torrent throwing water out of the river only so it can run back into it again. My eyes were wide, unable to take the view in. My head jutted upstream, then downstream, then straight ahead. I realized the severity of what was in front of me. It was only when I started to speak to Red that I realized how loud it was. We were both yelling at each other in order to have a conversation. He put his hand up to stop both of us from speaking, and motioned for me to come close. He explained the rapid in extreme detail. "It will be three big moves. Think of nothing else. Between the moves, you will be moving too fast to think and you will be through the rapid before you know it. But, whatever happens," Red continued, "you have to make the last move. Timing is everything." This was Knife's Edge on the Black River. This was why we were here.

As we reentered our boats my legs were shaky. I was practicing angles and torso shifts in my mind. I had no idea what this rapid looked like from the center of the river. Getting ready for the run, we each stretched our spray skirts over our cockpit rim and snapped them on. Red looked at Bow and pointed at himself and said one, he pointed at Bow and said two, then he pointed at me and said three. "Make sure you give each other room," Red said, before sliding quickly over the slippery algae and into the river. Bow gave Red about five seconds before sliding in behind him. I gave Bow about a ten count before I pushed forward.

The words of this morning echoed in my mind once again: *Today you are on your own.* My eyes went to the left side of the river, the same side we went out on. The trail we had walked on earlier had disappeared behind bushes, tall grass, and scrubby trees. It was as if it had never existed. I glanced to right of the river. There was no way to make it over there without getting caught in the first big hydraulic. My only choice was to go down the river. Red was now thirty yards ahead, and I was amazed to see how the speed of the water was becoming exponentially faster. The waves were getting steep, and at the bottom of the trough it was becoming hard to see over the next wave.

At the top of the wave I could see Red and Bow. Bow was paddling too fast and was too close to Red. They shot past the first wide hole on the left side of the river, and started picking up speed just as I was behind them. I needed to stay in control as my boat was being pushed around by the pulsing column of water. My stern was beginning to dig in at the midpoint of the waves so I increased my power and found myself shooting off the top of the wave with purpose. Looking down river searching for the guys, I saw they were now next to the huge wave hole, the K2 wave that we had stood in front of earlier. Red headed toward the left side of the big wave hole and was able to shoot past it without getting sucked in. He disappeared behind the massive wall of white coming back into sight on the right side of the hole. Bow clipped the hole but he managed to get through it, and ended up low in the eddy. He turned his boat upstream and struggled to get back into the slower moving water. He was finally able to get close to Red. As soon as Bow was stable

23

but low in the eddy, Red took off down the river to make the last move. It was now my turn to make the first big hole. I was looking at my line to get around the K2 wave while simultaneously watching Red's line. He was on his way through, and was making threading the needle between the two holes look easy. I was fifteen yards from the K2 wave and was watching Bow. He was not looking up steam, but was hurrying to get out of the eddy to run the line. I disappeared into a trough of waves and emerged to see Bow no more than ten feet directly in front of me. Not only was he way too far out into the river, but he caused me to cut the line short. I almost went into the K2 wave, but I hit the very edge of the K2 wave instead. I blasted through the edge of the hole as water pounded my chest. I corrected my angle and powered into the eddy that Bow had come from. I went into the eddy at very high height, much higher than Bow did. I turned my boat around on a dime and shot a look downstream. I saw Bow paddling hard, his head looking back and forth at the shelf. He was looking for the line of Knife's Edge. He was way too far left and was directly in front of the shelf. He wasn't going to make it.

When Red ran the true path at Knife's Edge, I saw him the entire time until he was well past the shelf on the left side of the river. Bow also disappeared the moment he went over the shelf. Then all of a sudden, there was an explosion. I saw Bow's blue boat in the air, it looked like it was thrown by a catapult back upstream and over the shelf he had just gone over. He landed above the shelf with a huge splash, upside down, and backward in no more than three feet of water. The fast-moving water drug him back over the shelf and he disappeared. Bow might be dead! I continue floating downstream and still have to make the line! I turned my boat and fixed my eyes on the spot I thought Red went through. I had to keep a left angle, but have a right angle to the shelf hole, and power through the foam. The foam was getting bigger and bigger as I drew closer. My boat rose in front of me as I was lifted by a fountain of water shooting skyward. I felt my boat level out before the nose took a downward angle. I shot down the face of this zenith of water into the trough below the shelf. I was through!

The waves were peaking at eight feet and rolling at the top. I leaned forward again and pointed my boat to the center of the river.

Almost sideways at the top of the waves I slipped over the peak and dropped into the trough. The only thing I could see was water. Three paddle digs up the face of the next wave, and I flew off the peak. I felt my boat leave the water and then slap down on the landing as I head toward Red in the middle of the river.

As I got closer, I could see Bow swimming with his left hand over his boat while holding onto the paddle with the same hand. As I pulled up next to Bow and Red, Bow looked at me with big eyes and a gaping mouth. Something was definitely wrong. As I took a moment to focus on him, I saw his other arm protruding into the blackness. He raised his hand from the depths of the water and as it got closer to the surface of the river, it looked like a shark attack had taken place. There were clouds of blood being ushered downstream by the current like a chum line. He threw his right hand over his boat, and blood quickly covered the surface. Bow's hand was shredded. I could see cuts that went down the length of his fingers. It looked as if a dull fillet knife was pulled down his fingers sideways. There were pieces of skin and meat hanging out of the cuts. Then I notice his left hand was cut as well. He held his hands up and splayed out his fingers to survey the damage. Red yelled at him to grab onto his boat so he could get to shore. A hundred yards later, Bow was standing on the shore dripping blood off his fingers into the cracks of the rocks where fossils have been embedded for thousands of years. I thought about that blood working its way down into the small crevices as if it were an offering to the gods as the earth drank it in. There was always a price to be paid, I thought.

Red pulled out his first aid kit and bandaged each finger; giving Bow instructions to look for any black specks of rock in the cuts. The sharp rock in the river is called Chert. It's a sedimentary rock with a hardness of seven on the Moh's scale of hardness, which makes it a form of quartz. It breaks off just like flint, only much smaller, and is sharp as a razor. You will see ribbons of plastic on the Black River that were peeled off effortlessly by the Chert. Bow had experienced it up close and personal. Red put antiseptic and gauze on Bow's cuts and wrapped it in hockey tape. With both hands taped, Bow looked like a prize fighter. We slipped back into the boats and headed down the river.

25

The water here felt alive, like it knew I was there. It pulsed and opened up below me, making me feel like I was sinking. It pushed me around, put my boat up on edge, and made my control seem minimal. This was what I always thought a river would feel like. At the end of the day, I had run Black River and knew I was a kayaker.

In the years to come I would run the Black River, sometimes seventy-five times in a year, at water levels ranging from the summer 2000cfs to spring runoff at 12000cfs (cubic feet per second) and everything in between. In all that time, I never received a cut. But I have had many other things happen. The river still seems to know that I'm there and there is still a price to be paid.

5

Letchworth

I grew up twenty miles from Letchworth State Park. It is also known as the Grand Canyon of East, and is home to the Genesee River which is a class III river. Over the years, I have paddled the Genesee River hundreds of times and consider it my home river. Besides its overwhelming beauty, there is little else remarkable about it. The only time the river is risen up is in the springtime, and even then, the water is full of silt. It's so full of this fine mud that the river looks like a chocolate milkshake. This silt is impossible to get out of clothes; with a grain much finer than sand, it gets into everything. The Genesee River is one hundred fifty-seven miles long; it starts on the Allegheny Plateau and dumps into Lake Ontario. It runs over one hundred twelve miles of farmland. You can immediately smell cow shit in the water, and if you have the unfortunate opportunity to taste it you will retain a metallic aluminum aftertaste on your tongue.

The Genesee River in Letchworth was the most highly regulated river on the east coast. I have been hassled more in Letchworth State Park than anywhere else I've paddled. The rules of the river were written by a conservative canoe club back in the nineteen seventies and, regardless of the forty years of boat evolution, the rules had never changed. The park police will ticket you for everything, even if they think the tinting on your car windows is too dark. If you don't have a license plate light, if your car or bike is too loud, or if you drive a mile over the incredibly low speed limit, they make you pay.

One day two friends and I went to the park because the river was up. The rules stated at that time that there must be three boaters in a group in order to gain access to the river. We simply called it the three-boater rule, however, my friend Little Red was only seventeen. When the park secretary found this out, she asked us if we were the legal guardians. After answering no, she stated that we could not go because a legal guardian was required if our third was under the age of 18. I asked if I could use her phone to call his mom, but she told me I had to use the pay phone outside the park office. We went and called his mom and gave her the park secretary's number. We watched as the secretary picked up the phone, received permission from the minor's mother for him to paddle, and still told us that we could not go. No matter what his mom offered, the park refused to let us go. I stated that the next time I was in the park it would be with a lawyer. This was the end of the constant string of harassment that I had received from the park since I had started paddling.

I was tired of getting punished for not doing anything wrong. I called a few friends and put a team of people together. We came together for a meeting and decided we were going to change the rules. If New York State Park Letchworth did not comply, we would sue. It would be a class action lawsuit that would involve every kayaker who had ever been harassed in Letchworth. We needed the help of a good lawyer. There was no one better to ask than the official American Whitewater Affiliation (AWA) lawyer, who had worked on water freedom cases all over America. He resided in Buffalo, NY, which was only an hour and a half away. One of my guys knew him well and had paddled with him in the past. After a phone conference, he was in.

We arranged a meeting with the Captain of the park police, the head of the park itself, the head of the rangers, and their lawyer. We sat down in the park's administrative offices and started to talk. Our AWA lawyer had read every detail of the rules and started by motioning to have the capacity plate rules removed. The capacity plate controls how many people can be in a boat and the maximum total weight the boat can safely handle. The Captain of the police immediately started giving Bob, our lawyer, pushback. Bob defended his position. He stated that if every boat on the river was held to this capacity plate, then kayakers would no longer have access to the river since kayaks did not fall under the same jurisdiction. Bob pushed a stake of neatly bound papers, six inches high, to the middle of the table. He said, "These are all of my winning case files from the last couple years working on river freedom cases just like this one. If you want to go to court, that's fine with me."

The Captain of the police backed down and the rest of the staff tactfully took over as he sat brooding. Over the next hour and a half we discussed the laws versus the rules. We changed every rule except two. The one requiring people to sign in and out and the on requiring people to sign a waiver. We made sure that anyone under eighteen was accompanied by an adult, whether or not that adult was their legal guardian. We raised the maximum water level and established a high-water team that could go on the river beyond the maximum water level restriction. There was no longer a three-boater rule. We cleaned house.

6

Genesee River, High Water Team

Through great efforts, we had established the new high-water team for Letchworth State Park. During the previous administration meeting I was asked to give a list of qualified kayakers for the high-water team. Of course, I gave them a list of every decent kayaker I knew, including all of my friends. The stipulations of a feasibility study were straight forward. To determine if the river was safe for a novice boater to be on at the current water level without being in a life-threatening situation. A detailed report of the river was to be submitted with any issues that may cause a threat to life or limb. This was to be an ongoing study at different water levels.

I invited two great friends of mine, Bugsy and Tad, to participate in the first High-Water Feasibility Study. Basically, I asked them if they wanted to kayak the Genesee higher than they had ever done before. Of course, they couldn't get to the park fast enough.

I stood at the New York State Parks Letchworth administration counter with a smirk on my face as the same secretary that had turned me away over the three-boater rule signed my personal high-water feasibility team onto the river. The Genesee River was not only above the previous max water level; it was above the new Max level that we had established during the last administration meeting! It had rained all week; the Genesee River was running at a level of 16ft, and the secretary never said a word as we signed in at the Letchworth administration park office

I asked Tad and Bugsy why they brought their creaking boats to a much higher volume river, and they looked at each other in a puzzled manner. One of them replied, "It's 16ft." I had brought a play boat because my boat floats on TOP of the water.

We descended into the canyon as if it were any normal day. There was no plan we were just going to have fun. We worked our way out into the main flow. At this level there was no ascending up the river. We shot the first rapid and caught an eddy or two on the right side of the river, until we got to the rapid known as Red Ball. It was massive; we were able to get to the left of the river and evaluate the magnificent surf waves. Each one from about six to ten feet high or higher! They had a rolling white crest on the top of them with a long smooth steep lead in face to surf. A kayaker surfs on a wave in a river like a surfer on a wave in the ocean. The main difference being that the ocean wave moves forward, while a wave in a river is stationary and is resupplied with water by the oncoming current. The only thing I really remember is this; I was surfing what I felt was the biggest wave on the river, my kayak was facing up stream as I slid back and forth on its face. The wave in front of me was almost as high as the one I was on making it hard to see upstream. All I could see was water in front of me when I was in the trough of the wave. I was working my way back to the top of the wave when I heard something. I glanced to my right and saw Tad and Bugsy pointing upstream. As I looked upstream, I saw a large branch sticking straight up toward the sky out of the wave in front of me. Calm and collected I thought, "wonder if that is attached to something?" Just then a root ball at least twenty feet in diameter broke through the wave right in front of me. My heart leapt into my throat. I thought, "If that thing touches me, I will be driven under water, out of control, and tangled up in a rats' nest of roots." I leaned forward, lifted my right knee, and leaned my body left. The wave I was on was nearly as wide as the river, and I was in the middle of it. My kayak shot to the left while I was still on the massive wave, and the root ball went flying by me with a thirty-foot tree attached to it! I paddled my way back to the center of the wave and glanced at the guys with a big smile on my face. I was thinking to myself, "I'm going to call that "debris" in the report."

We all had great surfs that day and continued down towards the take out point called St. Helena. Just before the take out on the left side of the river, Tad pointed out a massive whirlpool. Bugsy and I raced at the opportunity. Bugsy was there first and while he was spinning around, he got sucked down into the whirlpool up to

31

his chest; in a creek boat! At that point, I was spinning around the outside of it, trying my best not to do that. We had great fun all day, the river was now definitely worth the time.

We wrote a trip report that all of us approved of and I sent it to the head of the park. I sent it to Bugsy in digital form and asked him to put it on the local Paddlers Club message board. Bugsy published it and received an outpouring of hate from nearly everyone. You would have thought that Bugsy was Benedict Arnold, Genghis Khan, and Hitler all rolled into one, as he has come to make the rest look small and weak like helpless simpletons. At least that's how they took it. The reality was it took a lot of people to make this come together, and without their help it would have never happened. We had adhered to the new rules and guidelines, we had also written a comprehensive trip report, and shared it with the world; and the world hated us for it.

But most people did not really know about our meeting with the park, and the normal whitewater kayaker had no concept of the rule changes. We had not written a pre-trip report explaining the situation. In hindsight, that might have been a good idea. This caused a quiet feud between the conservative kayakers and the free boaters that would go on for years. But on this one I was not the front man and I had never officially belonged to any kayaking club, so I did not care. I had become the behind the scenes guy and that's the way I liked it. I just wanted to kayak down rivers without being hassled. Of course, a year later all the cool kayaker dudes wanted to be on the high-water team. As far as I know there has never been another official trip report written.

At one point someone posted a letter on the local chat board about the rules of Letchworth. They were wrong in all of their assumptions, so I corrected them with no uncertain terms. The backlash was extreme once again I had become the villain. My retort came in this letter:

I would like to sincerely apologies to you, and any other sensitive soul person that may have felt accosted by my words.

My handsomely rugged manly exterior has seldom allowed me the luxury of sensitivity. You see, I've had a rough life. All of my life people have told me what not to do. They would say things like "Marty, don't chase the cars" I never caught one. "Don't hang off the diving board with your toes". But it is closer to the water that way. "Stop making the teachers cry" I can't help it if they don't have the fortitude to not become emotionally involved in the argument. "Don't shoot the animal out the truck window" Why will it hurt the animal less if I am standing in the field. "don't have sex with a man's girlfriend or the neighbor's wife. Especially together." But it sounded like a good idea to me. Then there was kayaking, "don't run the water fall Marty" "You can't do 300 feet a mile Marty" You can't change the rules at Letchworth, Marty."

Luckily, I had decided long before that the people that were telling me not do to it couldn't do it themselves.

I spent five years in Letchworth trying to change the rules. Then with a small band of rebels, and googly eyed misfits we put the pencils behind our ears walked into chambers. Park police, administration, government lawyers (all of which did not want us there.) We emerged days later. Victorious, not just for us, but for kayakers in generations to come. Long after I am gone, someone will be at the bottom of the canyon looking up from a kayak. The thought makes me smile.

So, I was justifiably upset when I saw the rules being tossed back and forth on the abyss of hearsay. Then I felt the scolding however subtle it may have been was unnecessary, I felt that I needed to stand up. The idea of Kayaker being prosecuted for kayaking is not what I believe in. I don't think you do either.

"You could run the loop, but if they catch you, fines will apply. I know your boating experience is Class V boater status, but examples should be made, especially on a heavily paddled river like the Genny, Lehigh, Salmon Rivers." Quoted buy a friend of mine.

I believe I helped us all pay a little more attention to what we say and how we think. I knew this backlash would come; the risk was worth it.

What I wanted was for all of us to have the freedom to paddle, anywhere, anytime, and under any conditions we want. Without persecution of any kind, what I wanted is for some little kid to wave to me from shore so I could roll over for him and come up with a smile on my face, and that kid can say "that was cool, I want to do that" because that is how I became a kayaker.

After I posted that letter I was scolded again of course about "pounding my chest too much". But my point was received and after that I no longer posted on the message boards. Soon after that I ended up working up north, Watertown and Old Forge, as a professional kayaker. Red once told me, it's not bragging if you can do it. Well I did it, against all the odds that once held me back. Just like changing the unchangeable rules at Letchworth.

The Letchworth Ghost

How big was Letchworth 19? A little above the legal limit at the time. I decided that I was going to run the loop, meaning the first quarter of the river at Letchworth regardless of the rules. I dressed in my kayaking gear at home before putting a big sweatshirt and some sweat pants over it. I stuffed my boat with my life jacket and helmet, and threw it in the back of my minivan. I covered it with a tarp and tried to make it look inconspicuous. I drove into the park and pretended I was a tourist looking for relaxed recreation. I drove past the administration building where I was supposed to sign in, and I worked my way down to the lower parking lot below the last falls. I backed my van as close as I could to the bank that lead down to the river. I casually got out of the van and looked around for park police. No one was around so I quickly opened the back of the van, grabbed my kayak, and tossed it over the bank.

I watched as it careened down the steep hill, pinballing off every goddamn tree on the way down. My paddle, life jacket and helmet fell out, strewn across the landscape. I started back to the van, ripped off my street clothes, and headed back to the woods. I jumped over the edge and disappeared out of sight. I slid down the bank about twenty feet before I grabbed a tree to slow me down. Looking down into the ravine, I could see the tip of my kayak. I worked my way down, zig-zagging to pick up my gear. I put on my

34

life jacket and helmet when I got to them and then picked up my paddle. I worked the rest of the way down and found my boat T-boned against a tree. The boat had a big dent in its nose that wrinkled back about five inches. I put the boat on my shoulder and walked across the plateau to the final descent.

This was a steep bank that ended at the cliff above the river. If I lost control of my boat this time, there was a good chance I would never see it again. It had been raining hard for the last three days. The gully was muddy and slippery as I stepped off the plateau. I immediately lost my footing in the slick mud. I grabbed a tree and stabled myself for a minute. I took a strap out of my boat and used a carabiner to hook the strap to the boat. I let the boat lead me down the hill, slipping and sliding all the way. I was now covered in mud.

Finally, I find myself at the edge of a cliff. I could hear the river raging below. It was much too high to launch from where I was, which was about fifty feet above the river. I needed to move toward the regular put in at the end of the trail head without going all the way to it for fear of being discovered. I paralleled the river until I came to a suitable launch point, about ten feet above the river. It was a straight shot to the edge of the cliff then out into the river. But there was one small tree in the way. If I could get past the tree then I would be okay. I positioned my boat so the tree next to me would hold my boat sideways as I got into it. I set my paddle on my right and put the left side of the boat against the tree to hold me. The bank was slippery and I only had one chance to do it right. I eased myself into the boat and flipped my spray skirt over the back of the lip of the kayak. As I shifted my weight back, I felt the boat shift. I grabbed the tree and steadied myself. Once I was stable again, I put the front of the spray skirt over the front of the lip. I picked up my paddle and peered past the tree to the edge of the cliff. The river was a churning cauldron of dark brown mud and debris. But I was ready, and now only one tree stood between me and the freedom of the river.

I picked up my paddle and put it across the tree next to me and wrenched my body forward. My boat immediately took off down the bank. I turned and slid down the bank as if I were on ice. The only thing I could see was that one lone tree. I was careening

35

towards it as if my boat was a magnet. When I was two feet from impact, I twisted my body and legs to the right as hard as I could. The front of the boat missed the tree but the back end glanced off of it, which changed my angle just as I shot off the edge of the cliff. I did not float through the air like I had anticipated.

It was as if I was plummeting down a mine shaft. Time slows down when you do something wrong in your kayak, especially when you know pain is coming. I violently struck the water, my boat pointing upstream instead of downstream. I was nearly vertical as I entered the main channel of rushing water. The moment my bow touched the moving water, I instantly flipped. As my face slammed into the river, my head simultaneously slapped the back deck of my kayak, almost ripping me out of the boat. I was now under water being handled by the current. Beneath the cold water of the Genesee River, there was no light. I did not know if my eyes were open or closed, but I knew where the surface was. I rolled up on the first try and found myself twenty yards down the river from my launch point. Caught in a big wave train, it was time to paddle.

I blinked my eyes several times, trying to get the grit out and began paddling. I worked my way over to the right of the river into a big eddy and evaluated my situation. My heart was pounding and I was breathing heavy. I could taste the adrenaline and what I think was cow dung in my mouth. I spit into the water to get the taste of cow shit out of my mouth. As long as I didn't get swept passed the loop take out point I would be fine. I could see where the river split from there causing an island in the middle of the river, I definitely wanted to be on the right side of that island. I drove myself out past the eddy line feeling the warm wind as it worked its way down the valley and headed to the nearest wave.

The waves were eight to ten feet high with white rollers of foam at the top. I backed out into a wave and paddling as fast as I could, I cut loose and surfed down a smooth sheet of fast brown water and did a flat spin and back surfed up to the foam pile and flat spun again. Now surfing forward, I casually cut back and forth on the face of the wave lifting one edge of the boat then the other. I worked my way down the river to the wave train known as Red Ball. High and fast with almost no eddy service. I surfed for about an hour on top of the curling waves, flat spinning and shooting down the face before cutting into the wave and working my way back to the top. I was elated floating on a cushion of air, grinning ear to ear. The adrenaline had waned and I was suddenly at peace. I was alone in the canyon with a warm breeze in my face and nothing to prove.

Eventually I noticed people watching me from a great distance. It was the park police. I had overstayed my welcome. I knew they would be waiting for me at the take out of the loop so that was not an option. In Red Ball, I moved a couple of waves back out of sight of the coppers. I surfed for a bit before beaching myself on an island in the middle of the river where no one could see me. I contemplated my situation pictured a map in my mind. If the police wanted to catch me, they would have to get downstream of my current position. I was closer to my van than they were unless they were watching my van, in which case I was screwed.

I shouldered my kayak and walked upstream on the island I was on back in the direction I came from. At the tip of the island, I followed the river to the right. I was too close to the woods for anyone to see me unless they were at water level. I hopped into my boat and ferried from my little island across a small branch of water to the shore. If I wanted to get out without being arrested, ticketed, and having my boat confiscated, I had to go out the way I came in.

I hopped out of my kayak and ran upstream, past the normal put in, and into the woods toward the cliff I had launched from and I started to climb. On a normal day it was possible to climb back up but today it was incredibly difficult due to the muddy earth. I started up the gully face using every tree and root I could grab onto. My feet dug into the mud and leaves, and a few times I dug my hands into the mud-covered face of the gully to get enough grip to lunge forward and grab a branch. Once one of the branches broke and I slid five feet back. On my second attempt I made it and pushed myself to the plateau before the ascent to the parking lot. I peeked my head over and scanned the area. Luckily, I did not see anyone. I pulled my boat onto the flat area and dashed across it. Then I started up the bank on the other side. As I looked down from where I had come from, I could see a solid trail of slide marks in the mud.

37

Finally, at the rim of the parking lot I took off my bright blue helmet so no one would notice the flash of color at the edge of the woods. There were a lot of cars in the lot now but there were no officers to be seen. I jumped over the lip and hustled to my van with a trot, my adrenaline peaking again. I opened the back of my van and threw in the kayak and paddle, closed the door, and hopped in the driver seat. I started my van and drove off trying not draw attention to myself. I wasn't safe until I was out of the park. I threw my baggy sweatshirt on over my life jacket and headed to the closest exit. I went up to the hill past the administration building and drove toward the Perry exit. I waved to the attendant stationed at the gate with a muddy hand and a big smile.

I drove to the nearest kayak shop, grabbed a bag of dry clothes, and headed into the shop. The owner was a friend of mine. When I saw him, I said, "Hey, I have to use your bathroom for a minute. You don't mind, do you?" I never paused to hear his response. In the bathroom, I quickly changed and put my wet, muddy stuff in the bag. Then I calmly walked out to say a proper hello. His first words to me were, "You didn't run Letchworth, did you?" I shook my head yes and firmly said, "No, it's way too high for the rangers to let you on. But if anyone asks, I have been here for a couple of hours, okay?" He laughed and shook his head yes. "Thanks. Now I need to go have a good shower and wash this silt out of my hair."

7

The Moose River

No shit there I was about to run lower Moose below Old Forge. I was working for a popular raft company. I was the raft company's primary kayaker and had started the previous summer working as a full-time kayaker. I received a call in the middle of the winter and was asked if I could start working in early spring on the Moose River, of course I said yes. This would be the first time I would run the Moose River as a safety kayaker.

It was April 1st, and I woke up in the back of my truck to a fresh blanket of snow covering it. There was about three feet of snow in the woods. By the time I crawled out of my truck there was a misty cold rain. I was the safety boater that day. By 9 am we were next to the river, I had six rafts to look after that day, which was about fifty people. The river was not too high. The spring thaw had not really happened yet, but the river was still pretty big for the crews. The crews consisted of the average Joe, they were adventurous people that want life to be fun but safe. Most of the crew really had no idea what they are getting into, or how hard they are going to have to work. They are going to be cold, tired, hungry, and when they swim, they will have a story about how they almost died.

Each raft will always lose a minimum of three people into the river sometime during the day. That's if the raft doesn't flip, which three out of six usually flip. The Lower Moose is a highly regarded class V for rafters.

On that cold day, I was literally the only kayaker on the river, there were no other raft companies on the river either. So, the day was going ok, it was very cold, and my hands had lost most of their feeling except for the pain I felt by the third rapid. This could cause a problem because the colder your hands are the harder you grip the paddle, which causes the muscles in your arms to cramp up and you eventually loose mobility.

This section of the Moose was 12 miles long and not at all fast moving. Sucked, but it paid well. It had been some time since I had run this section, and I came to a rapid known as Rooster Tail. The lead into Rooster Tail was littered with lines. You could go left, right, center, just a multitude of choices. I decided to work my way down the center of the river going toward a diamond-shaped rock that was sticking up about eight feet out of the river and then shoots left of it. You would then have to navigate around the big hole that it caused, and then work your way to Rooster Tail wave. There was a long flat section before the wave, so I was sprinting down the river to get warm. I ended up quite far ahead of the rafts, but that was ok or so I thought. It would give me time to set up safety someplace good.

When I started the line I was doing well; I was all alone as the river necked down and continued to pick up speed. There was a lot of navigation around holes and pore over. It was a little bigger and faster than I remembered. I shot back and forth across the river. There was an eddy out behind holes, and I was having a good old time.

I was picking up speed while working my way to the diamond rock. This was the biggest move of the rapid and I knew I needed to go left of the rock. My eyes widened when the line that I wanted to run came into view. There was a tree in the middle of the river on the left where I needed to go! Holy SHIT! I couldn't stop, I couldn't back up, and I couldn't get around it! I was on a downhill slope with water raging beneath my kayak pushing me with great hostility. I needed to get around that tree. But that ends up putting me on the slope that leads into a big hole at the base of the diamond rock. This was the second biggest hole on the twelve-mile run. I knew I couldn't make it. I looked at the hole and in the fraction of a second I had turned my boat so the front was facing towards the small end of the hole which had less foam spitting out if it. I dropped into the hole sideways. It was massive, and towered above my head as I dropped in. I slammed into the diamond rock with my shoulder and water was shooting up over my head. My boat was jumping up and

40

down like a bucking bronco that never stops. I violently flipped and rolled up, flipped and rolled up. I couldn't see anything; I could only hear the water pounding against the granite. I could feel my helmet and boat slamming into it over and over again. I thought, "I am going to be pounded into pieces! If I don't break my paddle in half first! If I don't regain my composer I am a dead man!" The violence of the hole was astounding. Water was flying over my head, and I could barely breathe in without sucking water into my lungs; the water was freezing. The big granite that was causing this mess was smooth from a thousand years of water slamming into it. I was pretty sure it was not going anywhere anytime soon. I knew that because I had already slammed my body into it several times and it didn't seem to move at all. I gained stability by leaning into the granite as hard as I could. I was stable for now, if you could call being continually thrown up and down five feet stable. I needed to do something and there wasn't a soul on the river to help me. I was completely alone in the middle of this raging river. I was a blip in the middle of this rapid, barely noticeable, and captured in this hole. This felt like a continual car crash that wouldn't stop! I felt myself lurch to the peak of the water at the top of the hole, and I knew this was my chance. It could defiantly get worse, and I knew it would if I didn't get out of here. I would lose my boat and I might never be seen again. I leaned forward as much as I could and started to dig my left paddle blade as deep as I dared, and I jerked my body back to the center of the boat. I moved! So, I kept doing it, the water started to fall away, it was becoming less violent, and I could see. I did this several more times, gaining about a foot every time. This took a while; water was still throwing me up and down, and I had a death grip on my paddle. The hole was about twenty feet wide, but now at least I could take a breath without water being a part of it. As I was working my way out of the hole the rafts came around the corner.

I hadn't even run Rooster Tail yet, and now I had to set safety for the rafts. I had to hurry; the rafts were on their way. I was completely exhausted and freezing cold. I had no adrenaline left. Hopefully, the rafts didn't lose anyone. As I hit Rooster Tail itself, I put my paddle down and floated over to the wave almost sideways with my bow angled left. On the back side of the wave I threw a few hard paddle strokes and shot into the eddy on the left of the river. I

41

made sure I was in front of the rafts. There was a rock past the Rooster Tail wave on the right that could be bad for a swimmer. I wanted to be able to get to it if I needed to. Being on the other side of the river I was not only above the rock, but the position allowed me a clean entry to shoot across the river and help someone. As I sat in the eddy with one hand over the other on top of my paddle, I tried to present myself as calm and confident as the rafts went by one by one. Most the guides gave me a nod of some kind. I gave a big thumbs up to the middle raft guide with a big smile on my face; noting that I was happy with his line. I took off down the river again after the last raft went by. We had about five miles and three rapids to go, and I needed to get in front of the pack. I took off in a sprint, more to warm up than anything, I passed all the rafts again and hung out with the lead raft. Noting to myself that I should not have so much time between myself and the rafts, just in case.

About an hour later the lead raft guide said "you know Mart, I have never seen a kayaker play in the hole before. You were popping up and down in there like five feet. I am glad you are working on the river with us today". I smiled and nodded and made a comment like "yeah, it was getting cold in there," and it was. Word had gotten around about my escapade in the hole to the raft guides, no one knew that I was fighting for my life, or maybe they did. Either way, that day was a good day, and my employment with the rafting company was solidified.

Me and Twitch

I met a guy who knew a guy that ran the Bottom Moose, so eventually we got together. The Lower Moose is a destination river, and I considered it one of the big five on the east coast. It was a release river, meaning a dam that was holding back water would be bypassed, allowing the water back into the river and bringing the water level up. This meant that on a release date there would be guaranteed water in the river. The Bottom Moose was a class V river with big drops and significant must make moves.

The first drop on the Bottom Moose was intimidating. It was forty-five feet high at a forty-five-degree angle that dropped into a hole, that at higher water levels could be very bad for your health. I once saw a boat stuck in that hole for eight hours before it was flushed out. But this was my first day, and I was about to fling myself off this thing.

Twitch looked like Frankenstein, all he needed was bolts in his neck. Square jaw, blocky head with jet-black hair. He was skinny with an abnormally large head for the size of his body. If you ever paddled behind Twitch, you would notice that every few paddle strokes his shoulder would jerk like electricity was being shot through it. He had more stories than you could shake a stick at, and they must have been true because even I didn't believe them.

Twitch and I slid into the water above the first drop and floated toward the falls. He explained the line to me, it was going to be easy. There was a small drop we had to run before going over the falls. Above the waterfall, we were going to drop in on the right of the river, turn sideways, and drop into a hole that would keep us from being swept off the falls. We worked our way out of that hole and into a small pool of water about six feet from the edge of the falls, and above the worst part of the hole beneath. We then ferried across the top of the falls, to the other side, heading to the rock island in the middle. Then we went past the rock island on the downstream side of the river, turned downhill, and went off the falls. All the while the water was screaming by on both sides of us.

It sounded fine until I looked at it, later I would find out this line is called The Suicide Line.

So, the first day on the mighty class V Bottom Moose and I was following a psychopath. Great...

He went first and did exactly what he said he was going to do and waited for me in the small pool of water. I followed with my heart in my throat and a gallon of adrenaline in my veins. I dropped over the shallow shelf, turned sideways half way down, bouncing along, and then I dropped into the hole... you know sideways. I flipped and I braced up so hard I nearly broke my paddle. Next to

43

him in the pool he gave more instructions. He told me to aim at the rock island and not to go too high coming out of the pool. He made the move and went below the small rock island, across to the other side, off the ledge, and disappeared. My turn! I tried to go high out of the pool just like he said not to, but I just wanted to be as far away from the falls edge as possible. It didn't work though, there were too many rocks just under the water and I ended getting tied up in them for a minute. My heart was pounding, the water was so loud it was defining, and I ended up back where I was to try again. Off I went working my way across the top of the falls. I was paddling my ass off. Looking over the falls, the only thing I could see was the tops of the trees forty yards away, and I was starting to rethink this Twitch guy. But now it was too late, I was in the middle of the river above the waterfall and couldn't go upriver or get out. My only option was down!

I get to the rock island, but I was a little low in the line. My angle was a little off now. I was paying for it! I was swept over the falls sideways! The falls were at about a forty-five-degree angle slide, and I was careening down it sideways with no chance of recovery. I was looking at the hole at the bottom (why not there was time). I was about to hit a wall of water five feet high at a staggering speed. Then pop! My boat hit the bottom, and I was engulfed by the hole. I was blown underwater still in my boat and rolled up past the big hole. Twitch was directly in line with me just a few feet away.

"You did good," he said "you just went over too early, about twenty feet too early." He turned and darted away. The rest of the day was a blur. He would tell me the line and I would follow him down. I did not know it at the time, but Twitch was practicing for the downriver race that takes place on this section of the river. He was showing me the RACE lines.

I never stepped out of my boat except for the at portage, and to look at the last rapid. The last rapid was, is, and always will be Crystal (the name of the rapid). It's beautiful and freaking BIG! It had three drops. Basically get to the trough of water above the big drop, it doesn't matter how. Try not to get caught in the Horseshoe hole. Then when in the trough of water go left around the rock wall with the flow of water and go off the 16' waterfall. Twitch waited for me in the trough of water just below the Horseshoe. As I went off the edge of the horseshoe, I realized it was higher than I thought. I did a melt down into the hole. That was my angle, I was pointed down too much and went completely under water. I popped out of the hole upside down after getting worked a bit. Again, Twitch had lined up with me and was only a few feet away when I rolled up. I knew swimming was not an option. He said that he was going to push me back into the hole, if I did not roll up, to give me time to try again. You know, I thought that was nice of him.

The water in the trough was moving quickly, you only have time for one attempt at a roll, two if you are lucky. So, I guess he was going to do me a favor? With a ten-second head start, he took off around the bend and disappeared. My ten count was fast, I was sure, but I followed his line. It was an eye-opening experience going around a corner and seeing a bunch of confused water dropping off the edge of something. Looking at it from the edge of the river, you couldn't see the bottom of the last waterfall. All you could see were the entrails of bubbles. It did not look overly inviting, but rounding the corner and seeing the confusion of water with a boulder on your right and a rock wall with water pouring over it on your left, the only thing I wanted to do was get away from it. That meant driving myself forward to the edge and dropping over the falls. As my shoulders pulled my boat, I felt like I was driving myself over a waterfall that slammed into a cliff! But, just before the cliff I dropped and looked down at my landing zone. I saw white as my boat slides like a dart into the aerated water. Then I saw dark, really dark, I was a long way down under water. The buoyancy of my boat took over, and I felt myself shooting upwards. I was upside-down of course, but I knew that air was in that direction, so I didn't care. I settled at the surface and rolled next to the pothole like everyone did. I took a deep breath and saw Twitch paddling away. I had to hurry to catch up with him.

We shuttled back to the put in where a friend of his was standing; he turned to me and asked if I wanted to run it again. I hesitated but said yes, this time I would run the falls on the left of the river. "You didn't like the suicide line?" I remained speechless, just learning it's called The Suicide Line!

That was my first day on the Bottom Moose. After that, I became addicted to the Moose and spent a lot of time on it.

During my kayaking career, I have run the Bottom Moose a hundred and sixty times as a conservative estimate. This sounds cool but trust me, there are people that have run it much more than myself. I have met a cast of characters and had a great time on the Moose River. Running the Moose became a lifestyle. Every Friday after work during the spring and fall releases I made the pilgrimage north, to the Bottom Moose. I would make a camp fire and then eventual sleep in the back of my vehicle. Rain didn't matter, snow didn't matter, the only hope was that the next morning people would show up to run the Bottom Moose. You know, so I could have a shuttle back to the truck. Every Sunday afternoon I found myself dirty, wet, cold, tired, a little beat up, and hungry. I couldn't wait to do it again, so I did this for years at a time and learned invaluable lessons. The Moose was a great teacher for me and humbling all at the same time. Just when you thought you had it down, your complacency would destroy you. A thought that had always spilled over into the multitude of other rivers I have done. No matter what, I had put myself there, and everything I did on a river was my fault. I didn't have to be there, if I was not willing to accept the consequences of my actions, then I shouldn't paddle. The same goes for everyone else.

The Powerline experiences.

I had paddled with Shae almost since the beginning. We went to Madawaska paddling school together; at the onset of the courses I was taking. I did not feel that it would help me at all, but in hindsight, I did learn a lot. Midway through the week at Madawaska Shae had a horrendous shoulder dislocation. That put him down for the count for about a year. A few years later he was back on the river, and it was always fun for me to run into old friends. Shae never aspired to be some awesome kayaking hair boater. He was a conservative kayaker and has spent most of his time kayaking on class III water. Once in a while I would see him on the Black River in Watertown fooling around, but his goal was to run the Moose and I was more than happy to take him.

Shae and I hit the Bottom Moose with an old school boater friend of mine, Jim. I did conservative lines all day just having a fun day on the water. We did the sneak route on Knifes Edge by taking the easy line. Still, a class IV and he was doing just fine on the Bottom Moose as we worked our way down.

Powerline Rapid was a class IV rapid and was easily the most underestimated drop on the Bottom Moose. Nearly all of the water on the Moose moved through it at an alarming rate. But at the same time it was just an eddy hop situation, it was no big deal. As people looked at it, nothing really stuck out like the rest of the river. Powerline didn't have a big waterfall or a bunch of tricky moves to get through it. It had a multitude of lines that looked fun, and they were. All you needed to do.... was pick one.

At the beginning of the Powerline there is an eddy on the right side of the river, a big eddy that most kayakers stage in. Myself, Shae, and another old school friend of mine sat in that eddy as I gave Shae direction. I explained, "So here's the deal, ferry out PAST the center line of the river, then turn downstream with the angled toward the right of the river. There is a big hole down there, go around it to the right."

Shae repeated my instructions, "So ferry out and then go right."

I restated, "No, I said go out PAST the center line of the river with the angle of right. You are going to go around the big hole to the right; there is a small hole on river right above the big one. You need to miss it because it wants to shoot you into the big hole."

Shae "So go to the center of the river then go right."

Jim then said, "No, you have to listen to Marty he is right about the approach." "

47

ld him, "Shae watch my line and you will understand,
ng for you just below the big hole."

nt out and ran the line as tight as I could so when he
he would have room for small mistakes. I ran the line
well and stayed in a small eddy on the right of the river just below
the big hole. I was hoping that when he saw me he would naturally
come toward me, leading him to the line he needed to take. Shae
started the line and did not go out into the river nearly far enough. I
will say that the river was pushy and getting out of the eddy is
sometimes a struggle, but from the center of the river you can
recover your line. Unfortunately, the way he came out of the eddy
he did not have a chance. He was too far to the right of the run, and
he hit the small hole which bobbled him and shot him into the big
hole. He dropped into that big hole with a look of total confusion on
his face as if to say, "But, I did exactly what you said!" That was
really the last time I saw his face for a while. I did see the ends of
his boat quite a few times as it cartwheeled like a throwing star
spinning through the air.

He flushed from the hole upside down and quickly set up for
his role. He failed at his first roll attempt, so I went up close to him.
His face was only inches underwater as he was already set up for the
second roll attempt. I was about a foot away from him screaming,
"Roll up, you're OK, just roll up!" He was flushing downstream and
being pushed to the left of the river. He was hesitating and I did not
know if he had had a chance to breathe since he had gone into the
hole. I was now only inches from him looking at the bottom of the
boat with his face next to the boat still under water, his paddle in the
setup position for his role. Then he got pushed into a shitty rock
sieve. This was not violent, but when he felt his boat hit the rocks
he pulled the spray skirt and got out of his boat, and he grabbed the
rocks and stood upon them. I had great concern for his shoulder and
I asked him if he was ok. He was, but he needed to get his wits about
him. He had been under water for a while and needed some recovery
time. A few moments had past and his boat was upside-down in front
of him, and next to me. It did not appear to be going anywhere. The
moment that Shae reached down to pull his boat out of the water, it
disappeared. It had been filling with water and finally sunk! (I was

48

now a huge advocate of float bags to keep the kayak high out of the water). It bumped my boat as it went underneath me and shot off down the river before I could get a hand on it.

The chase begins…

This all took place in a matter of minutes, so buy now Jim was on his way down to us and I knew that Shae would be taken care of. I now needed to get his boat; I thought this would be easy… I took off after the boat as it worked its way through a shitty tight boulder garden. I kept getting tied up, and the boat kept getting farther away. The loose boat hit open running water before I did and it took off. I clambered through the boulders and I hit the main flow. I made good time getting to the boat. The problem was this, on the left of the river was a rock wall where the main flow was going and there was very little chance of pushing the boat to the right. Most of the water was flowing in from the right side of the river, coming in through a variety of small streams coming from the main flow. The farther down the river I got, the more water there was. I tried to push the boat to the left of the river into a small eddy, but with it full of water the boat sunk again and continued on.

Another attempt finds me on the downriver side of the boat trying to direct the boat to the slower water. Didn't work… I decide to grab the loop on the bow of the boat which was made from a climbing strap (it's on all boats). I was still in the main flow with my paddle over my shoulder and one blade in the water, I was attempting to pull the boat into another eddy I saw coming up. I dropped into a hole, the hole looked small, but for some reason it liked my boat. I hit it sideways and stopped, still holding onto the boat, I flipped on the downstream side. My paddle was in my right hand and the boat in my left. I had flipped to my left, and the boat was on the downstream side. So, I was underwater thinking, "This is good, the boat will pull me out of the hole." So, I waited for it to do so, and I waited and waited. Yea… "This plan sucks!" I thought. I had to let go of the boat and get some air. I let it go and rolled up still stuck in the hole. I had to actually work my way out of the hole. I was in a hard side surf and had to paddle backward then paddle forward to get a running start to get enough speed to break out of the end of the hole. I did this a couple of times and finally broke loose.

I looked downstream and the boat was thirty yards above the next rapid. That next rapid was called Crystal and its BIG class V. I shot off toward the boat

By the time I got close to the boat, it was at the top of the first drop. Then it occurs to me, "Holy shit I'm too close to this boat!" The first thing was, there was no chance of boat recovery in this rapid. The second was if I got tied up with this boat not only will it throw me off my line that I have got to make, but it may start to cartwheel and hit me or I could drop in on top of it. Now I was above the first drop of Crystal back paddling like a mad man trying NOT to go over, and the boat disappeared over the edge. But I couldn't go over the edge until the boat was clear.

There was a guy standing on the rock island that we stand safety from, and he knew my predicament. He yelled, "It's in the horseshoe." I was finally able to go over the first drop. Just above the horseshoe hole there was a small slow-moving pool. I rested there for a moment as the boat played around in the hole. Again, he yelled, "It's free and in the trough." At that point, I could see the boat taking off down the trough, and I shot over the edge of the horseshoe. Now I was in the trough myself and I sat back paddling as I watched the boat go around the corner and disappear. Now with the guy on the island next to me, I asked him, "Can you see it?" He shook his head no. I had to go around the corner and go off another waterfall, and I didn't want to land on the boat. After a minute or two, he pointed, "It's free, go ahead." I made my way through the trough, around the corner, and powered toward the falls only yards away. I went off the falls, went deep into the water, and flipped over. When I cleared the falls, I rolled up. Now there was a long flat spot before a dam, but I still had to get the boat. I was not going over the dam drop known as Migilla alone and unsupported. I could see the boat; it had a huge head start on me. Then someone came out from behind the Rock known as spectator rock. He was in a kayak and he scooped up the boat and took it to the left of the river. He and the boat were safe from going anywhere, THANK GOD! I paddled into the eddy and thanked him. He asked, "Where did the guy swim?"

I replied, "Powerline,"

"Holy shit you chased this boat all the way from Powerline? That's like a mile away." he said.

I was exhausted since the episode took a long time. Shae made better time by walking, so it only took a few minutes for him to get to me. He arrived at the edge of the water and kneeled down to grab his boat and said: "That's, ok I wasn't going to run Crystal anyway."

I had a hold of his boat at least three times, been stuck in a hole, stopped myself from going over three waterfalls by paddling backward as hard as I could and busted my ass trying to get that thing out of the river and he wasn't going to run it anyway! I laughed and shook my head, a least his shoulder was ok! But he definitely owed me a beer!

Me and Dr. H

So, I get this phone call one day and this guy asks me if I am Marty the kayaker from Upstate New York. I replied that I was and he said that he had gotten my name and phone number from someone on the Ocoee River in Tennessee. That guy said that if I was going to kayak in New York that I had to kayak with you.

I thought that was pretty cool, but Dr. H couldn't tell me the name of the person. So, I shot all the standard questions at him. He said that he was paddling class III-IV rivers and did have a pretty good roll. In my mind that meant he was a liability, so I told him that I was paddling above his level and gave him the name and phone number of a bunch of people that I thought he would fit in with. After that, I never gave it another thought. About a year later I was kayaking on the Ottawa River up north in Canada. It was our annual Fourth of July trip. One night I was sitting by the campfire, and I overheard my name. Something like I heard that Marty paddles up here a lot. "I'm Marty," I stated as I walked over. High I am Dr. H I talked to you about a year ago I got your name from a guy on the Ocoee, he told me to paddle with you. Of course, I remembered the conversation.

Dr. H was skinny, tall with big ears, a long face, and what seemed to be oversized glasses for his head. He was funny, sarcastic, and seemed pretty crazy. He had led an adventurous life, and I liked him right away. We told stories and shot the shit most of the night. I told him of some plans I had to run some rivers coming up later in the year, and he was going to see what he could do to be available. He was a Med. student in Rochester, NY, and time for him was tight. Over the next year, we paddled some fun rivers. We did some creaking and might have gone to the Black River a few times. He expressed his interested in the Lower Moose and said that he was going to go the Moose Fest in the fall. I was going to be there too, and I told him that if we could meet up, I would take him down the Moose.

The Bottom Moose was not super close to anything. Old Forge was where most people hung out. Several people had asked me that year if I was going to go to Moose fest and if so, where could they meet me to go run the Bottom Moose. So, I started giving a general statement, "The Red Barn in Old Forge serves breakfast, I will be there about 8:30 or 9:00." I thought to myself there will not be anyone there, but just in case I better show up. I also told Dr. H and a few good friends that I would be there. As I walked in, I heard a crowd of people collectively yell my name. I stood there in awe, nearly everyone that I had talked to had shown up. They all figured out that they were waiting for me and pushed a bunch of tables together. There were fifteen people! That's fifteen people that I now needed to take down the Lower Moose. I had drunk a "little" too much at the pre-Moose Fest party the night before; I was concerned about getting myself down, much less fifteen people. Not all of these people were new to the Bottom Moose, some were old school friends that had run it several times like I had and thank god. That helped break up the crowd. We put on and, in a loose pack, worked our way down the river. Dr. H and his good friend stuck close, and I gave them directions on how I like to run the drops. But I stressed there were always options and you can run it any way you want.

It was nerve-racking having several people asking you how you think they will do in a drop. On the other end of it, knowing that someone not only has your back and has the confidence that you will do fine was reassuring.

We waited in line to run the first drop, Fowlersville Falls, with hundreds of people watching. After that, the crowd began to thin out, and the Moose River became the beautiful scenic river of folklore. It took forever to run a river with a lot of people. Everyone had to contemplate their line, skills, the possibility of life and death, and procrastination is a killer. We were working our way down to a rapid known as Funnel/diamond splitter. In class III water well above the rapid Dr. H and his friend were fooling around. Dr. H flipped, no big deal until he rolled up, "Marty," he yelled, "I need help, get me to shore." I paddled over to him and asked him what was up? "I blew my shoulder; I need to get to shore." I ushered him to the right shore of the river above Funnel in a nice stable eddy. I asked him what he needed me to do. His left arm was sitting in front of him. He said, "Grab my arm and bend it at the elbow, easy." So, using both my hands I put my left hand below his elbow and the other I grabbed his wrist. I pushed his wrist up so that his elbow was bent at almost a ninety in front of his chest. His arm was in front of him. I asked, "Now what?" he told me to slowly pull his shoulder to me and push his arm out to his side at the same time. He was still in his boat at this point, and it was difficult to get leverage. But I could tell his shoulder was not attached. As I pulled his shoulder out I knew he was in agonizing pain, and he put his head down but sat up straight up in his boat. I pulled his left arm to me and slowly pushed it to his side with his wrist in the air. I did this slowly and got to the point that I was wincing and did not want to go any farther. I had his arm past his back. "Dr. H are you ok, is this right?" He looked up and over to his arm and replied," No, no, that's not going to work. I need to get out of my boat." I placed his arm back into his lap and stabilized him as his friend helped him get out of the boat. He tried a couple of ways to get the shoulder back in on the side of the river, but no dice. He told me to go ahead and run the river since I was with so many people, his friend would escort him to the road. The only problem was that the road was more than a mile away through rugged terrain. Apparently, he made it fine and ended up getting his shoulder to pop back in by walking his fingers up his chest and past his chin and over his head.

He told me that he blew his shoulder, trying to roll. Dr. H and his friend were just fooling around above the rapid running into each other and trying to knock each other over, and he flipped. As he was sweeping his paddle across to do his role, he hit a rock. He ended up rolling up fine, but his shoulder was out. Being a climber he had shoulder issues before. I have had many experiences with dislocations and broken people on rivers. Working for the raft company's and running with kayakers for years I was usually the first person to get to and deal with people in pain. A quick assessment of where they are in the river, if the person is in immediate danger, how much pain are they in, how easy will extraction be and a host of other things were going through my mind. I was glad Dr. H was an MD. I must say his pain control was impressive! I had seen several shoulder dislocations that did not go that well. A shoulder dislocation on a river was going to do a couple of things. The first was it completely stops the group; the second was it was going to change your life forever. Dr. H quit kayaking whitewater about a year after that incident. He went into a different discipline called squirt boating. You are still on rivers, but it has a much lower impact on your shoulders, but you can still have a great time. He ended up making a movie about it that sold worldwide.

Never Break Your Own Rules!

The rule was simple, rule number one about Knife Edge on the Bottom Moose was never run it under 2.2. Just do the sneak. I told this to my good friend Bugsy looking down at the run.

Two weeks later I had gotten to the Bottom Moose and hooked up with the regulars. They were old school boaters that had pioneered and run the Moose more than anyone on earth mixed with a few newer hardcore boaters. The water was running out, and this was the last creaking water left in three states.

Running a river with these men and women was an interesting experience. They were very good, very fast, and seldom scout anything. Their lines were tight, and paddle strokes were strong and well placed. We were on our way down the Lower Moose, I wouldn't say we were sprinting, but we definitely weren't stopping. At Knife Edge, they went through on a ten-second count. Allowing ten seconds from the time a person dropped out of sight to the next person entering the run. Allowing the person to clear the drop before the next person entered it. This was standard timing on most rivers depending on if there was a person standing safety to signal you.

The standard line was to paddle in on the right of the river two feet from the wall, with the bow slightly pointed left. You would find yourself on a shelf and launch yourself off that shelf into the middle of the cauldron of whitewater. With three paddle strokes leading to the next drop, get to the left of the river, straighten out your boat, and go over the next drop. As you went over the drop there was a big rock on your right in the center of the river. On your left there was a rock wall with Potholes in it. You had to angle your boat slightly right so you wouldn't end up in one of the big potholes. Then you had to scoot out between the wall and the big rock, and you had to make it. This was the classic zigzag line.

Easy right? Except when it was low it was super boney. It was hard after you went off the shelf to get to the other side of the flow, it was not very far, it was just slower getting there. Getting you closer to the rock in the center of the river, which intern slows you down, going over the next drop. You wanted speed to get you out of the way from the hole at the bottom of the last drop. "I know that NOW!"

Several people went before me and seemed to do fine, and as I entered the drop everything was going well. I shot off the shelf into the cauldron and got bobbled on a small rock that was usually completely under water. As I went off the second drop, I had no speed and dropped off the ledge at the same speed as the water. I went in pointed down, total meltdown. But what I did not realize was that drop became much higher and skinnier with less water in it. I had to angle slightly right going over it, but I hit the rock and it pushed me back to center as I dropped in. I dropped into the slot deep and as I surfaced I tried to paddle, but because I had nosed in my buoyancy had stopped any forward momentum. I was caught in the curtain of water coming off the drop. It threw me up in the air and flipped me over backward. I rolled up in the very skinny slot, and was now facing the waterfall that I had just come over. It pulled me in and shot me up in the air again, driving my body through the

55

curtain of water, and hitting the rock ledge behind it. It was an extremely violent slam against the wall, and at this point, I had little to no control. I knew I was in trouble.

I was upside down, under water, directly under the waterfall, and getting pounded in a slot about five feet wide. I was being pushed down by the falls only to have my shoulders slammed into something that stopped me from going down any further. I was desperate now, I pushed away from the falls with my paddle and rolled up enough to get a breath. I immediately went back underwater. I set up for a roll, this was absolute survival. This was extremely violent; I was being bashed back and forth between rocks on both sides of me. I felt like a piñata being hit from both sides. I rolled up again and was immediately flipped and blown against the left wall. My body was now being sucked into the pothole! It was like a trap waiting for someone to get close enough to suck them in. My paddle was across the hole keeping me from going in any further. I was pushing with everything I had away from the underwater hole. I could feel the water rushing down the bottomless hole past my head even pulling at my helmet. My bow was pointed downstream at this point, I could feel and hear my paddle hitting the rock on both sides of the hole.

I was able to get a breath by pushing on the edge of the pothole with my paddle blade, and then it slipped… back underwater. I went in with it. I knew I could not swim here. I also knew that someone died in this very same spot. If I got sucked into that hole I was monumentally fucked! I took my paddle and placed my blade on the edge of the pothole and pushed. It had seemed to work, but the paddle slipped again. When it did part of the paddle went into the pothole giving my boat momentum towards the waterfall and the back of my boat went under the powerful curtain of water again. It threw me up in the air and cartwheeled me so that I was upright facing the waterfall. At the same moment, the paddle had been ripped from my hands. I felt like extending my arms and saying, "the sacrifice will begin now" Yea…this is going to suck!

I tried to back paddle instantly with just my hands, guess what… that didn't work. I was drawn into the curtain of water again and again. I was thrown through the curtain of water into the rock wall behind it. Then I was upside down with no paddle, and trying to doggy paddle my way out of this mess. I was still being slammed back and forth into the rocks, and was now clawing at the rocks with my bare hands trying to get anything to help me. If I could feel a crack or the edge of a rock or handhold of any kind, I might have a chance. But the rock was smooth from thousands of gallons of water running through it nonstop for hundreds of years. I could feel myself being drawn back once again into the waterfall, and I was starving for air and starting to get tunnel vision. I just need one more breath. My adrenaline was maxed out, and I was doing the breaststroke underwater in an upside-down kayak trying to get away from a monster that wanted to rip my limbs off. Obviously, I was losing this fight. I could feel the rumble of the waterfall hitting the bottom of my boat as I was losing ground. I felt the back of my boat drop, and I was violently lunged forward. With my bow pointing downstream, I was finally able to push myself out of the hole and slot, upside down with no paddle. I could tell I was out, the water was not dark anymore, and the violence had stopped.

I pulled my spray skirt and swam. As I surfaced, I saw everyone gathering getting ready to save me. I was immediately helped to a small rock on the left side of the river not more than a few feet past the end of the slot. There a friend sat with my paddle, and he grabbed my boat as I scurried up onto the rock. He told me something I will not soon forget, "Dude, you were in there for more than a minute without your paddle!" Only a minute I thought, felt like half a day. It was cumbersome getting my stuff together. I was out of breath, dizzy, and in a lot of pain. I was in there for a long time, the dues were paid, and now I needed to get back into my boat and go down the rest of the river. When we reached the rapid known as Surform, I nailed my line! It felt great, the guys with a watchful eye on me even cheered and clapped for me.

It was hard to leave it behind me. When something like that happens, it eats at you. At the end of the day or the beginning of a run, there was always that time you got beat up. The truth will set you free. It will also scare the ever-living shit out of you. I couldn't say I almost died, I never said that. You would hear people say that from time to time, but I was not even close to dying. I did not need resuscitation or a shock to the heart, I didn't need a stretcher, and I did not even go to the doctor's office. I took some Advil and went and got a sub, drank some scotch by the campfire, and slept in the back of my truck that night. The next morning I ran the river again, but that time I did the sneak at Knife Edge, you know… because you never break your own rules.

I ran the standard line for years after that at Knifes Edge on the Moose, and I never had a problem. I was not going to let one episode affect my day or my life. That was what I expected to happen from time to time, kayakers swim, sometimes class III sometimes class V.

8

The Blue Line

If you look at a map of New York State, you will see a pale blue line running through the upper right quadrant. Inside the blue line lies the Adirondack Park of New York State. Also known as The 46 (referring to its 46 peaks), The Adirondack Park covers 18,702 square miles. It is the largest publicly protected area in the United States, greater in size than Yellowstone, Everglades, Glacier, and Grand Canyon National Park combined. It is world renowned for its exquisite scenery, hiking trails, and ski slopes. To the locals, it is known for excessive taxes, outrageous building codes, unemployment, black flies, and harsh winters.

No one knows how many rivers run through the Adirondacks (ADK). New York State itself holds approximately 119 true class V Rivers and hundreds of class IV rivers, the vast majority of which are in or near the blue line. The ADK and outlying area hold a lifetime of good whitewater. In the spring you can kayak for a week without ever seeing another kayaker. Typically, river releases occur in the summer and fall. At this time, several kayakers converge on one area. It's like a family reunion with a lot of family members you don't like showing up. Show-offs, geeks, newbies, loudmouths, vegetarians, the guys with the matching gear, cute couples trying something new, kid kayakers, know-it-alls, people who make their own paddles, the occasional kayak instructor masquerading as a guru, and the smelly guy. For the most part, they all begrudgingly get along because they have their own ideas on how to live life, and life on the river are two completely different things. When the ADK is roaring, you drop everything and go.

The Beaver Keeper

The Beaver River was a well-known kayaking spot that had been running for years. The water was controlled by the "Beaver Keeper," who was in charge of opening the dams and releasing the water. I had known him for years and always had a good conversation with him about hunting, fishing, and of course the Beaver River. He told me many of the secret facts behind the Beaver. The facts that many people have strived to know but never quite get a grasp on, like the Beaver runs all the time in early spring simply because of overflow, the intakes can only handle so much water, after that the water goes directly to the canyon. If you know how much the intake can absorb and subtract that amount from the overall CFS of a river gauge below the output, you can get a handle on how much liquid is in the canyon. The real trick is finding out how much the brim can hold back before the runoff begins; surface area, barometric pressure, humidity, spring growth rate, and loam moister retention all come into play. But that is a secret that only the Beaver Keeper and I know, it's much too complicated to explain.

I worked hard to acquire a friendship with the Beaver Keeper. Knowledge is power and power has a quiet way of getting things done when no one is looking.

The night before I was going to run the Beaver River, I broke two cardinal rules. The first was to never get to a river on an empty stomach, and the second was to never drink whiskey directly from the bottle. The Beaver Keeper himself had stopped by, had a few drinks, left me a bottle of whisky, and promised me a breakfast pizza for the next morning. Regardless of how passive one may think the Beaver is, the Beaver can turn on you and you will be left with what is called 'a yard sale.' All of your gear gets strewn about in the waves and you're left hoping your friends will pick up the pieces and throw them to shore. But the rules had already been broken; it was too late for me now.

The next morning, people were filing in on a single lane dirt road to hit the Beaver before the crowds. After eating breakfast pizza, I started my transmogrification from ordinary human to gnarly kayaker dude. As I pulled my kayak off the roof of my vehicle, my mind began to focus. All the noise faded into the distance, my view narrowed, and I became pointed. My hands and face were scarred from previous encounters; there was no consideration for the pain, the weather, the chaos, broken paddles, broken boats, or broken people. It was the discipline of living at the edge of fear and pushing through.

"I will live, I will perform, but right now I really have to puke!" I ran to a tree that would hide my face and spewed breakfast pizza from my gullet. I returned to my platform, a piece of plywood that I stood on to finish getting dressed but ended up running back to the tree. After the fourth time in the woods, my friend Bugsy came over to me. "Marty, why don't you sit this one out man? You don't look too good." I was pale, sweaty, and felt like I had swallowed too much Adirondack granite. I nodded my head yes and pursed my lips together, partly to keep from vomiting again. I grabbed a bottle of water, a throw rope, and a chair and started walking toward the river.

I walked down to the Taylorville section of the river and set up by the first hole. The first big hole had a new name every year depending on who was running it. The first person I ever saw get destroyed in it was a friend of mine. Ever since then, I have called that hole, Caine's House. I sat in my trusty chair, practicing deep breathing exercises while in an existential meditation. I was jolted awake by the screaming of several people giving advice to someone above the hole. I looked up just in time to see him try to pull into the eddy above the hole. He flipped, washed into the middle of the river, and swam. I realized someone was about to have a worse morning than me. Fearing imminent death, he stood up and tried to hold himself from being pushed downriver into the hole. He was losing, inch-by-inch, as the gap between him and the maelstrom closed. I ran forward with my throw rope and yelled in a low controlled voice, "Hey buddy, rope." Only feet from the abyss, he looked over his shoulder and extended his hands. I threw my rope in with an underhand toss; it flew in slow motion as it came out of the bag and seamlessly landed across his chest. He grasped it with both hands and, as soon as he did, I ran backward. The rope grew heavy and taught and his body became long. I pulled him as fast as I could away from the hole, but he still dropped into it.

I managed to get him to the shallow end, but for a moment he disappeared. I kept pulling until he emerged again. I worked my way

61

down the rope toward him, hand over hand, until he was a few feet from shore. With my rope still in his hands, he stood up and walked out of the river. He looked me dead in the eyes for a brief moment and said from his heart, "Thank You." His friends gathered around him and thanked me as we stood almost shoulder to shoulder. "Wasn't that bad," he said, saving face. I promptly told him what I thought of him and said something to the effect of, "get the fuck off the river and stay off." After that, I repacked my rope, sat down, and chugged half of a large bottle of water. I closed my eyes again and wondered if perhaps there was a higher order to things that we really did not understand. No one else in the area even had a rope. What if I wasn't there? With my eyes still closed, I smiled at the sun and drifted off to sleep.

Eagle has Talons

There is a section of the Beaver River called Eagle. Eagle drops around 475fpm and it's one mile long.

My friend EK and I decided to run Eagle again because we thought it might be high enough to be fun. Walking into Eagle next to the dam, the first thing you will notice is the serene lake to your right. If you are a normal person and not a whitewater kayaker, it may catch your attention. A typical small ADK lake, nothing spectacular, and honestly most people are looking at their feet making sure they are not going to fall. The rock was very slippery, especially after it rained. As you approached the dam itself at the beginning of the run, it didn't look like much. This was because you were on the same level as the top of the dam. When you looked across the dam to the other side of the river there was a vertical rock wall. When you turned left and worked your way downriver, you were immediately taken back by the angle of the run. It looked like a fault line with water running through it. Granite slabs descend at a forty-five-degree angle from the left of the river, the side you were on, directly into the rushing torrent. The next thing you may have noticed was that you were looking across the creek at a wall of rock that went up a few hundred feet. That wall started at the waterline, and even though you were much higher than the water at that point the granite wall on the other side of the river still towered above you. It was impressive. Looking to your left and your eyes widened. You were looking at the whole run, and the angle of it was truly impressive. From a kayaker's standpoint, well ok my standpoint, it looked like a bobsled track with big fucking rocks in the way and water was slamming into all of them. The run dipped and dived out of sight and with every perfidious step forward it became evident. This was an impressive set of drops.

When EK and I got there, we simply dressed not thinking about the weeks' worth of rain that we had. I had paddled with EK for a while now; he stood six feet tall and had a thin muscular build. His hair was short and his face square like a boxer from the fifty's. He was dependable and strong, and I trusted him when he sat in a kayak.

We quickly noticed that no one else was even taking the boats off their vehicles, but we were already dressed. We had not pre-scouted the run, when we put our boats on our shoulders someone asked: "are you going to run that?" Kind of a stupid question really, we have all our gear on and kayaks on our shoulders why would anyone think otherwise. When he turned around and walked back toward the run, we looked at each other puzzled. Maybe we should look at it. We left our kayaks by the head of the trail and walked down in. There was no reason to waste the effort of taking kayaks, just in case we did not do the run for some reason. When we got there, the river was full. I mean full of water! Normally this run supports two or three hundred CFS.

The first thing we noticed was that the sluice and the water release channel were FULL of water. Then we saw that the dam had a lot of water going over it, normally it was dry. We had no real idea how much water was in the run, maybe between seven hundred and a thousand CFS; closer to one thousand I'd say. It was a rushing torrent and loud. Standing thirty feet above the river, we were getting misted with water and had to yell at each other to be heard. The water at the normal put in was easily five feet above standard. I looked at EK and said, "It's up to you, I will run it if you want to" he clenched his lips and shook his head yes. I felt my adrenaline jump, holy shit he said yes!

63

EK was super athletic and a decent kayaker, but one of the most emotionally needy people I ever met in the kayaking world. There were about a hundred other kayakers around and NO ONE wanted to run this river. I thought he would bail for sure. A guy stood next to us as we looked at the dam, "Let's run the dam," I said to EK. He smiled. As we turned to go to our new put in, the lake, the stranger standing next to me turned toward the growing crowd of spectators and yelled. "They are going to run the dam!"

We put in on the lake and paddled over to the dam. By the time we got there, several people were gathered around to watch us. Looking at the dam from the lake, we slowly worked our way past the safety buoys; you know the ones that said whatever you do don't go past these. A few feet away from the edge of the dam with water pulling us forward, we back paddled and surveyed the edge. I couldn't see shit! The only thing I could see was the tops of the trees that were at least thirty yards away, and a good view of the valley that looked like a view from an airplane. I paddled back to EK, who gave me a good ten count and looked for the crowd's reaction. I had a good friend in the crowd Tad, and I knew he had my back. EK nodded; we were both too nervous to spit. I really only knew one thing, I had to be square to the dam when I started over it. If I was sideways at all, I could flip, if I flipped it would be on the downstream side and might snap my neck on impact or be pushed down the coarse face of the dam and have my face ground off. My heart was pounding, and I could taste the adrenaline in my mouth as I charged toward the dam's edge and followed the water over it. The moment I hit it I realized that my boat was halfway over the lip and I still could not see the bottom of the dam. Then my boat tilted, straight down and I leaned as fucking far back on my boat as I could get! I felt that my boat and myself were going to cartwheel off the edge. Just then my bow slammed into the face of the dam, and I picked up speed. The dam was a little concave in the center of it, so it felt like I was free falling, and my heart went further into my throat. Simultaneously, I looked at the bottom of the dam and could see a giant rooster tail of water spraying up into the air eight feet. I was headed right for it hoping I didn't get rocketed up in the air and flipped. I had so much speed that I zipped through the spray like it was not there. The main flow of water shot me forward away from the bottom of the dam toward the wall on the right. I found an eddy behind a rock on the right side of the river next to the wall. I turned upstream and waited for EK, he seemed to take forever. Finally, over the edge, he came with the same breaking hinge action of his boat. His eyes were big and his mouth was wide open as he careened down the face of the dam hitting the eight-foot rooster tail. He zipped through the spray with as much speed as I did and shot in my direction.

He dropped into my eddy beside me and over the roaring river, we heard the crowd whistle and yell. Looking over we saw the spectators clapping. My friend on shore gave us the thumbs up, turned, and walked downstream to watch us on the next set of drops.

Now we were across from the normal put in and we paddled out of the eddy. Normally there was nothing significant, except for one pour over between the put in and the first big drop. Only that pour over was now FULL of water and became a hole about six feet high that went all the way across the river. Albeit one spot that green water seemed to be shooting through on the extreme right side of the river. I hit it with as much speed as I could get and shot off the edge of the hole while leaning right on a hard brace. I hit the eddy so hard I almost flipped. EK was a ten count behind me and came into the eddy with BIG eyes. When we looked at this drop from the top of the dam on the trail it did not look anywhere near this big. I knew what he was thinking, "The rest of the run is going to be huge." We had only looked at this drop, not the rest of the run! But now we were into it and this was our life for now. Besides, I saw a few girls in the crowd and if I lived I might have a chance.

I thrusted out into the main flow of the water and headed toward the next drop. This was the first big drop of the run. At the top of the drop from the boat, I could see a granite slab on the left of the river that was going toward the base of the wall. The water was fast and high. Not only was there water going down the run next to the wall where it always went, but the slab of granite next to the river was also covered with water now and it was flowing into the crevice that I needed to be in all the way down the wall. The water was slamming into and piling up on the wall, which caused a rolling boil of white water six feet high or higher down the length. There was

65

also a bus-sized boulder at the bottom of the wall that most of the water was crashing into. It didn't look as bad as I thought.

I nodded at EK and he nodded back. I looked at the crowd and received another thumbs up from my friend. I moved from the left of the river to the right. I wanted to start the run close to the wall so I had less of a chance of flipping when I hit the maelstrom of water bouncing off the wall. The whitewater was your friend. If you leaned into the bubbles, it would deliver you from evil. I leaned into it hard, lifting my left knee, with my elbows tight, I dropped into the mix. The massive boil was on my right, and I was surprised at how tall the pile was. I went and I was nowhere near the bottom of it. Halfway through the drop I leaned forward and pushed my right paddle blade forward from a hard brace so I could turn it into a forward paddle stroke. I shot down the run headed straight toward the massive boulder. There was a pile of cushiony water on the boulder that was seven feet high. Just as I was getting to the boulder, I pulled my right paddle blade back taking a strong paddle stroke. It shot me down off the pile. The front of my boat was now pointing toward the left of the river. I shot across the front of the boulder, missing the boulder all together. I quickly paddled over to a big eddy on the left of the river and looked up the river at EK. He was in the run and eclipsed by the breaking wall of whitewater falling back into the main crease of the river. He rode the tube out, ending up a little higher on the boulder than I did, but made it without flipping. He was breathing heavy when he came into the eddy and I could see the blood pulse through the veins in his face. He was worked up! His nostrils were flared and his eyes were dilated. I probably looked the same way! There was a bigger drop in front of us, and we both knew it.

We turned around in the eddy and looked downstream. The river necked down, and the only thing we saw was the skyline. On the left of the river was another big boulder with water slamming into it which caused a big curling wave that was being pushed toward the right of the river. The only thing was that I remembered the line ran through a small hole next to the boulder, and I would have to stay towards the left of the river so I could make the slide. The entrance of the line was half as wide as it normally was in the river. Meaning there was twice as much water and power and I thought, "yea this should be good!"

The crowd worked its way past us, but no one said a word. Many of them were kayakers, and they knew distractions could be bad. People lined up looking at the drop and pointing down at it. "Geeze I'm glad that's not distracting!" I thought to myself. I looked downriver at that wave and the copious amounts of water pushing its way through the drop. I could almost feel the rock that I had my hand on vibrating. I looked at EK and yelled, "I am going to start on the right side of the river. T up to the wave and see what happens." The right side was usually full of a shit ton of rocks just sticking out of the water that screwed up your line, but today everything was under water. The adrenaline was using oozing out of my ears!

Behind that wave was a slide that I had not yet seen that day, but I did know that at the bottom of it was one big motherfucking hole. The slide was tight and fast, and it dropped directly into that hole. This was important to get through. We were both in big creek boats today and if we got stuck in that hole, we were going to have a short day and a long time getting to the end of it.

I looked at EK after telling him my plan, and he looked surprised but nodded his head yes. He knew that my line was my line. He did not have to run it, but he was a little insecure, so he would probably just run it like I did. You know if I made it. I glanced at the crowd and they looked nervous. Most were unshaven wide-eyed men. The women were clenching their fists. One thumb was up, and I nodded and thrusted myself into the main flow. I shot across the creek almost instantly with my ferry angle, and I turned downstream on the extreme right side of the river. I was surprised at the power of the creek; it was moving me much faster than I had anticipated. My bow was pointing left and I needed to get ahead of the water, which meant I needed speed. I was aiming directly at the boulder that caused the wave. If I hit that boulder things could go badly for me. I could get stopped, sucked under water and pinned, or flipped and flushed down the slide upside down. But it was time for the push. I was paddling hard at right of the boulder. When I was five feet from the boulder, I hit the massive wall of water that was being redirected by the boulder. I leaned forward and paddled. I was

67

instantly thrown five feet to the right as I made it to the peak of the wave. As I broke through the peak of the wave, the boulder was now only feet from my left shoulder, and I was leaning toward the right. My line was good as I dropped the eight feet to the beginning of the slide. I couldn't see shit, the slide was full of water, and it was shaped like a U. I basically disappeared into a tunnel of water. There was no paddling there, no fancy moves, and no showboating for the crowd. There was only one thing to focus on, and that was hole at the end of the tunnel of water. I could see it now spitting water about eight feet in the air. I couldn't go deep. The left side of it was a rock wall. I pulled a move that I had done here before; just before the hole, I thrusted my legs to the right and lifted my left knee while keeping my left paddle blade in the water. As I approached the hole, I could hear a hollow sucking sound of water pouring into a deep cavern, but I refused to look at it. My eyes were fixed on my line, as I hit the hole my boat skipped through the edge of the hole on the right, and it pointed me directly into the eddy. I turned on a dime and stopped a few feet from the hole. I executed it perfectly, and the crowd literally cheered. I was now in the biggest eddy of the run. I was in control and happy as I breathe a sigh of relief.

The thumbs up went to EK, telling him all was good. I moved away from the hole back into the eddy so I wouldn't distract him or get in his way. When I saw him come over the wave next to the boulder, I noticed he was late. He ended up lower on the run, which caused him to go into the slide at more of an angel from right to left. He dropped into the slide and went up onto the left side of the slide. He was high because that was the way he was pointed. He hit the hole dead center and was consumed by its depths. He completely disappeared for what seemed like forever. He rocketed out of the river and his boat came completely out of the water. The crowd gave a collective loud, "Whoa!" As he landed clear of the hole, they cheered once again. He paddled over to me and we high fived. He immediately mentioned that he couldn't see shit in the slide and had no idea where he was. He wasn't overly happy with his line, but at the same time he was relived! We retreated to the back edge of the big eddy and let the crowd work their way down to the next drop. We talked about how pushy the creek was and how hard it was getting through the wave at the top without getting handled. After he saw my line, he was afraid of hitting the boulder. I had only missed it by a foot, so he came in later than I did. I told him that I honestly went into the wave really early. I was a little afraid of hitting it myself.

Looking downstream, we could see the crowd setting up. The next drop was fairly high, but it was a point and shoot. I looked at EK, and he said he wanted to go first. That was fine with me. We let ourselves float slowly toward the next drop. We briefly looked at the crowd for the thumbs up and then EK took off toward the left of the river. This drop was always a dirty bouncy line. You had to start on the left and work your way to the right, don't hit the wall, don't get caught in the death-defying recalculating eddy, and whatever you do, DON'T FLIP! If you flipped you would get pinned on the two rocks that you had to go around at the end of the drop. But today there was so much water that the wall on the left side of the river was half covered, and was pushing all of the water to the right just like the drop above. It looked really nasty, like a brown boiling soup. But when EK went into it, he skipped right through it! He grabbed an eddy on the low side, pointed himself upstream, and waited for me. I worked my way over to the left of the river and pointed toward the right of the river as I went over the drop. I was concerned about the bad eddy and wanted to get past it with vigor. I pounded over the drop and started paddling hard. I shot down past the wall of boiling water and then through the shitty water so fast that I hit the wall on right of the river. My bow stopped and I almost flipped over, but I pushed off the wall and bobbled downstream.

When EK saw that I was ok he took off down the river, and I dropped into the same eddy he was previously in; after all the choices were limited. After that drop the creek was amazing, and there was only one big drop left at the end of the run. But the creek was full of holes, heavy eddy lines, and confused water. Every rock that was once in the way was now under water and had turned into a hole, a sticky hole! I followed EK as he worked his way back and forth across the river, avoiding these pour over-holes. I was picking my own lines and having fun. The only thing was that I was moving faster than EK and I needed to slow down. He had a tendency to float sideways a lot, but I had been pinned too many times and liked to keep my boat pointing downstream, so naturally I moved a little faster. I back paddled a few times and let myself get caught in an eddy line to slow me down. I Looked upstream and saw people filtering away. Not many people cared about the last drop, so they decided to cut and run, but I saw my friend walk by with a few people toward the waterfalls. I was not in a hurry. I eddied out and held my position for a little while. As I took off downriver again, EK was taking his sweet fucking time. I had to stall again! I hated that because it screwed up my rhythm. Now we were getting close to the falls. Normally it was not a big deal because you could run it left, right, or center. It made no difference really. At least when the water was at a normal level.

EK turned downstream and was ready for the push. He pointed directly at the center of the falls and paddled hard in order to lung himself forward. Just before the falls in the middle of the river was a rock. Usually we would simply go to the right or left of it, but today it was underwater. EK went right over the top of it! Of course, it was a pour over now! EK disappeared for a moment and was completely out of my sight. I back paddled because I was too close if there were issues. Then, he literally flew up into the air and never touched the lip of the waterfall. He flew over it! I had never seen anything like it before or since then! The remaining crowd went wild and erupted in cheers. I was happy for him, but I needed speed. My plan was not to go over that rock into the hole, but to flank it just to the left and use the water coming out of the hole to help push me over the falls. I picked up my pace and pounded toward the falls. I pointed my bow just to the left of the rock by about three feet. Thinking that was enough to catch the downstream flow coming out of the hole. When I got there I was really fucking wrong! It stopped me dead and turned me into the side of the surf. I was five yards above the lip of the falls and not moving on a hard-right side paddle brace, this was bad! The water was POUNDING over the falls just in front of me. I had to get out of this. I reached forward with my right paddle blade and buried it into the water and pulled while simultaneously lunging my torso forward, in order to gain an inch or two. I did it again and again and was inching forward. Further from doom closer to hell! The falls in front of me was roaring. I was finally out of the piece of the shit hole and I had nearly snapped my paddle trying to get speed with the two paddle strokes I had. I slid over the falls with no speed and did a complete meltdown.

I was completely vertical and completely underwater. I was upside down beneath the waterfall. I was getting pounded by so much water that my boat was being pushed under water five feet, and was popping back up only to be pushed under again. I was holding my breath and it felt like I was in a washing machine. I was being flung back and forth with no control what so ever. I couldn't see anything but bubbles and the occasional rock wall, which I assumed was the waterfall. What did I know? I knew I needed air, I knew my bow was facing towards the right of the river, and that was the way I wanted to go to get out of this fiasco. I extended my left paddle blade forward toward my bow and rifled it across to try to roll. My head charged out of the water and I took in some air. I guessed I was not dying in there, but it was really unpleasant! I tried it again and rifled my paddle across my left side while I snapped my hips. I got another breath. I was getting closer to the right side and it was becoming less violent. Again, I got a breath and pushed off the wall underwater. Again, and again I rolled up, and I was being sucked back into the waterfall. Underwater I paddled hard and slow with a backward movement. I could feel the water starting to batter the back of my boat. Oh no, oh no, my front end was starting to lift. I leaned forward and paddled. All at once I got airborne, I came completely out of the water, and I got kicked away from the falls and landed in relatively calm waters. Just like EK, I shot out like a watermelon seed! The crowd went wild as I made my roll. EK was shaking his head with a big smile on his face. "That's not even possible," was his only statement. Haha, that's when I knew the truth, I had become immortal. I always knew it, but now it was evident. My friend Tad on shore told me that he had never seen anyone, "paddle underwater to their destination before." But I was lucky, and I knew it.

For years after this run on the Eagle this occasion was mentioned to me, sometimes by people that were there and sometimes by people that had heard about it. There were photos and fireside stories about the day the Eagle was big and out of all of the kayakers only two ran it.

71

Today Eagle has been run by hundreds of people. Some people trying to see how many laps they could get in an hour. Other people stood on the granite slab, a slab that was older than man himself. Tourists standing around drinking a beer and hoping to film a crash and burn.

Where once stood a Church there now stands a playground. Opinions varied, of course.

Hulls Falls, Ausable River

It was another spring trip with the A team: Bugsy, Carpenter, Si, Warden, Lew and myself. We were trudging north to the Ausable River. Our goal was to run five new rivers, which four of those rivers were class five. The Ausable was a class IV+, but the definitions varied depending on the water level and mentality of the boaters. The thing about the Hulls Falls section was that it descended into a very steep canyon. The canyon very hard to ascend out of if not impossible.

As we arrived, we walked out onto the bridge. We were excited to look at the river, and I was amazed by what I saw. Most of the ADK rivers were stained brown. The brown color came from water that sept through the pine-covered forests of the ADK. The tannic acid that had accumulated in the pine needles would wash into the rivers. The rivers usually looked like root beer, but the Ausable River was crystal clear. Looking upstream from the bridge you could see a snow-capped mountain, and looking downstream you could see the river descending into the canyon with sheer granite rock on either side with clear mountain water carving its way unimpeded through the canyon. The average gradient of the Ausable was 70fpm, but down in the canyon before and after Champaign Falls it became 165fpm. The whole run was only about three miles long and could be run in a few hours.

I was standing on the bridge and was looking directly down at the first real drop, Hulls Falls. To me, the line was evident. You simply had to go over the right side of the fall and not hit the really big granite boulder on the right. The water would direct you where to go, so you just had to go with it. I mentioned the line to one of my comrades and he agreed. But here was the problem, the bridge was quite high over the falls, and I was looking directly down at it. I also had very little depth perception since one of my eyes didn't work properly, but I had lived with this issue all of my life and it very seldom came into play. I never looked at the drop standing at the edge of it. I always looked down at the drop from the bridge. For me it was like looking at a painting at the bottom of a set of stairs for anyone else. It looked flat. However, it was not flat! I probably should have considered that, especially because my face was being covered with the mist from the falls!

By the time I was dressed and ready to go, some of my guys were already on the water and working their way toward the drop. As I worked my way through the boogie above the drop, I started to realize that some of the holes were very sticky. We had already done six rivers that week, and we were tuned up and sharp with our skills in order. I was not really concerned. As I worked my way down, I watched Carpenter and Bugsy disappear over the drop on the right side of the river. They dropped where I thought they should be so I headed that way. I knew that as I went over the falls I needed to point my bow to the left and hang on for the ride. As I headed to the ledge, I suddenly realized that the falls were MUCH higher than I thought. I leaped off the edge and my adrenaline spiked! I had the speed I needed but I did not anticipate the free fall! The river was all white as I flew into the foam and disappeared. I couldn't see anything! I landed in a cushion of water only to hit a piece of ADK granite that shot my boat to the left of the river. Halfway across the bottom of the falls I still couldn't see anything because of the despotic whitewater flying up all around me. I hit another boulder somewhere in the mess and flipped! I flipped to my left, and I knew this was going to be bad because I did not want to be thrown into the curtain of the waterfall and be trammeled to death. I honestly didn't know how I did it, but I rolled up using my right paddle blade so quickly that no one knew that I had actually flipped. I was still in the mix of the white foamy mess and ended up flying out the other side of it to the clear green water. I was now on the extreme left side of the river looking up at the twenty-foot falls, but I was upright, and nothing was broken! I honestly thought the falls were like eight feet high and was surprised when I had the chance to look at it.

I looked at the guys in the pool below, and they gave me a casual thumbs up as if I had run my line perfectly. Maybe I did, I didn't know since I had not seen them run it. I worked my way over to the guys and waited for Warden, Si, and Lew. They did not run it the way I did, but it all worked out. We worked our way down the river, and started boat scouting through the next two rocky drops. As we were scouting, the walls around us continued to ascend and became higher and higher. The water was fresh snowmelt from the mountains and it was really cold. As we continued our descent into the canyon, I could almost see my breath. Lew commented to me that the canyon would be a great place to fish. As much as I loved to fish, it was the furthest thing from my mind at that moment. The first drop was an eye-opener for me, and I was no longer complacent about this river as it started to narrow. We spread ourselves out as we worked our way down the river. We snapped into a creeking mode. We gave each other room to perform by slipping back and forth across the river and dropping in every eddy we could find as we boat scouted our way down.

In front of us we saw a skyline, and we knew this was the beginning drop to a waterfall called Champagne Falls.

It was called Champagne Falls because of one factor. As the water careened over the falls it landed on a plethora of granite boulders. As the water worked its way through the sieves, it became aerated and was forced out at the bottom of the river with great downstream force. The bubbles would re-emerge up to twenty yards below the falls in the clear river water. This caused the Champaign bubble effect in the water. It was beautiful and mesmerizing to watch. The downside was if you were in a kayak and went over the falls in the wrong spot you could become part of the sieve. The water would pound on you until you broke up into little pieces like the bubbles and it wouldn't be beautiful anymore.

We stepped out of our kayaks on the left of river and scouted the lead in drops to the main drop at the falls. But from there we couldn't see the line over the falls itself. There were two drops above the falls. The first one was simple, just stay centered with the angle of the left of the river. The second was a little trickier.

Generally, when I looked at a drop, I wouldn't look for the fear in the drop. In other words, I don't look for something to be afraid of. I look for the "fun" part of the drop, as in, if you messed this up, you were going to have "fun" in there. Some people didn't see it the way I did. Some people looked at a rapid and said to themselves, 'don't go there, don't do that.' Your mindset could make you or break you. The more you'd think about something, the more your mind would play it up into something it wasn't. This happened to everyone at one time or another, and it affected your performance on the river.

We all carried some sort of superstition with us; our rituals to kept us safe. Years ago, I had a paddle that was an awesome blade but had a slipper shaft. I went through a rapid with it and just as I threw one critical paddle stroke, my hands slipped together on the shaft and I flipped. After that, a friend of mine introduced me to kicker wax. Kicker wax is made for the bottom of cross-country skis to help gain a grip on the snow. When it is put on a paddle shaft it stops your hands from sliding. Though that paddle was long gone, I still used the wax every time I went on a river because I believed it kept me from making bad moves. The second ritual I had was to get dressed slowly. There was no reason to be in a hurry. I was there to have fun and not to be stressed out. I dressed in the same order every time. By the time I put my helmet on, my mindset had changed. I became a quiet fighter. I was impenetrable through the clothes and safety gear I had on.

So, as I was looking at the set of drops I said to myself, "Go down here and turn left and shoot out into the slow-moving pool of water above the waterfall." The guy next to me, however, might say to himself, "Yeah, I am going to go through the first drop picking up speed. Take like four paddle strokes picking up more speed, careen off the second drop, and follow the water. Then I will hit the big fucking granite cliff that goes up two hundred feet from the bottom of the river. When the river catches the back of my kayak because I'm not pointing to the left, I will be driven to the bottom of the cliff eight feet under water. If I don't die down there, I will end up going over the waterfall sideways, if I do that and live, I will be paralyzed for life." But not me, I used kicker wax that day so I was going to go down there and turn left. What you believe in your mind makes all the difference. You could second guess yourself all you wanted, but it would not make you a better kayaker. When in doubt ask advice from people you trust on the water. People that would not get you revved up. People that made hard things easy, then say to you if you had any issues, "I will be there for you." With that kind of confidence you could inspire people to do great things.

So, the first drop was simple, but the second drop was a little tricky. Most of the water in the river cut to the right and went off the second drop. But at the end of the drop was the previously mentioned rock wall. The water was hitting the wall and going up the wall about six feet before the water fell back into the river. Some of the water rushed off the wall towards the downriver, the rest seemed to fall back into the rush of the oncoming water. The trick was you had to lean INTO the wall and hit the wave on the wall sideways. It seemed counter-intuitive to turn yourself sideways, but if you were in a play boat you could surf across the front of it. Unfortunately, today was creak boats because there was a possibility of your boat being driven underwater if your bow ended up being stuck on the wall for some reason. Leaning into the wall kept you from flipping, theoretically.

I dropped in first, excited to hit the wall and shoot off the top of the wave out into the pool. I was surprised at the speed of the river, and when I hit the wall wave, I went up the wall much further than I thought I would. I then shot down the face and jetted out into the slow-moving pool. For me, it was a great fun move. There were a lot of eddies in the pool on right of the river. It was like a boulder beach leading to the continuing cliff. The left side of the pool was just another cliff that went directly into the water. After I was through the wall wave, I worked my way close to the waterfall and found an eddy so the guys would have room to catch an eddy above me and we wouldn't become crowded. The slow-moving pool I was in was about fifteen yards wide and became faster the closer it got to the waterfall. As I watched the guys make their run, they were all looking good. I turned my attention to the Champaign Falls, the reason we were here. But the only thing I could see was a skyline with the fantastic granite walls on each side. I could see a little bit of the pool at the bottom, but it was just the outer edge of the pool. Directly below the falls, I couldn't see anything. As I turned to look upstream again, I saw the last guy working his way into the wave wall. He hit it sideways, was pushed up the wall, and flipped at the top! Now upside down the wave held him for about four seconds and shot him out into the trough of the pool. Ten seconds later he still hadn't rolled up! I saw his boat upside down take the familiar jerk; he was going to swim! Moments later, I saw his head emerge from the river. He was already halfway to the waterfall; Warden was in real trouble. I was the lowest in the river and had the best chance of recovery.

I quickly turned my boat and shot out into the river above the waterfall. I was screaming at him, "I'm here! I'm here! Look at me I'm here!" Warden was looking away from me and started to swim to the wrong side of the river. He was swimming toward the rock wall on left of the river and I was feet from him screaming at him at the top of my lungs. We were both closing in on the falls, but I was not going to fucking leave him! I was next to him still screaming "Grab me! GRAB ME!" He had let his boat and paddle go and was on a beeline to the wall, he was yelling "HELP! HELP!" I was pissed off that he was not responding to me, so I hit him on the head with my paddle blade. That action snapped him back into reality, and he turned and lunged for my kayak. I turned my kayak back toward the eddy I came from as he grabbed the loop on the back of my boat. My first thought was, "I'm not going to make it." We were about seven yards from the edge of the waterfall. I dug in my paddle blade and dove myself toward safety. As I did, I had so much adrenaline that I pulled myself from his grip. He was now floating free once again.

I felt the boat leap forward and knew something went wrong, so I looked over my shoulder. I was about five feet from Warden, he was just out of my reach! I back paddled two strokes, and once again he had me. I knew this was our last chance since we were about five feet from the edge of the falls. I drove my paddle blade into the river once again. I hit the water in triple time as my paddle shaft bowed

77

under the strain. I was pointed slightly upstream as Warden kicked and helped push me forward. I was not aware of anything going on around me, I had tunnel vision. All I knew was I was not going to stop paddling until I hit the shore. I finally hit the slack water created by the boulders and drove myself into the side of the river. Warden worked his way, hand over hand, up my boat. He touched the bottom of the river with his feet and liberated himself from the clutches of the river by launching himself up onto a small boulder next to me. He splayed his arms over the rock, I saw his hands grip it tight, he turned to me, took two deep breaths, and while still breathing heavily said, "Thanks for saving my life." I nodded my head and glanced back at the waterfall over my shoulder, his boat and paddle were gone.

Just at that moment, Lew ran past us with a throw rope in his hand and stood at the edge of the falls. He started yelling at me, "MART! Go over right there." He was pointing at the spot. He wanted me to chuck myself over the falls. We had to get his boat back! It had gone over the drop and was headed downstream. I pushed myself back into the main flow and lined myself up, pointing my bow at the end of Lew's finger. I had never seen this drop before and had no idea how high it was or what was down there. I just went! I shot past Lew's finger and became airborne. I landed with a good angle in a cushion of soft aerated water. I was followed by Bugsy and Carpenter, and we work our way into a big pool below the falls. Warden's paddle made it through seemingly unscathed, and we caught his boat before it got out of the pool. But the boat was busted up with a huge dent in the left side of the bow that was the size of a basketball where the plastic was caved in. But, it didn't look like the plastic was ripped at all. At this point, we didn't know if it would leak. But we had a bigger problem!

The swimmer was gorged up. My buddy Warden couldn't climb out of the canyon where he was currently. He also couldn't get down to us in the pool. He definitely couldn't get back to the put in. He was in a boxed-up gorge with no way out! Yelling back and forth, we established a few facts. He was safe and stable for the moment. He couldn't go up, he couldn't go back, and he couldn't descend, now what? Talking with the guys, I told them that if we had to rope him out from the top that it would take hours. We had to do the rest of the run leave him behind, and then come back and find him! It was late in the day, by the time we could get back to him, it might have been dark. No one wanted that. My mind was reeling and so was everyone else, we were at a loss. After a long pause, I looked up at him and yelled, "JUMP!"

Warden's reply was immediate, "t's too high!" My reply, of course was, "It's only as high as a basketball hoop!"

"You're full of shit," was his quick retort.

I explained it to him, "It looks high because you are in a gorge, the water is clear." I asked him if there were any rocks on the bottom of the river that might impede his jump into the water. Bugsy was behind me floating in his kayak talking into my ear, "You're going to kill him. Don't let him jump, you're going to kill him."

Warden tells me that he can't see any rocks in the water that he might hit. So, I say, "OK, then JUMP!" I could see Warden contemplate his options and struggled with the obvious answer as he looked for another way out. I saw his body relax, his face dropped, and he had excepted his fate. The only way out was down!

On his little ledge, he could take about two and a half steps. He walked back and forth to get his timing down. He needed to get a good push off from the ledge where he was perched to make it into the middle of the pool below him. While he was testing his legs, Bugsy was still behind me saying, "I don't know the man!"

"He will be fine," I say as Warden wound himself up. After two big steps and a great leap, he found himself in the air easily four times higher than the falls we just went over. He fell at maximum velocity; he was in the air for three seconds before hitting the water line and disappearing into the middle of the pool. I turned to Bugsy and said, "Wow that was really high!" I was thinking to myself, "Maybe the guy with no depth perception shouldn't be telling people what to jump off from."

79

Warden was underwater for a good eight seconds, long enough for us to paddle out to him just as he was rocketing up out of the depths. Good thing he had a life jacket on! He blew the water out of his nose and yelled, "THAT WAS HIGHER THAN A BASKETBALL HOOP!"

We helped him to shore next to his dented kayak and we eventually worked our way down the river. The kayak did not seem to be leaking, so all was good. We loaded up and headed to a campsite near the next river we were going to do. We broke into the whiskey that we saved for special occasions, like not dying, and did surgery on Warden's boat. Carpenter boiled water on the fire and gathered the wood chunks that he thought would work. He poured the hot water into the kayak and gathered another pot full from the lake at our doorstep and set it on the fire. The ADK loons were telling stories of legends at the edge of the sun, as the warm glow of the fire soften our resolve a bit. Carpenter poured another pot of boiling water into Warden's kayak and started working out the massive dent with the wood blocks he had gathered. Little by little the dent disappeared, leaving only a small indentation. We were happy the plastic had not cracked during the process. "A Basketball Hoop!" Warden would randomly yell, as the rest of us busted out laughing and would take another sip of whiskey. The loons had their own haunting story to tell as the sun faded quietly into the Adirondack Granit. The next day we went kayaking again because that is what we would do.

The Branch

The short run that lasted forever. If you looked at The Branch from a distance it looked like a well-done painting. Its continuously dropping water made rippling white lines that streamed down its tiered face among the small pools of dark green almost placid water. The shore was clad in dark gray granite boulders with an accent of green moss atop of them. At the edge of the granite stood the rich green pins with their fingertips that reached for every ounce of sunshine they could find.

It was a beautiful ADK river with class IV whitewater that lead to big class V drops. Making the line was important. It was always a big day on The Branch.

I had run The Branch several times, each time it was epic, and created memories that last a lifetime. The Branch would run in the spring or during heavy rain. With an average gradient of 140 fpm, The Branch would capture your attention, the pucker factor on this one was high. Every time I have thought of The Branch, one person stuck out in my memory. My good friend Si. On that outing The Branch was big and cold. You knew a river was big when you were next to a drop looking at the possible lines and you had to scream at the person next to you so they could hear you. You could feel the vibration through the ground as it worked its way through your feet, to your mind, and finally your eyes would widen while your breath quickened with your heartbeat. The moment you made your decision adrenaline would spew into your system, right or wrong, the decision was made. "Yea! We will run it big!" The lines looked soft and open, but the holes were tumultuous. We decided to set safety, we'd run one at a time as the rest of us watched on different tiers of the drop with throw ropes in hand. I was with My "A's": Bugsy, Carpenter, Si and a couple others that day and felt comfortable with the decisions. Among the first drops were a series of ledges and beneath them were the type of hole that changed your outlook on life. It was necessary to get a good pop; one good paddle stroke off the edge of the falls to boof the hole at the bottom. On the landing, it was optimal to be leaning forward, paddle at the ready for another hard paddle stroke to keep you from getting pulled back into the maelstrom.

It was a cold shitty day and the next river was not far away, so we were not in a hurry on this short run. I was the second or third to run the first set of drops. As I slid into the river, I could feel the cold radiate through my boat, it was pushy and fast that day. I felt I would ace this run, but I also knew that arrogance doesn't come with a snorkel. I worked my way to the center of the river above the series of drops to start my line. I glanced left and saw one of the guys, the skyline, and the tops of trees. This was higher than I remembered; I looked for the guide stone and the gleam of fast green water that would direct me with speed to the first big ledge. I was moving with motivation as I adjusted the angle of my boat. A big right sweeping paddle stroke to point left and then a big left paddle stroke forward to stay the proper distance from the guide rock that I would be on my left three feet away. As I got there the run opened up. The trick was to focus and only look where you knew you needed to go and not get distracted by the chaos to your left and right. One line and one line only. In the fast-green water my kayak tilted downhill and I picked up even more speed. Three hard paddle strokes and a big sweeping stroke on my left squared me up to the angle of the first ledge. Power, power, power through the confused water four feet above, four, three, two, one, BOOF hard left paddle stroke. Over I went landing in the aerated water in my creek boat. I nearly submerged, and the water rushed in over my head. As the cold ADK water slapped my face, my skin tightened, my eyes squinted, and my grip constricted. Fast strokes had me pulling myself away from the hole, I had to earn this one. Up on to the solid rushing water, I needed to get to the right. I picked up my left knee and leaned right paddling hard. I could see the next boulder to the right of my ledge drop; deep paddle strokes then ten feet away and I needed speed! Three feet above the lip, I took a right sweeping stroke and then squared myself to the drop. But I wanted to go over the drop with a little right angle. Two, one, BOOF off my big left paddle stroke I landed almost behind the boulder I passed on my right. Into a fast-moving strip of green water, I used a Duffek stroke to pull my bow to the left. I buried my right paddle deep to create more surface area and launched myself forward, knowing that after the next drop I had to get into the eddy on the left of the river. Still, in the strip of fast water, my boat planed out just before the lip of the drop. I threw a hard-right paddle stroke and caught air, landing with the front of my boat just inside the eddy I needed to be in. With my forward momentum, I took one left paddle stroke and leaned left, hitting the eddy at a blistering pace and used my left paddle blade on the top of the water to brace my boat up. In order to keep me from flipping, I came to an abrupt stop and looked upstream while sitting in the eddy. One of the guys grabbed the front of my boat from the shore; I pulled off my spray skirt, stepped into the shallow water next to the bank, grabbed my boat, and stepped out of the river. I turned my boat around and found a small plateau; the boat was safe and ready for a quick entry if necessary.

The guys all gathered saying that my line looked good and were inquisitive on how it felt. "The first hole was sticky," I said, "Tough entry, just make sure you have speed. I had a hard time getting out of the backwash." When it came time for Si to make the run. He looked good as he worked his way toward the rock on the top, but as he grew closer, I thought that he was too close. However, everyone ran lines a little different so I was not concerned. That was until he was next to the first lead-in rock, that rock tapered off slowly underwater. He bumped the bottom of his boat in the shallow water next to the rock, which not only slowed him down but it turned him a little bit as his boat took on a downhill angle. As he headed toward the next boulder at the launch point, he slowed down even more in the confused water just above the drop as he tried to square up his boat. Going over the first drop, he was a little sideways and did not get a good hard paddle stroke off the lip. With his angle too much left, he dropped into the disorderly hole that I myself had a hard time getting out of. He reached toward the foam free water and buried his paddle with a huge pull. But he did not go anywhere! He reached again and again with the same result; he was turning sideways and getting pulled back into the hole! His boat went vertical as the water from the drop pummeled his stern, and in an instant, he was gone!

Underwater beneath the falls we could only see pieces of him and the boat as the hole violently thrashed him about. In eight seconds, he had flipped five times and was being pulled out toward the middle of the river, away from us. With no chance of recovery, he swam, or at least we saw his boat without him in it. One of the guys stood poised with a throw rope, looking for signs of life as his boat thrashed about as if it was caught in a blender. This section of the hole was extremely violent; we could see that the lone boat was smashing rocks under the surface of the water and even hear the deep concussion. We glanced at each other, hoping that our man was not pinned underwater somewhere. Si surfaced like a yellow whale breaching just below the hole and started swimming toward us. The rope went out and found its mark; he grabbed it and was brought to shore. Climbing up the bank, I could see that he was out of breath, and as he looked up at us blood was streaming down his face; his helmet strap was around his neck instead of his chin. The helmet sat on the back of his head, allowing his forehead to be exposed. When we were safely on land, we quickly realized that the blood was from two small cuts on his forehead. Nothing to be concerned about, but the boat was a concern! He had held onto his paddle in the chaos, but holding onto the boat was impossible. So now the boat was dancing in the hole all alone, and we needed that back.

Bugsy and Carpenter worked their way toward a tree that lay below the drop. The tree had fallen and was half in the river. Just as they were working their way out onto the tree, the boat freed itself from its hostage chamber and set off to meet its fate. Luckily the boat kicked toward our side of the river and Bugsy ran down the remainder of the tree with Carpenter behind him. The boat was just outside of his reach and was moving fast. If we lost that boat, we might've never seen it again! Bugsy lunged into the river and grabbed the boat; Bugsy was hanging onto the tree with one hand and the boat with the other. With his body almost completely underwater, he ushered the heavy water-filled boat out of the swift-moving current onto the bank with Carpenters help. After a quick evaluation of the boat and emptying the water out; our attention turned to Si once again. He had wiped the blood from his brow, and we found that the damage consisted of two or three small holes in the skin of his forehead. Not deep, so he decided to continue the run.

We wanted to get back into our boats quickly; Bugsy and Si were cold and wet after being submerged in the river retrieving the boat. The easiest way to get warm was to get back into the boat and do some work. So, we set off down the river hunting and picking our lines. That day we ran the rest of the river without incident.

From time to time I would look over at Si to see his chinstrap tight on his chin and a small trickle of blood working its way down the right side of his face from the brim of his helmet. He looked badass, and only wiped his face when the blood went into his eyes. The only problem with this was that no matter what he did, even after we were off the river, it wouldn't stop bleeding. The traditional band-aid on the forehead looked cool but couldn't keep enough pressure on the nick to keep it from bleeding. We decided to get a motel for the night, it was cold and rainy, and the group and I had been sleeping in a combination of tents and trucks for a couple of days. It was going to be nice to get warm for a while. We haggled a price with the local motel owner, springtime in the ADK wasn't exactly tourist season. She gave us a good deal, so we procured a couple of rooms.

Run on the Boquete River

The day before we had run the Boquete River, it was a beautiful wilderness and one of our guys, Cook, had smashed his thumb so bad that he sat the day out. He said that he could feel his heartbeat through the thumb. It was now black and blue and swelled up. Now we had two injured, and surgery was necessary. Luckily, we had Beth with us, she was a vet and carried a med kit that would make EMTs envious. The first order of business was to stop the bleeding, so she sterilized the wound and put some numbing ointment on it. She pulled out her stitch kit and grabbed a needle and thread. She proceeded to put two small stitches in Si's forehead in two different spots. The bleeding stopped immediately. Cook, however, was not going to get off so easy.

Beth took a hypodermic needle out of her bag, Cook's eyes got big. The thumbnail needed to be lanced, rather than pushing a hot piece of metal threw it to drain the blood beneath it, she felt that a hypodermic would do just fine. Shit was getting serious, but we all joked that it would be less painful if you just cut the thumb off. Cook was drinking whiskey, and to him, the whole thing was sounding like a bad idea. We assured him that he would feel better to release the pressure. Really, we just wanted to see her slam a needle through his thumbnail! We gathered around and got really quiet as she touched the tip of the sharp needle to the nail. She started spinning it like a drill back and forth; she held his hand down as she started putting pressure on the needle. Cook's eyes began to water as the pressure increased. Suddenly, the needle popped threw and went in deep. Deep, deep; she quickly pulled it out and put pressure around the hole as the blood spewed out. Cook gave a sigh of relief, saying that it already felt better. She then turned to me with big eyes and

85

her mouth shaped like an O. She dressed the thumb up, and Cook drank more whiskey. Later she admitted to me that she had pushed the needle through a little hard and it went through the nail and hit the bone. But everything was sterile, so it would be ok. Cook recovered quickly as well as Si. We all went kayaking the next day.

Yet The Branch held our attention longer yet. The biggest drop on The Branch was a beautiful stair step. It was several drops strung together really, drop after drop. Individually each drop was challenging, but put together like they were, it became an epic run. You had to work your way from left of the river, then to the right of the river, and then back to left of the river again. It was not that the drops you were going over were really hard, it was the fact that if you missed the drops you NEEDED to go over you may end up in a heinous situation. It could have very well ended up being a flesh tearing, bone breaking, body wrenching, and boat splintering good time, if you didn't end up pinned under water and drowned that was. The granite on the ADK River had no mercy and frankly didn't care if you were there or not.

It was not a bad day for The Branch weather wise. The ADK in the spring could be terrible weather, but the sun was almost shining and it was not raining or snowing. We had worked our way down the river to a big drop. I was feeling good and the guys were looking tight on the river. When it came to this drop, we ran it individually. When my turn came up, I knew the most important move of this drop was a simple ferry across the river. The catch was that in front of you were waterfalls that you just came over, and behind you were bigger waterfalls strewn with granite boulders that you didn't want to go over. This was a high drop and the water in the run was flying by. It was loud, like standing next to a moving freight train loud. The trick was to get to the left of the river, past the terrible widow making waterfalls, to the more manageable falls on river left. In order to make this move, you had to start out next to a rock wall on the right side of the river with those terrible boulder-strewn waterfalls right behind you. They were ten feet behind you, and if you missed the move out of the eddy you were destined for greatness. Once you were out of the eddy and into your ferry across the top of the falls, there was another eddy that you went into. This eddy was an anomaly. Among all of the chaos, noise, and rapidly moving water, this eddy was almost sitting still! The water in this big eddy in the middle of this river was slowly moving clockwise and was nearly flat. Going into it with a lot of speed could cause problems such as overshooting the next move, or worse yet, being flipped. I slid into the river, it was my turn now. I looked downstream at the top of the first drop and I could basically see rocks on the skyline and the tops of the trees. This was nerve-wracking. Once you went over the first drop you were in the middle of the river and you were completely on your own. No one could get to you without a great effort. There would be no help on the horizon. I started my run and felt smooth over the first couple of drops. I knew I needed to make the wall eddy, and it weighed heavy on my mind. After the last waterfall above the wall eddy, I pounded toward the eddy and hit it with a lot of speed. When my bow crossed the eddy line, I leaned hard picking the boat up onto its side causing it to carve into the quiet peace of the water. Well maybe not quiet, it was heaving up and down three feet. I came to a stop next to the wall and started making small corrections with my paddle to not get turned around in the heaving eddy. I was now facing upstream and I looked to my right and saw one of the guys about fifty yards away on the other side of the river giving me a thumbs up. Behind me raged the gnarly V-shaped waterfall, which was now the ferry. I tricked myself into thinking this was just like any other river. I would just set my ferry angle and go. I kicked my front end out of the wall eddy with a left paddle stroke and calmly worked my way over a rushing column of water to the flat eddy in the middle of the river. Just before I got to the flat eddy I went over a small ledge. There was no turning back now. As I hit the edge of the flat eddy, I increased my lean in the boat. This brought the boat up onto its side and the boat carved across the eddy with about five paddle strokes. I lined myself up with a small shoot of water going off a drop next to a boulder. Behind it were two consecutive waterfalls, so I powered over the first landing and then threw a small correction line up with the second falls, and over I went! Landing, I went deep and my face was pummeled with water. I increased my power and pulled myself out with no problem. My heart was in my throat! My breathing was shallow, but as I leveled out, I once again took a deep breath. I knew I may need it for the next and biggest falls. Now in

87

the fast-green water, I picked up speed; it would take me seven paddle strokes to reach the edge. With a strong Boof stroke I flew off the lip of the falls. For a moment my heart completely left my body as I dropped eight feet. I landed well past the hole at the bottom, and I inhaled again for this part of the run was over. I worked my way to the left of the river and stepped out of my boat. My fingertips hurt, my eyes were dilated, my breath was quick, but I was not shaky. I controlled my adrenaline as much as I could as I stabilized my boat next to a tree at the edge of the river. I walked up to the guys, and the first thing I heard was "That was a hell of a ferry across there." The only thing I could do was smile and say, it felt good.

It did feel good; I was having a good day. I felt strong and sharp, but not everyone had a good day on The Branch. Every man or woman that paddled with our group had the opportunity to walk any drop without ridicule. It was easier for a person to walk than to be carried!

My good friend, Si, lined up for the same drop while we watched from the left side of the river. He looked strong as he pounded into the wall eddy above the waterfall. He hesitated to catch his breath for a while, and then he lunged forward pulling himself out of the eddy. He thrusted his paddle into the raging river driving himself forward toward the big flat eddy. In three strong paddle strokes he was at the edge of the small drop just in front of the flat eddy in the middle of the river. Going over the small drop with the flat eddy just in front of him, he continued with strong paddle strokes. He was powering into the eddy with way too much speed for the slow-moving water. His adrenaline had gotten the best of him, and he shot into the eddy and his boat turned upstream shooting him halfway through the eddy. At this point, he flipped! He did not just flip, he was upside down in an instant. The eddy was now drawing him downstream, and as he tried to roll, he inadvertently pushed himself even lower in the eddy. The first rolling attempt had him finding himself at the bottom of the eddy with his bow pointing the wrong way. With a moment of hesitation, his decision was nearly made for him as he was practically getting swept over the falls. He powered forward pulling himself away from the falls

1,2,3,4,5 paddle strokes and he broke the pull of the water and started edging forward. Still low in the eddy, he realized he couldn't get back to the wall eddy from which he came, but he went that direction anyway. There was a small boulder in the way as he shot across the green trough of water that lead directly into the V-falls. He instantly clung to the boulder on right of the river. The wall eddy that he wanted to get into was five feet away and he couldn't get there from where he was currently. He was clinging to the piece of granite protruding from the river by a single hand hold hovering above the V-drop. All the guys glanced at each other, we were helpless, fifty yards away and we knew that Si couldn't get the power or speed to make it back to the flat eddy in the middle of the river. We also knew he couldn't maintain the strength to hold on for long, as we could already see him struggling to stay tight to the cold unforgiving granite. It was time for plan B! Plan B consisted of four options; over it, under it, around it, or through it. As we grouped together watching this unfold someone said in a low voice, "He has to let go and run it." Our friend glanced over his right shoulder and looked toward us with a desperate need for inspiration. One of the group ran to the very edge of the river, cupped his hands around his mouth, and yelled at the top of his lungs "LET GO!" We never knew if he heard those words or not. But he let go.

As he released his grasp of the boulder, he glanced at us as if he was waving goodbye. He clenched the paddle with his free hand and pushed off the boulder into the fast-moving column of water. He buried his paddle and turned one hundred and eighty degrees, and then over the falls he went. A great volume of water whisked him over the falls into the first obstacle, and he landed on a boulder the size of a car. He got a paddle stroke in While he kept his bow up and followed the water off of it. He went onto another large granite round with a cushion of water careening over it. He kept his boat straight as he went air born off the last boulder into the big drop. The big drop was shaped like a V with a massive volume of water pouring into it from both sides, creating a cauldron of rushing water at the bottom. In mid-air he descended into the V confluence. He hit one thick curtain of water before the other and they flipped him violently while he was still in mid-air. He landed upside down in the cauldron at the bottom of the V with water pouring in on him. His

89

boat was jerked back and forth like a bobber, he may have been trying to roll, but it would not have made a difference. The water swelled up and pushed him downriver where the run narrowed. The water was still aerated with bubbles and we could see that his boat was barely afloat. All of a sudden, his boat jutted upwards again and again. He was getting the shit pounded out of him as he was hitting boulders from the bottom of the river with his body. The river was handling him as he tried to roll. He was slamming into boulders left and right with great speed. At the downstream end of the valley of water, the water swept to the left and moved around a low U-shaped island of rock that stuck up just above the water line. Si was now actively trying to roll the kayak as he approached the U-shaped peninsula. He had been underwater through thirty yards of hell, and he was now setting up for a final attempt at a roll. He badly needed air. He did the set up for his role and quickly tried it, and in the same moment he hit the U-shaped peninsula. He stopped dead in the middle of the U. He was Pinned! He was pinned with his paddle stuck against the rock. The paddle was lying across his spray skirt. If he pulled his spray skirt to swim, he would drown because he couldn't get out of his boat. If he let go of his paddle, he might get sucked deeper and drown. He was using all of his strength pulling up on his paddle to keep his face three inches out of the water so he could breathe while he looked at the sky. He needed HELP NOW!

Carpenter was closest to Si's boat. Carpenter turned and ran with five great strides and literally jumped into his boat. He stretched his spray skirt and snapped it over the lip of his boat. Without a thought, he launched into the river from the eight-foot plateau. He hit the river in slow-moving water at the end of the run. He set his ferry angle and took off across the river toward his friend fifty yards away. Si was struggling for breath and was quickly losing the battle. Carpenter sprinted across the river with shoulders of steel like a steam engine. His head affixed on his old friend. It took Carpenter maybe one minute to reach Si, but one minute was a long fucking time! He slammed into the shore just below the U, jumped out of his boat and launched himself toward his pinned friend. With inhuman strength he reached into the water and grabbed Si, literally pulling him and his boat out of the water and setting him upright on dry land. I could see Si shaking his head yes, and I could only assume that meant that he was all right. I could see his chest expanding through his life vest as the oxygen enriched his blood once again. The violence of the moment was over, and after a few minutes, they worked their way back across the river to us. We did not say much to him; some people would get mad at times like these and would hold people in contempt for missing a simple ferry. We just stood quietly and let him tell his story. Never in that story did he say that he almost died. He was sore and bruised, but he ran the rest of the river without incident.

Later that night, we ended up in Lake Placid looking for a hot meal and thinking about our next river. We did a little bit of light shopping and resupplying for the trip. I happened to see a can of BOOTS Oxygen, which I of course bought. Later that night beside the campfire I presented the can of Oxygen to Si, saying that if he was going to spend that much time underwater we would feel much more comfortable if we knew he had oxygen. We all had a good laugh and the next morning we hit the next river.

I have paddled with a lot of people in my life, hundreds in fact. The guys that I started paddling with were the same people I paddled with years later. I lost touch with many of the paddlers throughout the years but it turned out that the guys I called my A team picked me, or rather groomed me for their group. It was not an accident that they chose me, I fit into their group formula. When someone new was brought into the group we looked at them, listen to them, and made a note of their personality and their skill level. Skill was important, but knowing you were having a bad day and recognizing it, understanding and admitting that you were too cold or too hungry to run, was an important attribute that would save the whole team a lot of time and effort. We picked on each other a lot but we never chastise each other. We helped each other on and off the river. We didn't brag about how good we were, but instead we'd brag about how good the other guy was. We were all in pain in some form or another, but you would never know it. We made group decisions, even when it meant one of us was outvoted. Most of all, we had fun.

The Diver Got Me...

I was working in shipping and receiving at a metal shop on the west side of Rochester, NY, in 2001, during the early spring. My vacation was a week away and I was going north to the Adirondacks to kayak whitewater where the great rivers made legends of men in the cold still snow-covered lands of the north. Most people would cringe at the very thought of it, but my crew loved it. It was Monday and I was leaving Friday after work. By Tuesday, my lower left abdomen was killing me. By Tuesday night it felt like a red-hot poker was being stabbed in my side. By Wednesday, I couldn't avoid the doctor anymore. She asked me what my pain level was. I told her, "If a ten is me passed out, then at nine I would be on the ground screaming and writhing. During the day, the pain is a steady five to six under physical stress. When I lay down, it goes to eight, so I haven't slept in two days."

She stood in front of me astounded and said my description of pain was the clearest she had ever heard. She felt around my stomach and, when she hit the spot, I nearly went through the roof. She nodded her head and seemed to understand what was going on. "I think you have diverticulitis," she said. "Are you familiar with what that is?" My heart sank. I knew. When seeds get caught in polyps in your intestine, they can become infected. She wanted to schedule me for a colonoscopy. I told here, "Yeah, doc. That's not going to happen. I am kayaking class V whitewater in three days. Just tell me what the cure is." She tried to talk me out of going on the trip but, when I got up to leave she stopped me and said "Ok. Here is what you need to do. Don't eat for three or four days. Take in all the liquids you can drink, and take the antibiotics I am prescribing you. This will kill everything in your lower GI tract."

The next day I took a protein shake and a bottle of water to work along with my antibiotics. I was careful not to say anything to anyone about my condition. Weakness was frowned upon among the men at work, but I always ate lunch in my truck anyway so it was not an issue as far as anyone at work was concerned. By Thursday night the pain was already beginning to subside. On Friday morning I loaded the truck with all my gear and headed to work. I took off a couple of hours early to get a head start on traffic. By Friday night I was at the prearranged meeting place, the Beaver

River put in. The Taylorville section of the Beaver River was a good camping spot, and we were going to meet there Saturday morning with the boys. The next morning the guys trickled in one by one until the A team had assembled. By the time ten o'clock rolled around we were ready to go. I still hadn't told anyone about my issue and I had not eaten any real food in 3 days.

The Taylorville section of the Beaver was raging. It was easily three times higher than I had ever seen it. Once again that morning I had my daily meal of a protein shake and a bunch of water. I entered the river with a nonchalant attitude and worked my way down the river. Toward the end of the river was a small waterfall. When we were in full view of the falls, the A team were gone. It had become a massive pour-over. It was sucking water back into it from eight feet away, making it a drowning machine. If this was a sign of things to come, it was going to be a dangerous week.

Not to mention, it was the end of my third day without solid food. I was not a food connoisseur. I didn't live to eat, I ate to live. I could eat the same meal every day and be okay with it. If I could take a pill or get a shot that would fill me up for a week, I would do it. Throughout the morning and day, I felt shaky. I did not feel particularly weak during the day, I was just really fucking hungry. We pulled into Lowville and went to the local eatery for a nice meal. I ordered the Fettuccine Chicken Alfredo, thinking it would be a good combination of protein and carbohydrates. The rest of the guys ordered and we started our plan by spreading maps across the table. With phones, we used the AWA website to check the water levels. We decided we would work our way back to the west, and that we would look at the Cedar River first and go from there.

The food came, and when they placed the Fettuccine Chicken Alfredo in front of me it looked like a photograph. The aroma was a nutty combination of rich cheeses and chicken with a lingering hint of smoke. With my first bite it was as if I had experienced food for the first time. I had tasted the best cuts of meat and signature dishes from all over. All of it paled in comparison to the meal in front of me. I ate to my heart's content. I could feel the energy surge back into my body, my skin started pulsing with fresh blood. My vision

93

became clear and my hands became warm. My mind became sharp with intent. I hadn't felt this good in a long time.

We worked our way North East, and the closer we got to the Hudson River basin the deeper the snow became. The Cedar River was directed into the Hudson River by the canyon it flowed through. It was bordered by heavy woods and mountainous terrain. It held in the cold and snow like a cooler with a trickle of water at the bottom of it, only that trickle of water was now a raging class V creek. Our local expert and friend, Warden, checked the water level by looking at a rock as we crossed the bridge over the Cedar. According to his calculations, we were in the holy-shit territory. We put up camp near the take out of the class V section next to a small dirt road, which was a stone's throw from the river. Most of us slept in the back of our vehicles, so I unloaded my bins to make room for my sleeping bag. I took my antibiotic as the fire came into its own and the boys gathered around. The fact that I could see my breath meant that it was fifty degrees or lower. The fire chased away the cold for the time being.

Si was in quiet contemplation, he was answering questions that no one knew they had asked. Carpenter with his Zen-like quality was making hand jesters slow and smooth showing tomorrow's path. Warden spoke of the dangers and near misses, for he knew without a doubt that getting out alive wouldn't be easy. Bugsy with his chewing tobacco and a whiskey knew that we would be just fine, Mighty Fine. Then there was me with a cigar and a whiskey. I lived for this shit. But the bed called early when the weather was cold.

The morning brought sunshine and the hope of a warm day. We loaded all the boats onto one vehicle and tied them down for the bumpy ride, and then we proceeded to get dressed. I dressed for the absolute cold and emergency situations. I wore hydro skin long johns, rodeo pants, fleece pants over everything, and non-breathable waterproof pants with Velcro cuffs at the ankle. Wool socks, waterproof socks, and heavy creaking booties went on my feet. On top I wore another skin-tight hydro, over that a rubber fabric with short sleeves, over that a heavy expedition fleece, and finishing with a waterproof dry top with rubber gaskets around the neck and wrists. Standing in the sun I could feel the sweat dripping down my back.

We piled into the back of the truck and took off to the put in. We smiled at each other knowing it was too loud to speak and have anyone hear us. Twelve miles later, we found ourselves at the put in as we systematically filed out of the back of the truck. We dragged our boats to the river and made final preparations by checking throw ropes, airbags, boat adjustments, pin kits, carabineer straps, and pulleys. Eventually, we slid into the cold easy moving river.

The Cedar was listed as a class V creek and it was about six miles long, give or take. The first big drop was called The Undertake and it was a solid class V. We had about a mile to go before we had to deal with it, but the rest of the run was an IV to IV+ with normal water levels. As we rounded the slow sloping corner, we could see waves stacking in front of the beginning of the canyon wall. We went into the waves without hesitation, and started working our way through a peaky wave train that gathered in a large eddy below it. I stated that those were the largest waves I had ever seen here. It must have come out strange because the guys looked at me with shocked looks on their faces. I felt a little dizzy and almost flipped in the wave train. I needed to get my timing down. I felt awkward. A few small rapids later I started to feel better, until we rounded the corner to the first big drop, The Undertaker. We did not plan on running it, but you never knew until you got there. Now we were there, and I thought there was no fucking way.

Water was pounding into the drop with half of it disappearing under the wall to the right just after the big soul-sucking pothole. It was a no brainer. We walked it toward the left of the river. The rocks were shitty, sharp, and wet, not to mention half cover with snow. We were about to start our descent into the canyon, weather that was walking or not. I could see my breath again as I put my boat on my shoulder. I stumbled, slipping on the rocks. This was a bad place to fall into the river by accident. I pulled my foot out of the river hoping none of the cold water would find its way to the skin of my foot. I pushed myself up and worked my way along the side of the river to where we could put in again. I sat in my boat and flipped the back of my spray skirt over the lip of my boat. I then turned my attention to stretching the front half over the forward lip. This was always the hard part. I attained a perfect seal on my third try, the first two didn't

95

come close. Obviously, the skirt had stiffened up with the cold. I was struggling but felt better sliding back into the river. We worked our way down a little farther to the next big drop. We stopped at the corner before we could see the rapid. We were concerned about the water level. The guys got out of their boats and took a look. I stayed in mine and waited for them. They came back quickly saying that it was choked with wood and we needed to walk. I pulled my skirt with some struggle. Finally, it let loose. The Kevlar rim on the spray skirt doesn't help any, I thought.

The walk sucked, and we had to trudge up the side of the steep canyon hill through two feet of hard crusted snow with our boats on our shoulders. When we reached the top, I took a sigh of relief since it was all downhill from here. Only the downhill was steeper than the uphill, so we used our ropes to lower the boats. We descended to a small platform rock, and one by one balanced the boat and paddle as we slid in and snapped our skirts on. It was treacherous at best. I was tired, breathing heavy, and I could once again feel the sweat running down my back to the crack of my ass. We headed down the river again only to find the same scenario played itself out. I waited, and the guys came back with bad news, more wood we had to walk. I glanced up the same angle incline as we had ascended before; with both hands on my paddle I hung my head shaking it. The guys took it in stride and scurried up the ridge to a plateau and walked along looking for a way down. I struggled with the boat on my shoulder, and with the rubber soled booties I took one step up two back. I thrusted my paddle into the snow for stability. The guys waited for me through the woods at the other edge of the plateau looking at a possible put in. But at the top of the ridge I was not feeling good. I was dizzy, my vision was blurred, and I had all of a sudden become cold. As I took a breath on the plateau, I wiped my forehead and found it to be clammy and cold. Then a realization came over me, my heart was pounding, and I was breathing shallow and fast. I had stopped sweating!

I knew I was dehydrated. I hadn't taken in enough calories in the last few days, and knew that if I put back on the creek that I would be worthless. I was weak and knew I would be putting the guys in danger, myself included. I walked up to the guys and Bugsy immediately asked me if I was all right. "No," I said. "I am going to have to walk out of here." Carpenter added, "You don't look so good." Warden said that he had walked into this rapid from the road before and it shouldn't be a bad walk. Bugsy came back with, "Are you ok to make it?" "Yeah," I said. "I will be between that mountain and this rapid, I don't think I will die but if I pass out, come find me." They all agreed. They descended over the ledge and disappeared out of sight. I turned to see trees and glassy snow, above which loomed a white-capped mountain. If I walked toward that and eventually found the road. I took off my life jacket and then my spray skirt. I worked the neck gasket of my dry top over my head and then my wrists gaskets over my hands. I clipped my helmet to the rescue bar in front of the cockpit and stuffed the other stuff up into the boat. I unclipped my pin kit and retrieved my strap and clipped it to the front of my boat with a carabineer. I flipped the strap over my head and headed toward the unbroken snow.

Three steps in and I post-holed three times, breaking through the crust of the snow my foot dove through the snow. On the fourth step, I fell. I could hear the crust of the snow break as the weight of my body crashed through it. I got to my feet and was dizzy, so I sat on my boat and looked down the hill to where my paddle had come to a rest against a tree. My heart was racing and I was short of breath. Now I had to go and get my fucking paddle. I drank some water and took some gear off. I quickly assessed my situation. I deliberately walked forward, pounding my feet through the ice crust of snow. I reached my paddle and, with my boat behind me, I continued pounding my feet through the ice and pushing myself forward. With my paddle in my right hand I grabbed whatever tree was available with my left. Twenty yards later, I found myself at the top lip of a plateau. I held my paddle and looked up at the mountain in front of me.

There were two things that you never wanted to come across when navigating through the wilderness. The first was a swamp. No matter how long it took you or how far you had to go, you never walked through a swamp. The second was a blowdown, which was a massive area of broken trees twisted and tangled into each other lying on the ground. As my eyes surveyed the land, I saw a

97

blowdown. I looked left, then right, and saw there was no way around that I could see. Without a second thought, I walked forward into the middle of it. Toting around seventy pounds of gear, I pushed and pulled my kayak over and under tree limbs and used my paddle like a machete. I thought to myself, "Fucking peanuts! I will never eat peanuts again", which was the cause of all of this nonsense. While I was stepping over a tree, my foot slipped and I crashed into the snow face down. "I could go to sleep here," I thought, "The guys will find me." But if they took more than three hours I would be dead. I pushed myself to my knees, and yanked the strap. I drove myself forward through forty yards of bull shit until I was back into the regular woods again. With the blow down behind me, I continued to pound my freezing feet through the ice-covered snow. My shins were taking a beating and everything was sore. I had very little energy left.

Eventually I saw a steep incline in the distance. I was at the base, and I looked up to see a 45-degree angle up to the dusty dirt of the road. With my boat still strapped to me I slowly ascended the bank. I was grabbing at the grass under the snow to try and keep myself from slipping backward. Finally, my hands found level ground. I crawled on my hands and knees until my hands were covered in dust. Once on the road, I stood up and pulled my gear over the hump. I looked back in the direction that I had come. It had taken me a couple of hours to go three miles. I was safe and headed toward base camp. I had a long walk ahead of me, maybe seven miles, and my hands and feet were cold. I was shaky, but at least my stomach didn't hurt.

As I walked down the center of the dirt road in the middle of the ADK wilderness, I knew that there wasn't even a telephone poll within twenty miles of me. Then I heard something in the distance. A Forest Ranger pulled up beside me in a pickup. I couldn't help but think to myself, "There is something greater at work here than me, that's for sure." He rolled his passenger window down and asked, "You ok?"

I responded, "I just did not feel well, so I walked off the river."

"Hop in," he said, "I will give you a ride."

I threw my boat in the back and jumped into the cab. In no time I saw my truck. I thanked the ranger profusely, ran to my truck, grabbed a gallon of water, and started drinking. I pulled my white gas stove out and heated water, throwing any food I had into the pot for a stew. My gourmet meal was just starting to steep as the guys walked over the bank with boats on their shoulders. Fork in one hand and pot in the other, I said, "Where the fuck have you guys been?" Bugsy was obviously mad. Carpenter said, "You wouldn't believe it. There was wood in every drop. We had to walk everything." There was no reason to talk about what I went through in the woods. When I reached the road, I could barely stand, but I also knew the guys had gone through hell on the river walking around every drop. For the next six hours, I did nothing but eat and drink.

The rest of the week was epic. I grew stronger every day, my timing came back, and I was no longer clumsy. My boat and I became one again and every day we did something harder. That week changed my life. I started carrying around a magnesium flint stick in my life jacket along with my knife. I still dressed warm, but not to the point where it crippled my movement. To this day, I still evaluate the food that I eat. Most of all, I learned to listen to what my body tells me.

9

Black River Festival

I had been kayaking for several years. I spent a lot of time at the local paddling shop and had made friends with the owner and one of his employees, named Walker. Walker and I kayaked together on several occasions, and he always seemed surprised that I knew so many people out on the rivers. When I would run into guys that I knew in the paddling shop I would often talk to them about the latest festival or other kayaking event that was going on. The owner of the shop was oblivious to the whitewater festivals that took place in New York. I explained to him that the Moose Festival, for example, brought kayakers in from all over the country, including professional kayaking team members from the big boat manufactures. When the shop owner realized the opportunity he had to sell his products at a festival, Tom asked me if I would be interested in working one and sitting at his booth. He told me that I could run and play on the river as long as I helped him move the gear and set up the booth. I actually thought it would be fun so I agreed.

A few weeks later, Tom the owner of the shop gave me a call and asked me to stop by. When I did, he asked me if I would like to be a Pro. sponsorship representative for his shop and the boat company's they carried. Tom said he would give me the latest and greatest boat and that I could pick anything out of the shop that I wanted to use. I was astounded and beside myself. This was the deal of a lifetime for someone like me. All of my gear, including boats, spray skirts, paddles, helmet and whatever I had to pay for myself. Now, I was being offered all my gear for free. The next week I received a phone call from Tom again. The boat company Rep. was at the shop with my new boat and wanted to meet me. He had a Wavesport Triple X for me that fit me like a glove. It was customized to my stats exactly. I signed whatever pieces of paper he put in front of me without hesitation and shook his hand. I was officially sponsored to kayak. The Rep. and I talked about different rivers and people. He knew a good friend of mine from the Sacandaga River that owned a shop there, Jim. I said, "Yeah Jim calls me a couple times a year to paddle with him."

The Rep smiled and hesitantly said, "Marty, Jim doesn't call anybody to paddle with him. He only calls you." I was taken aback by the statement.

When the Black River Festival rolled around, I went early to the site with my van full of gear to help set up the booth. It was a fun atmosphere. I saw a lot of old friends and had the opportunity to paddle with a few of them.

All day we had a great time. I happened to see Lynn, Lynn had been a kayaker forever and she ran all kinds of stuff. I had run into her on a couple different rivers in a couple different states. She was always fun to be around. She told me where she was camping, and it happened to be the same campground we were in. I told her we would have a campfire later and told her to come look us up, she agreed. Then we went on about our day. At the end of the day, we loaded up all of the stuff from the booth back into the vehicles and went back to the campground. My van was once again full to the top, but a little more chaotic than before. It was getting dark and we started a fire. People started wondering the campgrounds. It seemed to be customary to take a walk around to see what was going on. It was readily accepted to walk into a kayaker's camp just to see who was around and hear the stories of the day. Lynn showed up at the campfire and we talked for quite a while about the rivers we had paddled for the last year. She told me she would be back later and took off to some other campsites to see some old friends. We had a lot of people around, and many of them were my good friends. So, I did not feel the need to wonder.

Much later in the evening, I felt like taking a walk. Most of the people had gone to bed and the fire was dying, but I still had some whiskey left and I knew I would not be drinking tomorrow at all so why waste it. I poured the rest of the whiskey in my empty Nalgene, which became half full. I then poured ginger ale into it to fill it up. A classy mixed drink! I walked around and noticed not many people were up. I saw a fire in the distance and heard laughing, so I walked over. Lynn was there with a bunch of people from the east side of the state, like Albany area, I knew most of them but they don't get out this way much. We talked for a while and someone announced that they were going to bed since it was late. This prompted every else to capitulate and everyone started to get up and head to bed. Lynn turned to me and said, "Well, I guess I will go sleep in my car." I, of course, being the classy genital man that I am said in retort, "I have a tent I just need to set it up that's all." She smiled at me and simply replied, "I will get my sleeping bag." I took a big gulp from my classy drink, kicked into overdrive, and double-timed it back to my van in as straight of a line as I could manage.

I opened the back of the van and threw some product off the box to the top of the pile. I opened the box and grabbed the tent. I could feel the stakes inside the sheath as I pulled it out of the box. My mind was racing, even though it was after two in the morning and pitch-black out. The old Boy scout in me was kicking in. "Do I need to put down a ground cloth? Nope, it hasn't rained in a few weeks. Do I need to put up a fly?" I glance up and see only stars gazing at through the night sky. "Nope, I'm good, not a cloud in the sky." I hesitate for a moment weighting for my friend Lynn. I wanted to show her my prowess with my tent erecting skills! I heard her coming and took a sip from my classy drink.

I unsheathe the tent onto the grassy ground with a dim flashlight in one hand. She approached and put her open sleeping bag on the box inside the van so she didn't have to put it on the ground. I was scurrying around the tent in order to prepare. I grabbed the steaks and threw the fly and the ground cloth aside. I pulled the tent out flat and arrange it into the perfect rectangle, and as if I was giving a lesson I said, "Let's see the sun in the morning is over there, the moon is over there the wind usually blows from there so it should face this way." I grabbed the tent and turned it appropriately. I looked for the steaks that I just had in my hand. I couldn't find those right now, so I scoured the ground with my waning flashlight. Finally, I look under the tent and behold, found them! I struggled to open the little bag that held them. My Dad had tied the thing in like four knots, because losing a stake could be the difference between life and death you know. I finally tore the damn thing open, and I had my steaks.

I walked to the corners of the tent with the stakes in hand. I was excited. I bent down at the corner, I stumbled a little at this point, and went down onto one knee. I was looking for the tab that contained the little brass ring that you put the steak the threw. Only I couldn't find it. Well, I thought the tent must be upside down. I expressed my concern to Lynn who was currently yawning. This was no big deal, I would just flip it over. I grabbed the tent and gave it a flip. It took four to five minutes to get her flipped. "Doing good," I liked to stay positive in times of great stress. I sauntered to the farthest edge, which was like four steps away. I knelt down again looking for the elusive tab with a tent stake in hand. Once again, no tab. "Well," I said, "I think I'll put the polls up first." Lynn seemed unconcerned now sitting on the back of my van.

I grabbed the polls and commenced assembling them. Four poles, old school and simple, all I needed was a string and a stake. "Let's see four poles have eight ends," so after I went through the 30 possible arrangements of tentpole configurations. I really should have taken physics. I finally came across the two that worked. Wallah, tent poles! I walked to the end of the rectangle and stood in the center. I was now looking for the tab in the center of the tent that would suspend the ridge center skyward. This would allow for adequate headroom, which I was pretty sure I was going to need. All I had to do was stick the poll through the tab and stake it down to the ground. But the elusive tab was nowhere to be found. So, I stated matter of factly, "Yup, I knew I had it right the first time," it was now upside down.

I gave the tent a good flip and over it went. Lynn was now standing next to me wondering what the hell was taking so long. "Well," I said, "There was no tab, and it's been a while since I put up this particular tent and I must have forgotten the poles go on the inside!" That made total sense at this point. So I had a tent pole in one hand, a trickling flashlight protruding from my mouth, and I was on my hands and knees looking for the opening of this flat tent. I found the opening, you know that was what I meant to do. The tent only had four sides. However, the opening contained a maze of

103

zippers that rivaled the maze in the Sunday paper. Unfortunately, I couldn't turn the page to give me a hint on what to do here. So I ended up opening them all. This seemed to work out ok, and I crawled my desperate ass inside the dilapidated tent. I was looking for a hole in the back of the tent, at this point, that I could stick my pole into. That elusive hole was about an eighth of an inch in diameter and should have had the same tab circle thingy in it. But this one went through the tent, "See that was my mistake earlier." I was thinking out loud, and I heard a muffled, "Uh-huh." Well, I was inside a tent that now seemed to be staticky and sticking to me. It was getting hard to maneuver the tent poles, and at this point, I was looking for this small hole by starlight because my flashlight was a dead soldier that had lost the fight. After a good inspection of the ridgeline and every other seem inside the tent, I concluded that there was no fucking hole. I did find a tabby thing though, and I thought maybe I had the wrong poles. I didn't want to poke a hole through the tent today. It was getting hard to breath in there anyway so I slowly backed out trying to get the tent to not stick to me! At the opening, I pulled the tent off my head. I realized I lost my hat somewhere in there, but at this point, it was also a dead soldier and I considered it lost forever. I took a deep breath of fresh air and consider myself born again. I like a new child, I was all sticky.

Lynn had the perfect suggestion, "Why don't we sleep in the van?" At this point, I was now finishing my classy drink. "Great idea!!" Why not, I slept in there last night. I explained to Lynn that there was limited space available, and she told me we could work it out. I said, "Hop in." We threw a sleeping bag on the wooden box and left the tent to rot in the warm stale air. She climbed into the van and crawled on her hands and knees into the confined space. The moment she got past the wooden box I heard a noise from the plastic boxes. Then I heard her say, "Um... I'm stuck." Then she said, "UUA what's in here?" She said this in a higher voice than normal, and I could only come to one conclusion. Her hand must have gone through the interlocking plastic box I keep my wet gear in. Then she came back with a panicky voice, "Seriously I'm stuck!" I was looking at her ass thinking to myself, yea this is going to suck. I jumped onto the pile of gear like a commando under fire and crawled between the top of the van and whatever I had in there. I could see just enough to realize that she was indeed stuck. She had her hand in the center of my plastic box almost up to the elbow. The flaps of the box were pointed down toward her hand. Every time she tried to pull her hand out the flaps tighten up, locking her arm in place. I was three feet above her pinned to the roof of the van looking down on her arm, and crushing the expensive product below me. She was saying loudly, "I can't get it out, it's stuck, I can't get it out!" Finally, I pushed down on the flaps of the box, opening the hole enough so she could extract her moist greasy hand from my wet gear box. She backed out of the tight grotto and landed on her feet at the end of my van. I followed her out taking half of the van's contents with me. As I stood at the back of the van with her, the van continued to unload itself at my feet, pouring stuff all over the ground. She looked at me sternly and said, "I am going to go sleep in my car." It was almost four in the morning at this point, and I had no other recourses other than to agree with her. She pulled her sleeping bag out, threw it over her shoulder, and disappeared into the darkness as she was trying to shake the moisture from her hand. I took out my sleeping pad, blew it up, and with my sleeping bag in hand I climbed onto my boxes and went to sleep.

The next morning ET, Walker, Cliff, and myself were standing around the picnic table discussing plans for the day, and I was doing my best to act as if nothing had happened last night. ET shook his head and started laughing. Then he started telling a story as we all looked at him inquisitively, "You probably did not know this, but I was awake last night watching you." My eyes rolled back in my head, and I thought, "Oh shit, here we go." He started with something like, "and the tent should be like this because of the sun and the moon." He ended with, "it's stuck and I can't get it out." The guys were laughing so hard they looked like they were going to puke. Yea, I was never going to live that one down.

I needed to pick up the remnants of my tent. So, I walked over to fold it up, and at a glance, I said out loud, "Who the fuck puts a tent away inside out!"

I threw all of the stuff back into the van and ET drove the Big van with the trailer on it. Walker and Cliff followed behind. On top of the canoe trailer, was a Mad River open whitewater canoe. As we

105

were going down the road, I was in the lead and I saw the whitewater canoe launch into the air about ten feet off the top of the trailer. It hung in the air for a moment as the wind held it there like a kite until the last tether broke. It fell to the road and bounced about eight feet back up into the air and hit the road again. It started tumbling until it stopped in the ditch on the side of the road. We all pulled over to assess the damage. Luckily it did not hit any cars or people, and the only real damage was along the gunnel and a small scrape along the bottom. We all knew we could say that someone tried it, and they brought it back like this. None of us were in any real trouble, I told Walker to tell the boss it was my fault. But he never said anything to us at all, so it was not an issue.

10

Colorado

A few weeks after I received the Triple X, I had the opportunity to go to Colorado with the cinema advertising company I was working for and I jumped at the chance.

I scheduled all of my work at a double-time pace so I could have a whole day off at the end of the week before I went home. We had a lot of work to do so they sent the guy that trained me originally to work with me. The company had just received a big contract, and my company wanted to make a good impression by getting the work done quickly and without any issues. Crain came with me, and we split up the work.

Crain was one of these guys that took life way too seriously! He always wore a long-sleeved, button-down shirt but never in a solid color. It might be 102 degrees out, and he would have the sleeves buttoned down around his wrists and buttoned at the neck. His hair was jet black and immaculate against the pale acne scarred face. He was nervous and jumpy, and always concerned about offending anyone or saying the wrong thing. He always did everything the same way every time. Working at a movie theater for most people meant that he would be in the movie theater until the last movie faded away and he would finish his work and training at around two in the morning. Me, on the other hand, would call the manager and would say, "Make sure the projectionists arrives there early so I can get this training shit out of the way and I want to get into the theater two hours before you open so I can have the gear ready for him." I would do the install in a couple hours and training in fifteen minutes. If the manager gave me a hard time, I would say, "Look, man, I am just trying to do my job and make it easy for you guys. I am only going to be here once, this is a two hundred and fifty-thousand-dollar contract, and both our companies are being a pain in our asses. But I don't want to be the one that is telling them it's not working out; you know what I mean?" Usually, the response

107

was, "Yea I know what you mean, what time did you want to come in?" It always seemed to work out for me, not so much for Crain. People hated him. Honestly, he was not a bad guy just awkward. The moment people saw him they loathed him, especially women. Crain could never figure out how I could be done with my work so fast. I told him what to do, but he never would since he thought that it was unprofessional.

We were going to be in Denver, Colorado for four days. We were flying back on Friday, I had Thursday off, and Crain was flipping out about that of course. But we only had one car for Thursday and Friday. Saving money for the company, of course. When Thursday came around, I had done my research about the area. There was a whitewater park and a kayak shop about a block from it. I called, and they rented kayaks for people to use in the park all the time. I was set, I was going to go kayaking in Colorado! What if it was in a whitewater park! I asked Crain to drop me off at the kayak park, and he asked me how I was going to get back to the hotel. I told him that I would work something out, get a cab if I had to. Crain took me to the park about ten in the morning, the moment I stepped out of the car he was so uptight that he said, "Ok, see you later and took off." Of course, he had my kayaking shorts and shirt with him in the car. I was left standing at the park with nothing. But I had a plan anyway! I walked to the kayak shop and walked in and looked around. The shop guy looked at me and asked if he could help. I said, "Yep rent me the smallest kayak you have I want to try it out at the park."

I knew he had to prequalify me to make sure I didn't die in the thing before he could rent me a kayak. He started asking me questions to do so. He hit me with a barrage of questions. Where was I from? Did I have a driver license? Did I have credit card? The standard stuff, until he came to a question that was actually relevant. He asked, "What kind of stuff do you run in a kayak?" The whitewater course that was nearby was made for slalom kayakers, however I was not a slalom kayaker.

So, my answer took him by surprise when I said, "I run rivers like The Bottom Moose, Oswegatchie River, the Hudson, the Grass River and stuff like that."

108

He looked at me with big eyes and asked, "You run the Bottom Moose and the Grass?" I said, "Yea, you have heard of them?"

"Are you kidding me, I read articles about them all the time in the AW magazine, and I have seen the videos, those rivers are massive!!"

I smiled at him and said "Those articles were probably written by a friend of mine, Dusty."

His mouth dropped open, "You know Dusty?"

"Yea," I replied, "I paddle with his group about once a month on the Bottom Moose when it is releasing, they are always there, and if I don't have a group going down, I hook up with them."

I gave him a bunch of names that hang with the group and people that might have shown up in a few articles. He was beside himself and asked me questions for about a half an hour about different rivers and people I knew. I did not realize that UP State NY was known for whitewater at all! But this guy knew everything.

It finally came time pick a boat, the shop guy remembering my original request said, "We just got this boat in it's a triple X." I smiled a big smile, and the shop guy said, "What?"

I replied that I have one of those at home on a Pro deal. He shook his head with a big smile and said "I should have known."

I told him that, "I have only had it for about two months, so I am still getting used to it, but it's really fun!"

He replied, "Yea cool, we just received this one last week, but you can take anything you want."

I thought this boat would be great fun in the whirlpool eddies of the slalom course. "Now," I said, "I have an issue, my coworker drove off with all of my gear, and I will have to buy some stuff." He asked me what I needed, I told him shorts and some sort of a top. I

109

had on my sandals all ready and they might fit in the boat. He looked at my feet and walked over to the rack and grabbed some booties, some shorts, and a kayaking shirt. He threw them at me and said, "Don't worry about it have fun, just give them back at the end of the day." I expressed my appreciation and suited up with everything I needed a paddle, life jacket, spray skirt, helmet, booties, and clothes. I put my clothes in a locker at the shop under lock and key. Then I put the kayak on my shoulder and walked to the park.

I arrived at the park and saw an old school slalom boater in a big boat running gates in his fiberglass kayak. We could not get any further apart, as far as kayaks go, and most would think mindset as well. I watched him until he came to the bottom of the course and I waded in the water a little. He looked at me with disdain as if to say, "What the hell do you want." I knelt down to his eye level and said, "Minus five for gate seven, but the attainment was awesome definitely a plus eight, so you are up by three."

He laughed and I said, "I don't want to be in your way, I'm just fooling around here today."

I smiled and said, "Me too, you can do anything you want it won't bother me."

We talked about his boat. I asked if he had had that made for him, I knew he had. I wanted him to know that I knew what was going on in the slalom world. I told him that I had spent some time on the Ocoee River on the east coast, but I was Not a slalom guy, I preferred creeks with much fewer people! Again, he smiled and stated that he knew what I meant.

After the short exchange, I wandered to the top of the run. There were several people milling around and some people with kids at the bottom of the run fooling around in the pool of water on this warm day. I dropped into the river and pounded into the first eddy. "Oh man," I thought, "This is going to be fun" as the boat went under water in the turbulent eddy. There was a bridge going over the park, and I saw some people watching me and waved at them to my astonishment, none of them flipped me off, and some waved back! This was a cool place. Around the river there were stadium style steps to sit on, and people were sitting there eating and enjoying the day. It was a nice facility, but I was here to say that I paddled in Colorado so off I went into the next eddy. As I pulled in, I dropped my stern, and my bow went up in the air. I spun around almost flipping over and braced myself back up. I sat up straight and drove myself into the oncoming water and sunk my front end. The river drove the kayak down as I sunk down to my chest in the water. I tried a bow stall, but that seldom worked for me, so I turned it into some acrobatic feet in order to try to keep my head dry. I did not have nose plugs, and I was thinking that this was not the cleanest water I had ever been in. I fooled around for an hour or so, and several people were watching me. I had given in by this point and was now flipping over, stern squirting, and throwing an occasional cartwheel, or at least I was trying to. It seemed to be closer to noon, I did not really know. The time change still had me messed up, but there were many people eating their lunch on the benches by the river and standing on the river walk over the park. I was feeling good and thought to myself these people probably only get to see slalom boaters and never get to have the experience of seeing someone in a small boat. I was also sure that this was the first time this boat had been here. I pulled out into a whirlpool that was just forming and did a big stern squirt. Well at least that was what I thought I was going to do. My ass went down as I looked at the sky and spun around in circles. I completely disappeared under the water. Just after my head submerged, I saw that I had been swept down river about ten yards in a complete mystery move. Then the buoyancy took over and I re-emerged slowly. It looked like I was in control and I did not have to roll up. My head came out of the water first and then my boat. I popped the front of the boat out of the water and jetted to the next eddy. All of the a sudden, I heard cheers and claps from the crowd surrounding the river. I looked around wondering what was going on. Apparently, I had done something pretty cool! I was pretty tired, so I worked my way down to the end and took out for a while.

I walked about half way up the course, flipped the boat over, and sat on it. I was getting warm again while watching the Old School boater do his thing. There were people and kids still playing in the pool. One of the kids, about seven years old, wandered up to

111

the river and was playing in the lower eddies. He was being spun around and was pushing himself up and down off the bottom of the river. After a while he moved up the river one more eddy, this was a much stronger eddy. One of the reasons it was stronger was because it was deeper. The kid obviously did not know that as he slid into the river off the stacked stones that lined the spillway causing the swirly eddy. As he hit the water, his head disappeared, and he popped up in the middle of the strong eddy. He was pushed downstream only to be drawn back into the eddy and sucked upstream past where he had just launched himself. He reached for the wall with no chance and again went under water, popping up in the center of the swirling maelstrom. He was pushed once again downriver and sucked back into its power. He had passed the point of no return. This kid was in trouble.

These courses were designed to do exactly what was happening to this kid. I was just underwater in a kayak with a lifejacket on for ten yards. In ten yards this kid would be dead. I saw the youngster's Dad panicking trying to swim upstream to get to him. But I knew that was not going to happen as he kept getting swept back to the pool. At this point, I was standing at the edge of the river staring directly at the kid, not taking my eyes off of him as I was trying to get my spray skirt off. He was on the other side of the river, but I knew I could get to him, just not with a spray skirt on. I would have to dive in as far as I could and make it to the eddy. This kid was struggling badly, and I was about to go with everything I had. Out of the corner of my eye, I saw the slalom boater shooting down the river. He turned into the eddy, and the kid emerged next to him. He grabbed the kid and pulled him over the deck of his kayak. He let the water pull him to the stacked stones and lifted the kid so he could get a grip. Then the boater pushed the kid up onto the edge of the river. His dad ran the last ten yards to scoop the child up in his arms and hugged him. I started clapping and yelling, "Woohoo!" The crowd joined in and we all clapped and cheered for the guy who deserved it. The Dad thanked the kayaker profusely and the pair quickly gathered their things and moved on.

I walked over to the benches and sat down. I needed a minute to get my adrenaline back into alignment. I sat adjacent to a very pretty woman who turned to me and said, "You were going to jump in and save that boy, weren't you?"

I turned my head toward her, "I wouldn't have had a choice," I replied.

She smiled and tilted her head, "You always have a choice."

We struck up a conversation and talked for quite a while. She told me that it was a nice day, so she had taken the rest of the day off from work. I explained my situation and told her I needed a ride back to my hotel at some point and perhaps we could get some lunch? She agreed to wait for me while I took my gear back to the kayak shop. I grabbed my gear and walked back. When I arrived at the shop, the Shop Guy greeted me with a smile and we spoke briefly. I gave him back the shorts and shirt and wanted to pay up for the rental. When he gave me the bill I told him that I did not think that it was enough. It was not even close to what a rental should be. He told me that he felt that I was an ambassador for the sport and because of that he let me have it for half price! "Well," I thought, "Who am I to argue with that?" I thanked him for everything and worked my way back to the park. My new friend was still there, and she smiled at me now with regular clothes on and she said, "Let's go to lunch, I'm hungry." We had a great lunch and a fun time. As she dropped me off at the hotel, she gave me her phone number and told me that if I was going to be in Denver again to give her a call, I assured her that I would.

Cain, for some reason, was at the hotel. Maybe he had not gone to work yet, I didn't know, but I did not ask either. He asked me about my day, and I told him all of the luck I had with the Shop Guy, kayaking, and then meeting a beautiful woman and having lunch with her. "Then she gave me a ride back to the hotel." I said. He was disgusted with me like always, I'm pretty sure he hated me.

Friday, we flew home. Luckily, I did not have to sit next to Cain. Actually, I talked to the secretary previously and told her that if we are sitting together and the plane crashed, we might both die. But if one of us was in the back of the plane and the other near the front, one of us might live, and it would be less expensive for the company in death benefits.

She smiled at me and said, "You just don't want to sit next to Cain, do you?'

My reply, "Nope, no, I don't," while adamantly shaking my head.

She smiled, "I will take care of it." From that point, all of my flights were happy ones, including this one.

All of the work we did that week went very well with no issues, and Cain had kept his mouth shut about me taking the day off. Really, it did not matter anyway I had already talked to the boss and he told me that as long as my work was done properly I could do anything I wanted. He and I got along great. About a week after we were back, the manager that had only let me go a half hour earlier when I wanted an hour to go pick up my boat was dramatically fired and walked out of the building. I had no idea why, but she deserved it.

After the Black River festival, we did a few more festivals where we raised awareness for the shop. I was able to keep my pro rep status for a few years until many of the boat companies merged and dropped their sponsors. I didn't mind. I knew enough people in the business to always get whatever boat I wanted for next to nothing, even without being a sponsored. I eventually quit the cinema advertising company that I had been working with for the last three years. I had not been given a raise in over two years and felt that I was stuck and would never be able to move up in the company. When I left, they hired two full-time people and two part-timers to fill the position I held on my own.

One week after I walked out of the company, I obtained employment at one of the largest gun stores in Rochester, NY. At the time, it was a great deal, and I made a deal with my manager I would work all of the hunting seasons anytime they wanted me to, in trade, I had the weekends off in the summer and worked up in Watertown on the river every weekend. I worked at the gun counter, but I also put together a few classes for kids about water safety that I did in the pool they had at the time. I worked there for a couple of years, and when I saw they were starting to go downhill, I quit and took another job. Eventually I ended up on the river full time and being laid off every winter. Many times, taking a temp job until spring then I would quit and start kayaking again.

11

The Pejibaye River, Costa Rica

I received a call from an old buddy of mine, Red. "I have a deal working to go to Costa Rica to kayak. You interested?" Of course I was interested. He had been called by a local adventure company to do an exploration trip through Costa Rica to run a bunch of the rivers. They wanted to find out if these rivers were feasible for their clients to be guided down. They needed a few kayakers that had experience and my name came up. We put a small team together, had a few meetings to discuss the intentions of the trip, and made a plan. Within a matter of weeks, we were on our way to Costa Rica.

Costa Rica had the same rating system on rivers that America did, but their rivers were much harder to run. Their class IV rapid might be a class V by our standards. This was important information since many people on our team were not class V kayakers. Terry was the least experienced kayaker but, politically, it made sense to take him since he had contacts with management in Letchworth State Park. Terry was not aggressive. On the river, we always had to tell him what to do and where to go. I had paddled with Fred several times and he always did fine. He had a laid-back attitude and was always consistent on the water. Debbi was one of those girls who would try anything once. She was aggressive on the water and didn't mind putting herself in danger. Sam was the leader. He made all the arrangements: flights, hotels, kayaks, food, and anything else you could think of. He was a kayak instructor, which meant nothing to me, but Red assured me that he was a good paddler. The next morning we met up with our driver, Henry, who doubled as our interpreter. We went and rented kayaks and outfitted them in about an hour. We loaded them in Henry's van and headed to the Reventazon River.

The Reventazon River was a class III and was a good warm up to test the boats. We were a bit nervous putting in on a strange river in a new country. The locals told us the river was cold from the rain, but the water was actually sixty-five to seventy degrees. Many of the rivers I had been on had ice floating down them. This was summer water to me. We set off down the river, and as we did so, I could feel the water working its way past my spray skirt to my legs. Water, as a general rule, goes downhill. So, as I felt a drop of water on my leg migrating uphill, I worked my way back to shore. I hit a small sandy beach, pulled my spray skirt off, and jumped out of my boat. I started shaking my leg like it was on fire. The biggest cockroach I had ever seen had been hitching a ride on my leg.

After my episode, we got back in the water. We were getting used to our boats and were starting to understand each other's skill sets. Although I had paddled with most of these folks before, I was now getting a better idea of what to expect later when we got to the harder water. Sam was a sharp paddler with clean strokes, but he never really concentrated on kayaking as a single discipline. One thing that struck me as funny was that Sam stopped in the middle of the river and ate a big meal. He had brought cheese, bread, different spreads, and fruit. I never ate on the river because it was counter-intuitive. All the blood in your body moves from your limbs to your stomach to help aid digestion. When you get back on the water, you would have to get your arms and legs going again and it could cause issues. I was concerned about Sam's idea of kayaking. I think he was concerned about me too, but what we had in common was that we wanted our people safe. It was the most important thing.

As we ran the Reventazon River, I was overwhelmed by its beauty. The river was bordered by rainforest and deep jungle. It was also at the bottom of a steep ravine. At times, sheer vertical walls would appear rising directly from the river covered with jungle foliage. The noises coming from the jungle were haunting. From time to time, you could catch a glimpse of something in the trees: monkeys, iguanas, and colorful birds of all kinds. This was a new experience for me, and I was humbled by it.

That night we went to the Pochotel, a beautiful hotel with an amazing view. The hotel was situated at the top of a ridge in the lush green mountainside. Looking down on sugarcane fields, your eye was led to the river at the bottom of the valley. Scanning the

117

landscape, you could see roads cut into the side of the valley's wall. The morning brought warm sunshine and the sound of toucans popping their bills and squawking as they flew back and forth from the jungle to their aviary. In the cafe, we found fresh ground aromatic coffee and a host of breakfast foods, all fresh picked that morning. We had a light, happy attitude and, with our taste buds thoroughly satisfied, we looked forward to the day.

We were running the Pejibaye River, which was a class V river, in the jungle that ran down into the Reventazon River. Terry and Fred decided to meet us halfway down the run, because the river was much bigger than we originally thought. They would be on the side of the river waiting for us. This river was harder at the top, as most rivers in Costa Rica were. The rivers started in the mountains, descend into the flat of the low lands, and got easier as you went. The Pejibaye was no exception. We all went up the river as high as we thought the van would go. We found an open spot and walked through the undergrowth to the side of the river. The river was littered with massive boulders and the drops that we could see were technical with a lot of water in the main channels. The river curved around a corner and disappeared behind a rock wall rising from the forest floor a few hundred feet with an impossible tangle of vegetation on it. Past that we couldn't see a thing. We could only hear the water.

We suited up and made a plan. I would lead and would go across the river into an eddy just above the drop. I sat at the edge of the river and peered downstream into the darkness. The jungle canopy was thick and the walls of the canyon were blocking most of the sun. The river was ripping by as I slid myself off the bank and shot across the creek. I dropped into the eddy and looked over the drop. There was a big eddy on the left side of the river that was created by the same boulder that caused the drop. The drop was about eight feet high and once you went over it, you were in the canyon. I gave my guys hand signals from across the river to show angle and direction. I peeled out of the eddy, gained speed, booked over the falls, landed in the eddy, and turned to look upstream. Sam, Red, and Debbi came over the waterfall one after the other. They were too close together and none of them made it into the eddy I was in. I was disappointed they had little to no control, "This might not go well," I thought. I caught up with them and we worked our way down the river until we saw the rock.

There was a house-sized rock in the middle of the river that split the water. Sam and I looked at each other and automatically got out of our boats to take a look at it. On the left side of the river we could see that there was a slot of water running between two boulders. The big one in the center and another boulder that extruded from the left of the river. The slot was about five feet wide with a lot of aerated water running through it. At the entrance, the water was building up on both sides of the slot, and the water was higher on both sides of the entrance than it was in the slot the boulders created. This was a concern because if a person did not hit the entrance straight on, they might end up sideways and a folded boat with the person in it. "What do you think, Sam?" I asked.

He replied, "I want to run it."

"No, I don't think it's a good idea with this group. I would like to go across the river and look at the other side to see if it it's more open."

As I said that, I pointed across the river to an eddy I thought I could get into. When I pointed, Red took off down the river. Just above the big rock there was a significant hole. Red hit it and flipped. He hit the house size rock upside down and immediately swam. The boat went to the left and ended up going through the crack on left side of the river that we had been looking at. Red, however, got swept to the right side of the river and disappeared behind the rock.

We were in the middle of a rainforest, in the middle of a three-hundred-foot canyon, in the middle of a class V rapid. If we lost his boat, we were fucked. I yelled at Sam do the slot or go to the right of the river. We had to find Red and his boat. I jumped into my boat and launched off a boulder six feet down into the river above the hole that had flipped Red. I shot through the hole and lined up with the slot. But on the way into the slot, I had to make a correction and water was building up on my back deck. In the slot I couldn't keep

119

my paddle across my boat because the paddle was too long. I had to point the paddle, the only problem was now I was moving the same speed as the water with my stern under water and my bow straight up in the air. My paddle was at my side, and I was trying to keep from flipping over backward by popping the paddle off the water behind me. But the water was so aerated it had no perches. As I came out the end of the slot and into regular water, I looked to the right for Red. He was climbing up on a rock in the middle of the river. He stood up and pointed down to the center of the river. There was his boat, wrapped around a rock in the middle of the flow of a class IV+ rapid. The cockpit was facing upstream and the boat was mostly underwater. I signaled the boaters behind me who then came through the slot just fine. Sam, Debbi, and I stood on the left of the river and Red stayed on the rock in the middle of the river. We were getting out throw ropes and carabineers when we heard Red whistle. We turned around as he jumped into the water and disappeared. He reappeared about ten yards downriver, swimming to get to the same side of the river as us. It was a stupid move and he was lucky it worked. Now we had to address the boat issue.

First, we would simply try to paddle up to it from downstream and hook a rope to it. Sam got to it once and I got to it once. But the river was too fast and neither of us was able to hook a rope to the wrapped boat. Sam wanted to string a rope across the river at an angle and have a person slide down the rope and hook the boat. I felt that was too complicated. When he asked me how I wanted to do it I said, "Put a man on a rope and pendulum him out to the boat, hook the boat, and go downstream with the rope. Then let the person slide down the rope using the water to help him get to shore." Sam felt that was too dangerous. I was agitated and wanted to get moving toward a solution.

Sam somehow got to the other side of the river, but the river was too wide for one rope to go across. The team had to use a carabineer to attach two ropes together. With a long hard throw, with the two ropes attached together, the rope arched up over the river and came down at the edge of the river where Sam scooped them up. He began pulling the rope taut but it wouldn't tighten. Somehow the carabineer had hit a rock just right and was stuck open. The ropes had come undone and now two people were left holding two different ropes on either side of the river. Neither rope was long enough to reach the other person. This set up of getting a person across the river took a very long time. In Costa Rica, it got dark at six o'clock. Being close to the equator, the sunset lasted about five minutes before it was completely dark. It was now two-thirty and we had an estimated three-hour paddle out.

After some time, everyone assembled on left of the river again. I was pissed off and laid it on the line. "You are putting my life in danger. I am not going to spend the night in this jungle. Red can ride on the back of my boat or we get his boat back. Either way, I am leaving you in thirty minutes." Sam was a bit taken back at my anger but I knew this was serious. Sam asked me what I wanted to do. "I want to pendulum a guy across." Red stepped up and said, "It's my boat. I will go into the river." Sam jumped over the slot we had come through with our boats with me hanging onto the rope. Sam wrapped the rope around himself before throwing the end to Red. Red, with a good carabiner, attached it to a strap that was around him. I fed the rope to Sam as Red worked his way into the river above the boat. Red was able to push off the bottom and direct himself to the boat. He reached it and hooked the boat to the rope with himself still attached. Sam let me have the rope and I ran down the side of the river below the boat and Red. All he had to do was simply slide down the rope to Debbi and me. Then we all pulled the boat out. It was a little out of shape, but after Red jumped on it, the boat snapped back into position. We quickly re-entered our boats and headed downstream. I was relieved to be on my way down the river. When we found Terry and Fred, they were happy to see us. They had seen someone's lunch and water bottle float by and knew there must have been a problem since we were taking too long. They had walked up the river and were stopped by the canyon wall, then they came back and walked up the road to the put in. They could not see past the canyon and saw no sign of us on either end. All they could do was wait by the edge of the river. We all continued down the river and arrived at the takeout at sunset. It was completely dark carrying our boats from the river to the van. We loaded our boats into the truck with a flashlight.

121

The next river was the Sarapiqui River, this was a very popular river in Costa Rica for rafting and kayaking. Sam had gotten in touch with the company that we rented our kayaks from and had arranged for us to follow the rafts. Specifically, one of their kayakers, and as he told us about the arrangement I questioned him about the kayaker that we would be following. Turns out he was the cameraman for the group. I said something to the effect of, "You do realize that that guy has to sprint past the rafts, set up at the rapids, take photos of the rafts, then get back into the kayak and sprint past the rafts again to the next rapid, and if we have an issue he can't wait for us. We have to be on his ass." Sam did not seem overly impressed with my view of the situation. Then we hit the water, we saw that boater for about five minutes and never saw him again. At this point, I was sure this was the last trip I would be on with Sam. He was still carrying a full lunch for everyone, and he had no knowledge of how to really run a river. He understood the theory of how to do things but had no reality-based knowledge.

Fred had to swim early in the beginning of the canyon and said his shoulder was killing him, but twenty minutes later he had to swim again. Fred swam at least five times that day. Later, when he was back home, we would find out that Fred had a bone spur rubbing on the tendon in his shoulder that he used use to roll with. He was in a lot of pain and was still tired from the day before, he did not have a good day. The river was fun and moving along pretty good. Many times, we would stop and talk about what we were going to do, in the upcoming rapid.

This river was much bigger and more aggressive than the first river. The volume of water and moves were much harder for Terry, and Terry wanted to follow someone, usually Red. I was leading most of the time, and we came to a beautiful spot in the river. Sheer rock walls with a rock pillar growing out of the middle of the river, it was about eighty feet high. Covered in green foliage and vines showing only pieces of the sheer granite pillar. The river necked down a bit here and picked up speed. Now we were in the canyon with a straight rock face that extended up nearly out of sight on the right side of the river, and the rock pillar in the center of the river made the river waves stack and crash over themselves. It looked intimidating, but we had to run it between the rock pillar and the wall. We had no choice, the other side was tumultuous, and if someone had an issue, recovery would be very hard.

I would run it first, followed by Sam and Fred. We would get in an eddy and Red, Terry, and Debbi would follow, that was the plan anyway. Sam and I took off, but when I looked behind me Red was on my ass, and Fred was behind him. Terry and Debbi were left in the eddy. Right next to the pillar, Fred flipped and swam, we were able to promptly get him into an eddy. Terry came down the river very pissed off with good reason. "We need to have a talk," he said. This was the biggest water he had ever been in, and he was afraid. Terry was counting on the group to get him through. Especially Red, but Red had left him and did not follow instructions. He was still shaken up from the day before, Fred and Terry really did not know what happened the day before other than the basic a boat got pinned. It took a lot out of Red, and he was becoming conservative when he should have been stepping it up. We rehashed our order, got Fred in his boat, and went down the river, it was a long run, and I did not want to stop. Of course, we had to stop for lunch. The lunch thing was taking forever. I was going past a big hole / hydraulic in the river, and something caught my eye. There was a dude on a Pyranha river board in the middle of the hole playing around. He and his friend were locals and ran the river all the time. They were happy to accompany us down the rest of the river and they weren't in any hurry.

These guys saved our ass, the 2nd guy was in a kayak. He ran lines tight and knew every turn and hole. This sped our trip up immensely; I was super happy to have them helping us out. We came to the one class V section of the river, the locals told us all about it then ran it as we watched. I ran it next catching eddies on the way through it. Both guys smiled and nodded their heads showing approval for my lines. Sam was next and took the standard go for the big wave mentality and crashed through the waves with no real issue. The rest of the group walked it.

The end of the river was like the end of a movie. Sheer rock granite walls on both sides of the river going straight up hundreds of feet, with a footbridge over the river inundated with vegetation.

123

With a slight rain starting, there was a misty fog that seemed to cling to the walls not wanting to leave the lush green vegetation. Kids swam from the shore jumped in the river and swam out to us and hitched a ride on the back of our kayaks with big smiles on their faces. They accompanied us to the takeout around the corner. I didn't care what happened that day, the view was worth it. Fred was pretty beat up though and did not look good at all.

That night we talked about the day and Terry reiterated that he needed more help on the river than he was getting. Fred drank beer and ate pain pills, his face was drawn and hollow as he rubbed his shoulder. I had my doubts about him paddling the next few days. We knew something was really wrong with the shoulder, but there was no way to know if he was doing more damage or not.

The next river was the Penas Blancas. This was a class III+ and the last river we would do. It had rained all night, and the river was pumping and was brown with silt. At the put in a local kid had come down to talk to us dressed in kayaking gear. He spoke no English at all, but Sam said to me that he was asking us if he could boat with us.

"How long had he been boating?" I asked.

"One year," was his answer.

"Has he done this river before?"

"Yes."

"I think that would be fine," I said, so he came with us.

The river was fun and playful, we surfed and played in the strong eddies. Then we came to the corners, on every big corner of the river the water was piling against the rock walls sometimes causing a breaking wave six feet high on the wall itself. Not knowing if the walls were undercut or what the hell was going on, I hesitated to go into them. Then the kid about ten years old singled me to come and turned and paddled right into it. "Yea baby... play time!" This kid was awesome, he was stern squirting and cartwheeling all over

124

the place. I will admit that the first time I dropped into one, I ended up cartwheeling by accident and flipped with little control. These were much more powerful than they looked. But the rest of the day I had a smile on my face, stern squirting, bow stalling, and surfing with my new found partner. The eddy lines were extremely powerful. With one paddle stroke backward your stern would be sucked underwater, you would be in a stern squirt with the bow of the boat pointing skyward, and because the water was hitting the wall and pushing you back, you could hold it for a long time. Every twenty minutes, the kid would stop and empty his boat because it had a hole in it.

But we had a great time. Sam at one time asked me to hurry up because we had to go, but I paid him no mind. I had waited for these guys all week and lead most of the trips, this was my time. At the end of the day I asked Sam to ask the kid how many days he had paddled in the year. His answer put me in my place, 365 days, every day for a year. That kid had paddled more in one year than I did in three years. Yea, we all think we are a badass until the badass shows up, then we are just like everybody else!

Sam had several things planned for the rest of the week, sightseeing stuff. Just the kind of thing I never want to do, I mean who really gives a shit about an oxcart? We went to the central market and saw the local shops. Wow, that was an eye-opener. If you had a piece of tin and some lumber to make a frame, you too could be a vendor in the central market. There were chicken guts in the muddy alleyways and stray dogs all over the place. Fish and meat hung on hooks in the open air. The air was humid and still beneath the hot tin, and it stung your eyes as the stench wafted into your nose from the small markets. This nearly caused my gag reflex to go into overdrive. Not a place I really wanted to hang out.

The Volcano...

Hey, there was a good idea, "Let's go to the volcano and take a hike." Now, this sounded good in theory, the only problem was the volcano was very active. Arenal Volcano was next to a national park by the same name. No access to the general public was given beyond a cretin point, but before that, you could do anything you wanted. We parked at the gate of the National park. Everyone wanted to hike up to the side of the volcano, but not me. The rest of the group headed into the jungle below the volcano while I catching up in my journal. Twenty minutes after they left, I felt the ground start to shake and heard a great rumble. I looked out the van door at the guard standing at the gate. He motioned for me to come, so I hustled over to him as he pointed up at the face of the volcano. It was erupting! There were boulders the size of cars flying off the top of the mountain causing landslides. There was a plume of ash shooting up in the air about three thousand feet. I retrieved my camera and took a few photos hoping that it would stop and that my people were ok. The guard at the gate explained to me somehow that this was common and happened all the time. It was good that he did that because I was starting to look for the keys to the van! I could still hear rocks crashing down the mountain, and the wind had started deforming the ash plume.

The funny thing about the whole thing was that I was the only one out of the group that saw the eruption. My friends were under the jungle canopy and couldn't even see the sky.

All and all it was a great trip, we walked through a rainforest park and saw both the Pacific and Atlantic oceans from the same point. I had smoked a Cuban Cigar every night of the trip except the first one. We had seen poison dart frogs, caiman, and a host of other wild beings, not to mention the cockroaches. The jungles were amazing and the food was much better than anything I had in the states. The rivers were impressive and fun. It was worth it, and I am glad that I had the opportunity to go.

I ran thirty different rivers that year and paddled over a hundred days. I had kayaked whitewater in Canada, Costa Rica, and America. I realized that really, it was the people you were around that made all the difference and helped you have a quality experience.

12

Henry the Optimist

I had known Henry so long that I couldn't even remember where I met him. Henry was tall, lanky, and didn't look like he should fit into a kayak. He was loud, fun, and usually the life of the party. When he sat in a kayak he was sharp and daring. The guy had balls, and I had kayaked with him on the Moose River at very high levels, Salmon River, Black River, and several creeks. He was a solid class V boater and I was lucky to have him as a friend. You simply never had a better time than you would have with Henry. He knew everyone and everyone knew him. One day, Henry gave me a call and told me that a mutual friend of ours, Beamer, was having a party. I immediately knew a party with those two shouldn't be missed under any circumstances. He told me that it was supposed to be good weather and that the he and I should try to run Mill Creek in Lowville, NY before the party. I called Jed a friend of mine that lived in that area, and asked him about the run. He told me that this was a great little creek and that I would have a fun time, but the snow was still deep and it might not be running yet. Jed would know, I had met him years earlier on the Moose River and he invited me to his home to change and get warm. We have been good friends ever since.

Mill Creek had an average gradient of one hundred feet per mile and a max gradient of two hundred feet per mile. It was only about four miles long, we knew we would run it later in the day when it was warmer and still make it back to Syracuse in time for the party.

The next day I met up with Henry and we headed up to Lowville. When we arrived, we were surprised to find there was still three feet of hard snow on the ground. Jed was right about that, that's for sure. The only thing we really looked at from the road was the waterfall below Rt. 12 Bridge. The drop did not look bad, it was clear of debris and looked like a fun line. So we found the put in,

127

which happened to be in a farmer's field. From this vantage point, the river didn't look like much. It appeared to be a little creek that snaked its way back and forth until it reached the first drop off. We could see that the river necked down to half its width and that the water was piling on the left and the right before the drop. We put all of our cold weather clothes on, but we were already sweating, it was about sixty-five degrees. That was very warm for a north country spring day. We walked through the snow to the put in.

The thing about spring paddling was that you had to have your shit together. It may be the hardest water you do all year, but you also hadn't been in a boat for a couple months. The cold weather gear we had to wear reduced our flexibility and range of motion, but it was a necessity. With no warm-up, we dropped into the river and headed down to the first bottleneck. Into the first drop I went and disappeared under water, which took me by surprise. I shot out in a tail stand with my big creek boat, unable to reach the water with my paddle. When I broke into the eddy with Henry, we were both taken back by how aggressive the water was. Before every drop, we parked our boats to take a good look at the rapids to make sure there was no debris.

With a multitude of slides at a medium angle it was like a bobsled run that ended with a BIG splash. Slide after slide the river grew a little faster, the hits at the end kept getting bigger. We caught the last eddy before the big drop below the bridge. It struck me that the bridge seemed much higher looking up at it. I instantly had a sense of foreboding. The drop was clear of debris but I knew that the water was continuing to rise quickly because of the warm weather. Henry smiled at me, "You ready?" With no sense of impending doom, he powered through the eddy fence and jetted downstream as I watched from the swirling eddy. It took him about ten paddle strokes to get to the drop above the waterfall before he disappeared. Suddenly, I saw the end of his boat, then the other end, then the other end. He was caught and cartwheeling end over end in his kayak until he ended up in a violent side surf.

"Holy fuck, he needs help," I thought as I slammed into the eddy fence and powered downstream. My plan was to slam into him and knock him out of the hole. As I drew closer, I saw how massive

128

the hole was. Getting closer to the hole I realized there was no way could I get through it. I was in a kayak that was over seven feet long. The hole was longer and higher than that and my friend was caught in the middle of it. I pulled the hardest Duffek stroke I had ever made. It drew me to the right of the river, far enough to make the gap next to the bank. I just missed the hole! Henry was in a hard-right-hand side surf facing away from me. He was paddling his ass off and going nowhere. I was in an eddy that was heaving up and down four to five feet! Henry tried coming backward toward me as I screamed at him, "Keep coming, I've almost got you! Paddle, paddle, paddle!" He was inches from my hand as I reached out to him, only to be violently cartwheeled back into the hole. Flip roll, flip roll, flip roll. He was getting beat up bad. I looked for a handhold or a tree or anything to anchor to. I had a throw rope between my legs in the drink holder, but it was impossible to get to. I had to paddle out into the river at times just to keep from getting sucked underwater or slammed against the wall. We were in real trouble. Henry disappeared and, three seconds later, his boat shot straight up out of the hole without him in it. I paddled out behind the hole facing upstream toward it. It would be my only chance to grab him if he came out. I paddled, paddled, paddled, and still no Henry. I paddled as fast as I could at the edge of the foam coming out of the hole, but I still lost ground. I was slowly getting pushed back toward the waterfall that was behind me. I was screaming, "Come on! I'm right here! I'm right here!"

I was now yards above the waterfall and needed to go over it on the other side of the river! With no other choice, I ferried to the left of the river, turned, and ran my line. I dropped over the edge and freefell into the wave below and I was able to ride the wave. It shot me into the air over the next drop without touching it! I followed the water over the third drop and got into the eddy on the left of the river. I looked upstream at the waterfall, and I was helpless. Henry was in a world of shit with no boat and I couldn't get to him! I hadn't seen him for over two minutes. If he was caught underwater, in another minute he'd be dead. His boat, now full of water, careened over the drop, hit the main flow, and worked its way down to me. I met his boat in the center of the creek, angled it toward the eddy, and gave it a push. Suddenly, Henry came over the waterfall on the right of the river. I watched him curl into a ball and free fall fifteen feet landing in the backwash of the waterfall. I watched him cartwheeling out of control before he disappeared and came over the next drop. I was in the middle of the creek and was going to get him no matter what.

I saw his helmet, then his face. I started screaming, "I'm here!" two feet from me. He realized I was there. He pushed off the bottom, went up into the air, and landed across the front deck of my kayak, gasping for breath and holding on for dear life. With great effort, I drove us to an eddy on the right of the river. I glanced briefly to the left of the river checking for his boat, but it was gone. Henry sat on a small shelf, half in the water and half out, shaking his head back and forth, looking down at the water, and breathing heavy. I said, "Tell me what's going on, man. Are you hurt?" He was definitely in pain. After a couple minutes, he determined he was good enough to scale the bank that led to the bridge. He told me to find his boat and to avoid going over the waterfall near town at the feeder stream. I shook my head yes and took off.

Around the corner, the creek canyon went up again and got very thin. As I looked downriver, all I could see was whitewater and rock walls. The fun bobsled slides had been replaced by a moving caldron of brutally unforgiving whitewater. The river had gone up exponentially and was getting bigger by the minute. I dropped into the canyon on a mission. I was looking for two things: big holes and my buddy's boat. I paddled to the low side of the river and broke through the holes as hard as I could. I tried to have a controlled descent, catching eddies where I could to read the next drop. I got handled, thrown back and forth across the river by compression waves coming off the walls which directed me to the center of the creek. I kept paddling and tried to keep my bow pointing downstream. I was reactionary boating at this point; brace, paddle, lean, paddle hard get over there! On and on it went, until finally, I began to see daylight again. More in control, I made it to a feeder stream. I needed to take out. In an eddy, I stopped and popped my spray skirt and stood upright in the river as fresh cold-water rushed into my booties.

I scurried up a muddy bank, leaving my boat sideways on a tree below me and pulling it up with my throw rope. I did this, again and again, using the saplings growing out of the bank until I reached the plateau. With my boat digging into my shoulder, I walked into the town of Lowville. I found Henry by my van, running up and down the river bank looking for me with a throw rope. He hugged me when I walked up to him, "I thought you had been swept over the waterfall, I thought you were dead!"

A police officer had picked him up just as he was limping across the bridge and gave him a ride to my van. He had been looking for me ever since. We quickly threw my boat into the back of my van and went down river looking for his boat. Still dressed in our gear, we followed the river out of town. Eventually, he called off the search. We were spent. My hands were still bleeding from being slammed against the wall in the crazy eddy and he hurt all over. Henry called "The Moose" radio station in Lowville with a report to look for his missing boat.

At Beamer's house, we evaluated the day and the injuries. Henry had cracked his helmet, lost his paddle, lost his boat, and was bruised all over. He had taken water into his lungs and had a broken toe. I was no worse for wear with busted up hands and sore arms. It was nothing that alcohol and Advil couldn't fix. Three days later, Henry received a call from the radio station. The water department was patrolling the river after the flood and found his boat at the confluence of Mill Creek and the Black River, five miles from where I saw it last. His throw rope had come unraveled and had gotten stuck in a tree. His kayak was half full of mud but would live to see a river again.

Over the years, Henry's near-death experience circulated around the kayaking community where it took on a life of its own. Even years later, I am still asked, "Weren't you the guy with Henry on Mill Creek that day?" Yes, yes I was.

13

The Salmon River

I never liked the Salmon River. The first time I ever ran it, I inadvertently slipped my new custom-made wooden Mitchell paddle into a crack in the wall at the end by the takeout. I was being pushed around by the current and ended up cracking the blade. The Salmon's riverbanks were sequined with hundreds of fishermen who wholeheartedly believed the river belonged to them. The fishermen left behind a host of garbage, from candy wrappers and beer cans to broken fishing lines and freshly sharpened hooks on the bottom of the river. If you were upside-down in a kayak the worst thing that could happen to you was to run into a taught eighty-pound fishing line underwater. The Salmon was usually a beginner river at class III. But when the river was raging, it became a class IV that no beginner should attempt. The eddy lines on a low water day could be tricky, but on a high-water day they became tumultuous.

Many years ago, my friends put together the Salmon River Kayak Festival. The Salmonfest drew in loads of people wanting to try the sport of kayaking. One night during the festival, I was jumping from campfire to campfire looking for people I had not seen in a while. I had been spending most of my time kayaking on bigger rivers so I had lost contact with many of the people I used to run with. I caught up with some old friends and told them I was going to do a quick run on the Salmon early the next day before going back up to the Black River where I belonged. The next morning, I picked up something to eat in town and headed to the put in on the Salmon.

Down by the ramp to the water I saw an old friend of mine, whom I always called Fingers. Fingers had gone to Madawaska kayaking school with me in Canada and broke his fingers. Now he gave lessons to beginner kayakers and looked like he was in the middle of a class when I came up to him. When he saw me, a smile shot across his face. "Marty, oh my god. Marty is here. It's a pleasure to be in your presence, all mighty 'Marty, The Kayaker."

He had dropped to his knees with both hands pointed toward the sky as he bowed down. He crawled over to me and touched my feet as if I were an emperor. I stood smiling, a little astounded, and said, "It's nice to see you too." This, of course, was met with much laughter from his students. I reassured his students that I had started kayaking with Fingers, and he knew what he was doing. We had a quick conversation before I jumped in my truck and went to the takeout.

I told the guys that gave me the shuttle back to the put in that they could follow me or not. It was up to them. They elected to keep up with me, so we went to the first big eddy and took turns playing. Somewhere along the way, I passed Fingers giving instructions. We played all the way down the river, surfing where we could and dropping into eddies. I did a bit of stern squirting, which was when your bow points to the sky and your stern gets sucked into a good whirlpool causing you to spin in circles. I started telling the other guys that they must have more power than the river, moving faster or slower than the water. If you travel at the same speed as the river, the river would handle you and you would lose control. For me, it was always fun to see people progress in a short time on the river, learning skills that would serve them for the rest of their kayaking lives. We continued down river, laughing and hollering at each other the whole way.

We made our way to an epic hole known as Titanic. Titanic, as the name implied, was the biggest hole on the Salmon River at this level. It was sticky and could be hard to get out of if you didn't have much experience. Several people had lined up on each side of it, weighting for their turn for fame. They would each try to get in and miss, or get in, flip, and flush out. Some swam while others surfed for a while before washing out. I watched as a kid got stuck in the hole. He was not giving up, but he wasn't making any headway either. Motor Mouth, as I liked to call him, was another one of my pals from the past. I saw him standing on the side of the river on a small peninsula ten feet away from the kid that was now stuck in the hole. The kid was getting tired and started to extend his arms and lean into the hole too much. Motor Mouth yelled out to him, "Guess what?" The kid's head snapped up to look at Motor

Mouth, no doubt looking for inspiration. Motor Mouth shouted, "You're fucked," as a shit eating grin formed on his face.

I looked back at the kid and knew that when he inevitably flipped, there was a strong chance he would hit his paddle on the bottom of the river and blow his shoulder. I wasn't going to let that happen if I could help it. With ten people in front of me, I powered out into the river and passed them all as fast as I could. I dropped into the hole and surfed in real slow to avoid slamming into the kid. He was facing away from me and did not know I was there. I eased up behind him and yelled so he could hear me. "Hey! I am right behind you. Keep your arms low. I am going to give you a push. Paddle hard on your right side. Are you ready?" He yelled back that he was, so I worked up to him and leaned hard into the foam pile. I grabbed my paddle in the middle of the shaft and put the right blade of the paddle into the foam pile. I grabbed the back of his boat, gave him a push, and he started paddling.

He was right up to the edge of the hole where I would let him go and stopped. He slid back into the hole and my boat ended up overlapping his. I tried again and was able to give him a better push and he popped out of the end of the hole without flipping. I raised my fist into the air amongst cheers from the crowd. The guys that had come down the river with me were whistling and clapping and everyone followed suit. I worked my way to the back of the line where the kid was catching his breath. I pulled in next to him and he began thanking me profusely. I told him, "You did a great job keeping your composure. If you had pointed your boat the other way in the hole, it would have been easier to get out of. Just practice and you will get it."

After that, I needed to go so I waved goodbye to the guys I had paddled with and took off on my own. I took off out of the river and walked to the parking lot. I walked up the stairs and was met with a beer and a, "nice save" from another kayaker. I did not even know who they were but I said thanks and walked to my truck. Motor Mouth was there looking disgusted at me for upstaging him. I threw my boat on the top of the truck and meticulously tied it down like I always did and took off to the north to play on the Black River in the early afternoon. I decided I would never go back to the Salmon during a standard release. The group mentality was as foul as the stench of the dead fish on the water. I didn't need to be around that.

14

Good People

There were times when information was critical; times when a small piece of information could change your life. Several times in my kayaking career, moments before putting on a river, I've had another kayaker come up to me and say something like, "Watch out for the tree in the second drop." This bit of information didn't seem like much, but in my world it could be the difference between celebrating with steak and beer or being on the slab myself. Although information was imperative, the character of every river was different. The skill level of each person was different, and one person alone could change the whole dynamic of a group. You had to remember that, no matter what you were told and no matter where you got your information, you had to look at your situation with an open mind. You had to set aside all preconceived notions and interpret what was in front of you. You should never assume that the information you have been given is completely correct.

When we pulled up to Lampson Falls on the Grass River, the falls were raging. I was with the A team with a few new arrivals. Bugsy, Carpenter, and Si were the standard but we also had Beth, Cook, and Greeny as additions.

We were on our way south after a weeklong trip in the upper ADK. We had run several rivers over the week, most of which were new to us. It had been a hard week between bad weather and bad areas, but this river seemed like a good one on which to end the week. It was a short fast run and would only take a couple hours. I had been fixated on Lampson Falls. It was an ugly slide that extended all the way across the river. Unlike many slides in the ADK, this one had rocks jutting upwards causing water to shoot off the rock flakes nearly eight feet into the air. It looked like a boat-breaking neck-wrenching good time. We decided not to run it, and this decision came with no protest from me at all.

The weather was cold and rainy, which was nothing new for the ADK spring. There was still snow in the mountains and the water was not getting warmer anytime soon. We had a swimmer almost every day of the trip. This was unusual for our group. We were usually tight and efficient on the river. But every time you added a new member, there was an adjustment period and on this trip we had three of them. We were beaten up, tired, and stressed. One of the new members wasn't up to our skill level and this added a level of stress, especially since we were stuck with them until the end of the trip.

We knew that a group of kayakers had run this river at 600cfs. We checked the current level with cell phones and we could see that 600cfs would also be our level for the day. We knew that the previous group had a much lower skill set than our group did. Even with our weakest link, we thought the river wouldn't give us any issues. We put in at the pool below the falls as the Cook walked out onto a peninsula below the pool to fish. He was sitting this one out because of a mishap earlier in the week, smashing his thumb.

The rest of us worked our way past the roaring falls, dwarfed in its shadow. Today would be a pool drop run. After every drop, we had time to recover. Also, there were easy take outs if we wanted to scout out the next drop.

We went through some boogie water and a small drop with a big hole in it that we skirted around. We approached the next drop and the group took out on the right of the river. My plan was to stay in the boat and wait for the guys to return with the low down on how to run the drop. I liked to run stuff like this blind with a little information from the group. With any other group, however, I always got out and looked for myself. From the first moment I pulled up above this rapid I kept hearing my little voice telling me to get out of the boat, after waiting for five minutes, my little voice was now screaming at me! I extracted myself from my boat and tugged it up onto the shoreline and secured it. I grabbed my throw rope and took my paddle with me on the short walk to the drop zone. The guys were lined up, wide-eyed with their mouths open. Bugsy walked over to me as I approached. "I don't know about this one," he said, shaking his head with pronounced wrinkles on his forehead.

137

I walked over to the edge of the river and looked down, holding onto a tree. "What the fuck is that?" I exclaimed. Before me was a Class V, possibly terminal hole, with rolling waves of water rushing into it from both sides. I stood there dumbfounded with my mouth open.

I immediately consulted with Carpenter. "I can't believe how much water is in it," I said.

Carpenter looked intently at the run. "If you miss one paddle stroke, you will be in the hole and might drown before anyone can get you out. If you run the left wall with the angle of left, you still need to break through the two rolling waves that are kicking into the hole."

I could see the line he was talking about. "I think you have to start in the center of the river and drive into the waves to make it through. No way could you get through it if you start on river left," I said as I glanced at Bugsy.

He shook his head no as he pursed his lips. We all decided to walk it rather than end up a skeleton by having the river rip the flesh from your bones before it was done with you.

As we walked around the maelstrom of absolute violence, we came to the next drop. We could see the beginning of a big drop at the end of the pool, but the cut through looked interesting. It was about eight feet wide but the volume and violence of the water running through it was astounding. We could feel the ground vibrating under its force. If anyone of us ended up sideways, our boat might fold with us in it. It was skinny and tight and the water was causing the holes to fold back on themselves. We did not even consider running it. We put into the pool above the cut through and went around it to the drop at the end of the pool. We took out on the right of the river to take a look. From the pool, it simply looked like at smooth drop with a significant elevation change. That smooth face of water ended up as a huge hole with rock faces on each side of it, with both of the rock slabs tapering into it. We stood shell-shocked. It looked runnable, but the problem would be getting to someone that might need assistance. Bugsy was unnerved. For the safety of the group we all agreed not to run it. We all respected each

138

other's opinion but we also knew the dynamic of the group had changed. It was enough to throw us off but, at the same time, the choices made in your mind would always reflect the choices made on the water. We didn't want to make the wrong choice.

We were halfway down the river and had not run a significant drop yet. Something was wrong. We paddled out into a big pool and looked back at the hole. It looked bigger than it did standing close to it and the noise from the hole took on an eerie deep hollow sound. It sounded as if air was being pushed deep underwater and belching to get out from under its clutches. No one said anything. We ran the next few rapids tenuously and scouted carefully. The next drop was going to be the last of the day and should have been a boof. I suspect the boof part of the drop was underwater because I did not see any boof opportunity. There was a boulder on the right of the river that was mostly underwater and I was sure I did not want to get near it. Water was piling on it and pulsing up and down its face but there was little foam caused by the rock itself. This made me believe that it may have been undercut. We ran the rapid three times each, running a different line every time. Bugsy even ran it from the right of the river all the way over to the left of the river through all the holes and waves it offered. He ended up on the left of the river next to the shoreline and nearly flew over the top of me doing it. He overshot his mark but made it look smooth. He looked at me with a big smile on his face. It was the first smile I had seen out of anyone that day. After repeated runs on this drop, we took off downstream. We dodged holes and surfed some waves and surfed some smaller holes for fun.

We had regained our jovial attitude for a little while and by the time we saw our vehicles at the takeout, we were drained. I pulled my boat up the low muddy bank and captured the smell of fresh earth. I stood on the gravelly road and stretched my arms skyward. I was relieved to be off the river. I looked upstream to see a few fingers of soft light illuminate the white in the river, then quickly close up as the tall deep green spruce that framed the river started swaying.

We had one more day to paddle but we could all tell we were done. Cook was hurt, Greeny had a business to get back to, Si was

139

concerned about infection around his stitches he received early that week. Carpenter, Bugsy, and I had frayed nerves. The rest of the crew did not have a clue what had happened that day and that was a major concern. The decisions we had made were good at the end of it all. At the end of a long week, it was important not to make knee-jerk decisions.

Two days later I received a phone call from Bugsy. All he said was, "It was six thousand." I said, "what are you talking about?" He explained that when the guys looked at water reading for Lampson Falls on their phones the chart cut off a zero. We had not run Lampson Falls section at 600cfs. We had run it at 6000cfs. It had ten times the amount of water it normally had but we had not idea. It wasn't luck that saved us that day. It was skill. With this small oversight, this river could have gone bad for us; we anticipated this was going to be an easy happy go lucky day, but that turned into a class V hardcore adventure. This was exactly the type of thing that would get people killed! I learned that being aware, adapting to the situation, and keeping it together mentally would keep you alive. That, and being around good people making good decisions.

15

The Fish

The Fish was spoken of in quiet tones with reverence as if it were some holy place. To a kayaker, Fish Creek or 'The Fish' was revered as one of the greatest play rivers on the east coast. If you ran The Fish long enough, one of the best days of your paddling life would be on this river. The Fish was a class III to IV continues run, play waves, and holes abound while trees that lined the banks, making strainers a daily occurrence. On The Fish, you needed to be aggressive and careful. If you mentioned The Fish to a kayaker their eyes would widen, their body would tense, and they would ask you…is it up? Running the Fish for me was always fun. One of the reasons was that you could make it as hard as you wanted. I was never a straight liner. A straight liner was someone that shot straight down the river without stopping to play or move in or out of eddies. Typically, straight liners loved to crash through holes and move as fast as they could over waves to create the roller coaster effect. It was fun, but I preferred to make things a little more technical. Rivers changed every year, but after you ran them once or twice, you had a good idea what was going on.

The Fish was up, and my new kayak and I were on the way. I met some friends at a Syracuse exit and we made our way north. Arriving at The Fish, we set the shuttle and started our descent. There was still snow on the ground, and the further down into the canyon we went the deeper the snow and colder it was becoming. As we reached the river, we could see that it was ragingly high. My new boat and I slid into the river with great anticipation. This was early in my kayaking career with new friends on a new river that I had never run before with a new boat.

I found myself breathing heavy and I caught a wave and surfed. I peeled off and dropped into the eddy next to Pencil, the one person I knew best. "Don't waste your time on the small stuff," he said. "You don't want to tire yourself out." I nodded my head and smiled while thinking, "Ha! The small stuff." The waves became bigger and bigger and so did the river. I held my own and surfed with a smile on my face. The river was fast with a lot going on. I thread my way through only to find myself upside down coming off the edge of the last hole. I tried to roll but I couldn't manage it. I tried the upstream side and the downstream side, gasping for breath at each attempt. I could barely see, and as the blood in my body rushed to my core, I started to get tunnel vision. Finally, I settled into slower moving water and took by my role using every muscle I had. Though I had righted myself, I had also rolled so hard that I pulled my knee out of the knee brace and it went through my spray skirt. Freezing cold water came pouring in and I began to sink. The river was high and my only choice was to head into the trees since there was no shore. I pulled myself and my boat from the water and emptied it out. My friend helped me readjust my boat so that I was more secure. Then we got right back on the river.

On the horizon line, I saw it, the top of a perfect wave. The river tilted a bit and seemed to pick up speed. The closer I got, the bigger the white line became. I suddenly realized it was a hole taking up seventy-five percent of the river. It was as big as a Grey Hound bus, and I was too close and moving too fast to get out of its way. I pointed my boat toward the left of the river and paddled my ass off. I hit the lowest part of the hole. It violently stopped me dead as I slammed into the pile of cold thrashing water. I leaned hard into the pile on my right side. Digging with my paddle, I tried to propel myself forward out of the hole with my boat still pointing to the left of the river. The water was too loud to hear and the six-foot pile of water adjacent to me seemed to be continually falling on me blocking my vision. I was being drawn backward and I was pretty sure there was nothing good back there. I took a moment to think and looked around. Straight ahead was where I had come in from. I had been stuck long enough for the gang to catch up. They were on the side of the river, warm, dry, and safe watching me. There was a white line of water in front of me that curved in an arch going upstream. Can't go that way, my options were limited. The right side of the river was behind me with a rock wall that went up a hundred feet or more. If I could get to that wall and hit it, I might not have gotten out of there.

But whatever happened, I was going to die in my boat so they could find the body. I started paddling backward and slowly started to move. Harder and harder I paddled as I found my rhythm. As I pulled my paddle out of the white pile of water for another stroke, I leaned the wrong way and flipped. I ended up with the front of my boat pointing up the river in what was called a Blast. My stern was under water and my bow almost vertical still at the bottom of the hole. I leaned toward the wall and rocketed across the hole. I hit the wall, flipped, and went underwater and rolled up at the edge of the eddy. I was freezing cold, gasping for breath, and trying to hang onto the wall. Hands too cold, head too cold, I put my hand on my ear to warm it up. "Holy shit," I thought, "I don't have a helmet on!" The hole had ripped off my helmet.

I needed to get out of there. I looked downstream. I saw a big hole, as big as the one I just came out of it twenty yards below me. I was getting cold, tired, and needed to do something, so I just went for it. I found myself facing downstream powering toward a hole that should open up and let me through. I made it through the hole with great relief and worked my way with the others down to the bridge. I borrowed a person's helmet that had decided to walk off the river at the bridge. Before me I saw a river full of holes and waves. I could have gotten out of the river and it would not have been held against me. I was cold, tired, and thought to myself, "I don't know how I'm going to get through this." But then I thought, "This is what I came for." I paddled well the rest of the day. As it turned out, it was one of the best days I had ever had on a river. In my moments of fear, I prevailed by a simple philosophy, control starts with me.

Another day on The Fish, I had hooked up with a small band of rebels and was in the middle of The Fish when we came around the bend that lead into a great rapid, one of my favorites. I had noticed that one of the guys was following my lead kind of close, and I felt that this section of the river may be a bit challenging for him. The line I wanted to take was very tight; I called this section of the river "The white mile." As we floated in the slack water before the rapid, I turned to Mr. Cool Guy and said, "Don't follow me

143

through this one ok, you can go down the left or the right with no problem."

He laughed and turned to his buddies and said, "Did you hear him? He said not to follow him."

I said, "Seriously, you don't want to follow me through this."

He laughed again and said sarcastically, "Yea right."

I shrugged my shoulders and said "whatever" and turned my bow downriver and started paddling toward the line I wanted to take. After all, he might be ok.

The river descended at quite an angle, and you couldn't quite see the bottom of the rapid from the top of it. Obviously, I already knew what it looked like, past several holes and decent size waves there was a bottleneck where the river narrowed a bit. Just left of the center of the river was a hole. This hole stood about five feet high and was about eight feet wide, it was EXTREMELY trashy. Not a friendly place by any means. Seven feet down past the trashy hole just right of the center of the river was another hole. It was a shallow hole and you could see the water running over the rocks with a BIG foam pile behind it. The water was flying in this section, so decisions needed to be made quickly. From a distance, it looked like one-hole half the river wide and it looked scary! So that's where I was going.

I was flying past the entrance waves paddling full out. I powered toward the trashy hole picking up speed, paying no mind that I had someone that wanted to follow me. I was ten feet from hitting the center of the trashy hole and angled my bow to the right and took four good paddle strokes. I hit the right side of the trashy hole at about a forty-five-degree angle with lots of speed. I took a hard-left-hand paddle stroke that threw me off the edge of the hole and toward the shallow hole. I just missed the shallow hole and used its foam pile to slow me down. The foam pile projected me all the way to the right of the river, where behind the hole was a good size eddy. Easy move, right? Apparently, Mr. Cool did not anticipate my left to right move, so as I sat in the eddy looking upstream, he looked a bit confused. I could understand his predicament. In a split second

I could see he was too close to the trashy hole to go left of it and too close to the shallow hole to go right of it. So, he went for the lesser of two evils and turned his boat to the right of the river toward me knowing he did not want to go anywhere near the trashy hole. Thinking he could bomb through the shallow hole he powered toward me in the eddy behind the hole. But at this point, his overzealous reaction had found him nearly sideways only feet above the shallow hole. Dammit, he forgot rule number one of hole riding. The foam is your friend, lean into it! He instantly flipped up stream. I couldn't even describe the speed of this encounter. I was hoping he did not break his neck and I didn't mean that metaphorically. As he flipped his shoulder, he hit the bottom of the river, and the boat was literally flung off his body. The boat then was loose in the hole, went up to the foam pile, stopped, slid back down the pile into the bottom of the hole, and hit Mr. Cool. He had the fortitude to grab it, a good sign at least his neck wasn't broken! I peeled out of the eddy and onto the downstream edge of the foam pile screaming "I got you, I'm right here." A hand reached up from the depths of the foam and grabbed the back of my boat. Officially I am calling that one luck, hell, we'll call that one dumb luck.

The swim began, you know the truth is, even if you were holding on to a boat and if you were in the water, you were now a swimmer. I was pointed the wrong way when he grabbed my boat. (Life in a kayak is all about the angles you know) so we flushed past the eddy I was in. But that was ok, I didn't like that one anyway. I did need to get to the right of the river though. It was not only closer, but the left of the river was full of the same stuff he just went through, and he didn't seem to care for that. So, I started pulling myself around and pointing my bow back to the right. We were flushing down the river quickly. I could feel him tugging at my boat and I knew he was hitting the bottom of the river. I needed to get him in, so my paddle strokes were deep and fast. As I looked back at him, I made eye contact with him for the first time. The moment I did, he started to get that lost look in his eyes. So, I scream at him, "Don't you fucking quit if we go around this corner you are going to have to swim a mile." And I meant it. There was a left turn coming up, the right side of that turn was a gorge wall, and we would have to go across the river to get him out. After my inspirational speech,

145

Mr. Cool turned into Mr. Mosses, and we were on shore in no time at all. He and his friends emptied his boat, and we stayed with him for a minute or two watching his condition. He was cold, and a little beat up but not bad at all. Back in his boat, he slid into the water without complaint, and we had great paddle the rest of the day. He recovered very well.

The next year at a paddling festival on the Moose he approached me. "Do you remember me? You told me not to follow you." I smiled, "Oh, I remember you; you had a great recovery when you got back on the water." I said. He smiled, shook my hand, and thanked me.

Mr. Brooks

One day out at The Fish, a tall and lanky man asked my group and me for a shuttle to the put in. On the way he explained that his name was Mr. Brooks and that he was from the area and had run The Fish several times. He put in after us as we shot down the river. The Fish was big that day. It measured six feet high on the old bridge gauge. After a while, we found ourselves at one of the biggest holes in the river. We all navigated around it and sat waiting for Mr. Brooks, wanting to make sure he did not get caught in the hole. He ran the hole on the right of the river while the rest of us had run it left with no issue. I saw a wave that was eight feet high and almost reached into the tree line. It was glassy, steep, and extremely fast with a small rolling line of white water at the top. Leaving the others behind, I shot over the wave and dropped into the eddy next to the wall. Mr. Brooks couldn't see me as he caught the very same wave. Most people were happy with a simple front surf, but I saw that Mr. Brooks went to the top of the wave and hit the foam pile. He broke loose, screamed down the face of the wave, and cartwheeled three times on his left side. He landed in a back surf, worked his way back up the pile, and repeated the move on his right side. He made kayaking look effortless.

I ended up paddling with him for many years. I never heard him say one bad thing about anyone, and his humble and quiet nature

146

personified what every whitewater kayaker should be. He remains the best kayaker I have ever met.

For me, every day on The Fish was an adventure. It was never ordinary and it was always epic. I learned an invaluable lesson during every run.

16

The Edge

Feeling bored and complacent is a bad combination on any river.

I was headed toward Knife Edge on the Black River for the fiftieth time that year. I was leading a rafting expedition for the rafting company I worked for. The water was low, but with the release it was okay, albeit slow for the rafts. I had several rules I was required to adhere to. All raft trips needed to have a safety kayaker, so no matter what I always went down the river. I was not allowed to put myself in more danger than I had to. In other words, I would not be running the sketchy hard lines that I normally would if I was there with friends. The company ran on a timeline with the guests so I helped to make sure everything ran smoothly.

There were lots of rafts and people bantering back and forth on the river that day. The guides were telling their usual stories and I was bored out of my mind. I decided to shoot way ahead of the rafts to kill time while I waited for the rafts to catch up. I was fooling around in the K2 wave when I came off it and shot over to the right. That's when I realized there was almost no water in the river. I had outrun the bubble.

The dam released water at a certain time during the day. All of the rafting companies had a time slot during which to get on the bubble so everyone had a good release. It was called the bubble because it was a moving unit of water, and when it had passed the river dropped back to the original level. Conversely, if you were moving faster than the water, then you could outrun it. That was what I had done. This was a real problem because I was also on the wrong line without the ability to get back to the line I should be on. I decided to go over the last ledge next to Mary's Hole, the biggest hole on the river. I scratched down the shelf cringing, knowing that the Chert Rock was shredding the bottom of my boat and pealing lines of plastic off it. When I arrived to the main shelf, I saw a trickle of water going over it. I literally got stopped on the small shelf. I wiggled around to release myself so I could slide into the river, unfortunately I ended up sideways at the edge of Mary's Hole.

Suddenly, I was pulled directly into Mary's Hole. Even though it was a low water day, that particular hole rarely changed in intensity. I felt like I was on my kayak in the middle of a car wreck that wouldn't stop. How bad could it be I thought, of course, that was before I was cartwheeling uncontrollably. Then, my boat stopped moving. I looked up and realized that my boat and I were under the waterfall against the ledge. My head was behind the curtain of water, I had only a small pocket of air in which to breathe, but it is full of bubbles. I was invisible to the outside world. The recirculation of the water was pinning me behind the waterfall. I was gasping for breath while getting pounded by the weight of the water, my boat flat against the ledge with me in it. I was writhing back and forth and extending my neck to try and get good clean air. The water was exploding over my head off the shelf was extremely violent and the noise was deafening. Even if I had been able to yell, no one would have heard me.

No matter what I tried, the boat would not move. I pushed against my paddle against the inside of the shelf as hard as I could, until I thought it might snap in half. I was not budging. I knew I would drown if I stayed there much longer. I took my hand off my paddle and reached up to find my spray skirt tab. I gave it a yank and felt my legs go cold as the water rushed in. All at once, I was violently pulled from my boat and thrown to the bottom of the river. I tried to get to the surface of the river but I couldn't get past the foam pile caused by the water coming over the shelf. I was sucked back into the hole and flipped, twisted, and turned through the hole which was no choice of my own. I no longer had my paddle and I was a long way away from where I thought my boat must have been. I could feel myself getting sucked backward as I tried to swim forward. With each attempt, my head went under and I was driven to the bottom of the river. I got my feet under me and kicked up from the bottom of the river bed to propel myself upward. My head came out of the water on the downstream side of the foam pile. I was free.

149

I was completely out of breath, floating down the center of the river. I looked around for my paddle and spotted it about thirty yards away from me. I was swimming toward it but the water in my lungs stopped the oxygen from getting to my muscles to make them work. My paddle ended up in a big eddy with a slow recirculation. I ended up there a few minutes after my paddle did. With my paddle in hand, I dragged myself up onshore and looked upstream. I could see that my boat was still in the hole, shooting back and forth, disappearing and popping up in a different spot just like I had. I checked myself for cuts as I continued to gasp for breath.

One by one, I saw the rafts work their way over the drops. Eventually, the lead rafter worked his way over to me and asked if I was ok. By now, my boat was starting to disassemble. Eventually all of my belongings came trickling down the river to me. The moment my boat was flushed from the hole, it was quickly scooped up by a good friend of mine, emptied out, and brought over to me. I was embarrassed and I knew this happened because I was being conservative. In hindsight, I had run the line at Knife Edge called The True Path more times than I cared to count and at much higher water. There was no reason that I would feel that I was putting myself in danger by running The True Path line on that day. After the swim I re-evaluated my time on the river. Once again, I went back to kayaking the way I wanted to, the reason I originally went there for. To have fun and kayak hard!

17

Doe River

For years my A team of kayakers and I would do a Sothern trip. We would shoot down south and chase water all over the east coast. From Tennessee to New York, sometimes we rolled with the punches but always seemed to have a great time no matter what the weather or situations.

The group decided to head south farther than we had been before. I did not want to go that far south personally but decided I did not want to walk out on the group. I knew they wouldn't walk out on me. Tennessee was the destination. We had been in West Virginia looking for water, but I felt that it was a long way to go moving all the way to Tennessee. But that was where the rivers were full of water, so our choices were limited. The agenda was to go and run this thing called the Doe River.

We were shooting down the highway, and we were about to turn off the main road when one of the guys in the group started passing a slow-moving tractor-trailer. The only problem with that was as he was passing the tractor-trailer, he also passed the exit off the highway. The rest of us filtered off the highway, and he never knew it and just kept going. We did not stop; the road system did not make that easy until we were well off the main highways. But we had discussed it ahead of time, so we knew that everyone in the group knew the directions and where the put in was. We thought he would simply catch up with us or maybe he knew a better way and would be waiting for us at the put in. Twenty minutes later, we found ourselves at the edge of a farmer's field seemingly in the middle of nowhere. We drove over to the put in a bridge and I heard my name being called, "Marty, Marty is that you" I looked over, expecting to see our lost guys. But even better luck! There at the edge of the road stood three guys in kayaking gear and I recognized the guy waving at me.

There stood a skinny blond headed short guy, George. The only vegetarian kayaker I ever liked. I had taken George down the Bottom Moose in the ADK when he did not know a thing about it. He was a good paddler and a fun guy to be around, we stopped the vehicle and talked for a moment. "George what the hell are you doing here?!" I asked. He told me that he had come down for Cheat Fest, just like the rest of us but there was no water, so he and his cohorts had come south. He asked me if I had run the Doe before and when I said no he jumped at the chance to take me and the group down. He had run it before and would take us down, and he already had a shuttle set up and told us to just hurry up and get dressed. My group scrambled around unloading boats and getting dressed. George had two guys with him, they did not look tough. But looks can be deceiving. Both of them looked college-aged, the first was a short rollie-pollie kid that talked a lot and the second guy was taller with an average build that looked a bit nervous. I suspected that George was as happy to see us as we were to see him. He knew that my group had a lot of creeking experience under our belt. We put our boats on our shoulders and walked to the creek.

This section of the Doe was a class IV creek, it was a little over five miles long and descended rapidly into a very steep gorge. With a max Gradient of 160ft a mile, it was very technical and good boat control was a necessity. There were small pools after most of the rapids, but in the middle of the rapids the eddies were small and the river was pushy. Not a good place to have a bad day. With rapids named Toaster Slot, Flag Pole, Bear Cage, and Body Snatcher the creek had an ominous feel to it. Looking at the river from a distance, it looked like a dark deep ditch through the earth. Somewhere at the bottom of that ditch boasted an extremely high vertical cliff that ascended up from the river hundreds of feet. The ecosystem inside the gorge was completely different than outside. There was a lack of sun and the high humidity allowed for interesting plant life. But this was early spring, and the only thing that was alive now was the water.

We dropped onto the river with a happy go lucky attitude, even though we were missing two of our guys. My group liked the way things were shaping up, and George's group seemed happy for the support. So, we headed into the gorge and picked our way down. We had about eight guys all together, so we spread out with George and his group taking the lead. I really should mention that one of our guys, Saddle was in a canoe. No shit really! He was one of the best technical whitewater open canoers I had ever paddled with. We loved to eddy hop together, I followed his line then he would follow mine, it made a fun game for us. George and I were sticking close to each other and eddy hopping our way down through.

I didn't like to get out of my boat. Honestly, I had a harder time walking next to the river than I did just running it. My depth perception was bad on land, but on the water, it seemed to be fine for some reason. So, someone in the group would come back to me with instructions, I liked my instructions to be vague but stern. Like, there were three drops go over the last drop on the left of the river. It was up for interpretation, but the last drop was important. But on this creek, most of it could be scouted in your boat. It was always a little risky scouting from the boat, but we do it often and never seemed to have many issues. But we were with people that knew the way and they had intel that there were no strainers in the river, it was a fast run. But what they looked at was worth looking into since the lines were more technical than the rest of the river. Every time we stopped to look at a rapid, one of my guys would walk back to me and tell me the line. Most of the day was pretty easy because the drops were only one or two moves. But the further down into the gully we descended, the darker it was becoming. The walls were getting more vertical on both sides of us. It was plain to see that there was no going back and no climbing out, there was only one way out.

Sitting in my kayak waiting for instructions above a drop, it seemed to take a long time for the scouting expedition to get back. Then George hopped in his boat and disappeared over the drop. Rolly Polly went next and had some issues getting tied up sideways on a rock, turned around backward flipped, and swam. The ropes went out, and he was recovered quickly, without much of an issue. The canyon was tight, and you could easily throw a rope across it. There were boulders all over the place to stand on or safety from. By then, I was being given the information I needed to make the run.

153

Apparently, there were three drops, and the last one was the biggest and I had to be careful of the last one. By then, George's group had cleared, and my turn was up. I pulled myself out of the eddy on a heavy lean and headed down the river. The angle of the river was very apparent at this point, the guys in front of me had taken about five paddle strokes and completely disappeared out of sight. Also, the river seemed to be picking up speed. All three drops seemed to be in succession one after the other from what I could see paddling up to it. I took a breath, drove my paddle in deep, and lunged forward into the first drop with my heart pounding and my eyes scanning the river for the next line. The first drop was only about five feet high.

I shot over the first drop, pulled my bow around to the right, paddled a few hard strokes, hit a skinny slot, zipped down into a section of fast-moving water, and picked up speed. I was a little confused at this point. I saw a small eddy and drove into it on a hard lean and eddy out. I sat there for a moment and looked at the guys. Their eyes were big and they looked shocked! I did not know it, but the last drop was behind me, like right behind me, about three feet! I had misjudged my instructions. I sat only feet above the biggest drop of the day. Looking over my shoulder, I could now understand why the guys were looking at me in such disarray with their eyes like saucers! I was in a tiny eddy with the river pushing past me, the only one the river provided before the falls. To my defense, no one told me that there was an actual waterfall in the river much less that it was ten-feet. No one told me to boof or talked about the angle or what side to go over. I was completely winging it at this point.

It happened to turn out that the eddy that I had dropped into only feet above the ten-foot waterfalls was stable, but getting enough speed to make the last move was going to be a feat. I couldn't just turn and drop over the falls without momentum. I would get eaten up by the bottom of the falls and definitely be trashed. I should not be in this eddy. I could see George past the waterfalls against the gorge wall in his kayak. Beside him the rock wall towered over him, over the river, and extended up hundreds of feet with only a small shaft of light trickling in at the top. He motioned for me to come over the drop. I looked at the drop and quickly interpreted it, the drop was at an angle to the river. If I pointed downstream going over it, I might get caught in the hole at the bottom. It was better to point away from the hole, I wanted to point toward the wall George was next to rather than downstream. This was counter intuitive but I had seen this sort of drop before. Then I saw a flake off the top of the drop, a piece of rock that pointed straight off with water going over it. It was halfway across the creek and I knew that was my ticket. All I had to do was get there. I leaned back in my boat and thrusted myself forward. I paddled like hell into the fast-moving water. I kept my ferry angle, which helped me get across. Still only feet above the drop I was facing upstream with my back to the drop. When I got to where I think I needed to be, I turned the boat downstream on my left side. Just in front of me was the flake, so I gave a few quick paddle strokes to gain speed, hit the flake, and threw a Boof stroke on my left side. I popped off the flake while pointing to the right of the river as I ran to the left of the river. I landed away from the hole and never got my face wet. The guys cheered and clapped and George gave me a big thumbs up. It was a hard move, it was a good move, and it was the only move I had! I found the nearest eddy, parked my ass, and watched the rest of the guys run it.

Saddle thought it was a cool move too. So he tried it, only there were a few complications. His boat was too long to fit behind the rocks that made the eddy that I was in, so the front of his boat was in the eddy but the back of his boat was OVER the drop. This caused the drag of the water going over the drop to slowly start pulling him back. He moved his single paddle blade with lightning speed popping the water, trying to keep himself from inching backward. From the bottom of the drop, I could see that he was losing the encounter. Slowly the back of his boat became more and more exposed to the air until he hit his breaking point and tipped over the edge. The front of his boat went straight up into the air and he plummeted over the falls backward! He hit a pile of rocks at the bottom, and his body violently lurched toward the back of his boat. His boat tipped sideways and quickly filled with water as he was being raked across the stones that had been pounded on by water for a thousand years. I was sure that the stones were going to be ok. The moment he swam, he was only feet from where some of the boys stood on the side of the creek. They grabbed his boat and collected him matter-of-factly. My good buddy Walker was the other swimmer from our group for the day in the same spot. As he came off the edge of the drop he was pointed too far downstream, a classic mistake. He launched off almost parallel to the drop and landed too close to the hole. He was drawn into the hole instantly and violently flipped. Stuck at the bottom of the waterfall upside-down and being pounded by hundreds of pounds of water, he had no possibility of escaping without swimming. Once again, the guys were ready, and the ropes went out. It was a fast save, but Walker was a little traumatized by the violence of the hole. He thought he was going to run a conservative line by pointing downstream off the drop. But kayaking itself was not usually a conservative sport. You cannot kayak down a river scared without getting beat up. He gathered up his stuff and no worse for wear slid back in his boat, giving me his classic shoulder shrug and hands out as if to say, what are you going to do.

The rest of the river was great fun, eddy hopping, punching holes, and picking slots. A classic creek run with a lot of great technical moves. The great canyon became a little wider as the daylight started to trickle in. It slowly opened up as the attitude of the river changed. The end of the Doe brought a light happy go lucky attitude. No one was hurt and most of us had a great time. The fun points on this creek were very high. Until we reached the takeout!

There stood the two guys that we had previously lost on the highway. They weren't happy, not happy at all! They bitched at us for not waiting for them at the put in, they were right to be mad. But we told them that the river sucked, we had a bunch of swimmers that had to be roped out, and we had to scout every rapid and that it took forever to run and we were happy to be off the river. Yea we lied, but it seemed to calm them down. It did not change the circumstances, but they seemed happy to not have participated in the carnage.

George's group followed us and ended up camping with us that night. Sitting around the fire, we talked about the day. The two guys that we had lost earlier in the day started to get the gist that we did not necessarily have a bad day, but they never said anything.

Saddle commented that I had a hell of a move above the drop. (The drop he swam on). So, I quickly told the story from my perspective.

"Yea, I never knew it was there, someone told me that there were three drops in a row. I thought I had gone over the last drop, so I eddied out. When I looked over my shoulder, I realized I had not gone over the last drop. I did not have a lot of choices after that, so I made the only move I could see."

Saddle looked disgusted at me, "You mean you did not plan that move?"

I shrugged my shoulders and said, "I never looked at it."

He threw his hands up and said, "Unbelievable," as he shook his head.

Now I was going to go ahead and take that as a compliment. It was not meant as a compliment, but that's how I was going to take it. Without the help of George, I was quite sure that the day would have gone differently. At the end of the day I was glad that I met George on the Bottom Moose, I was also glad I met him on the Doe.

18

The Kipawa River

There was a festival at the Kipawa River. It sounded like a good idea. It took about seven hours to get there from where I lived. I was in the river and it was raging at a hundred year high. This was the year to go.

Si, Carpenter, Bugsy and myself headed north. A friend of ours, Clergy, was going to meet us later at the campground. This was my first experience at the Kipawa River and one that I would not forget. After a long ass drive through Canada, we arrived to see a bunch of people in white suites. I asked, "Why are all of those people in white suits? Has there been a hazardous waste spill or something?" When we stepped out of the vehicle it took about thirty seconds to figure out what was going on. We were swarmed by voracious mosquitoes. All of the white jackets were bug jackets with a fine black mesh over their face. One deep breath in and I found the inside of my nose crawling with Canadian mosquitoes. In an hour I was exhausted from swatting at my face. I was wearing a coat, long pants, and hiking shoes. It was late summer. My tent was set up and I was inside it seeking solace. If I thought drinking Deet would work I would have done it, but I knew it would not work because the bugs were licking my skin like a lollypop. I had put so much of the stuff on, that my clothes were literally melting onto my skin. Our only saving grace was the fire we started and we stuck close to it!

We walked around and met the leader of the festival. He was a super cool dude as far as I could tell. He seemed to know my name, but I didn't know why. He would always say hello with my name included. We walked out onto the bridge to look at the first rapid, but it was late in the day and there was no rapid. I did not really understand, all I saw was a big dam. I was told that they used this crane and pulled out the beams that make up the dam. The Beams were about five feet high by five feet wide comprised of trees that were over a hundred years old. They pulled out the logs and then said "OK go ahead and run the rapid their A" but I didn't believe it when I saw it. Officially the festival had not started yet, but tomorrow in the morning apparently it would begin. The water from the lake was running over the dam creating a curtain of Canadian water covering and flowing over the dam. The head guru was saying that it had rained more this year than several years before and that the Kipawa Lake was way higher than he had ever seen it before. He also told us that this was a winter drawdown. They needed to take the water level in the lake down for a few reasons. The ice buildup here was massive; the average temperature of the area was -28 degrees Celsius in the winter. That's 18 degrease below Zero to us American folk.

The ice buildup was so heavy that it put the dam in danger of failing. If the water level was not taken down, the ice would end up ripping out all of the docks and would destroy the waterfront property with ice buildup. The ice would do a lot of damage, so draining the lake to a reasonable level was the only way to avoid the issue.

The next morning I woke up early with the sun's rays hitting my tent, lighting up the inside of my tent with a warm maroon glow. Yet at the same time, it sounded like it was sprinkling against the canopy of my tent. "That's odd," I thought "Maybe it's a passing cloud and the sun is sneaking in under it." But I could hear the distinct voice of my buddy Bugsy. The guys I hung out with were old school, and would always get up early. As I stepped out of my tent, I realized that the only cloud to be had was a hoard of mosquitoes that were bouncing off my tent trying to eat me alive. I hurried to my pack for more Deet and lathered myself in the mystical oil. I met with the guys and they had come up with a plan. As I walked up to them Bugsy said "We were thinking about going into town for breakfast." Although it seemed more like a statement, to which I wholeheartedly agreed to as I turned and started walking toward the vehicle. We hit the road and found ourselves in the nearest town, which took us about twenty minutes or so.

At the diner I noticed everything was written in French. The menu's and all of the signs, even the bathroom sign, was in French. It never occurred to me that it was French until the waitress started

159

speaking French. I asked for coffee and promptly ordered by pointing at the menu. Everyone at the table looked at me inquisitively. "Marty, do you speak French?" For a moment I was taken back, but replied, "Nope." I never said anything, but I read body language. As a kid every sign or written word was backwards, even the letters were backwards. Nothing ever made sense to me, in times like this my mind kicks back into interpretation mode without me even knowing it. I honestly did not know these things were in a different language. Maybe that's why I liked rivers so much, a river doesn't care what language you speak, it doesn't even care if you are there. We were just passing through, and all of the knowledge you would ever know didn't mean anything to a river. You were not judged, or laughed at, picked on, or held to some invisible standard set forth by a society that wanted you to behave and stand in line. Rivers had enough respect to not care at all.

After eating we paid our tab and headed back. When we arrived there were significantly more people there. Kayakers, open boaters, rafters, and spectators. A lot of Spectators! The workers had removed the wooden beams that held back the water. I do wish I had seen the removal of the beams, but now I was starting to understand what all the hoopla was about. The sound of thunder rose up from beneath the bridge followed by a swirling mist of steam. Hundreds of people cheered for the river goers that paddled themselves over the first drop as if they were cheering for gladiators in a coliseum. People with their fists pumping up and down in the air and clapping, dads carrying their kids on their shoulders, and from time to time you could hear a collective *oooh* ascended above the noise of the river when something went amiss. The shores on both sides of the river and the bridge were adorned with loud colors worn by people that had come to see the carnage. It looked like people from hundreds of miles away had shown up for the occasion. As I looked at the first drop, I noted that the water had so much power that it flew past the columns of the dam going forty feet before beginning to drop off, causing a literal wall of moving water fifteen feet high. It was impressive and the only thing I have seen that had ever come close was the release of the tubes on the Upper Gauley.

We quickly dressed and released our bug stained boats from the racks on our vehicles. As we walked toward the lake complete strangers patted us on our backs and enthusiastically wished us a heartfelt best of luck. This was disheartening at first, where I come from the locals would not even acknowledge your existence. But here they seem they genuinely speak as though they didn't want us to die.

As we glided into the cool clean water of the lake, my adrenaline went up, and the sound faded away. We paddled over in front of the dam well away from red the safety buoys That were put there to deter any boats from getting too close to the dam signifying danger ahead, but today this was our starting point.

As we floated closer to the buoys I noticed two things. The first was that the water we were in seemed to be pulsing. It was like someone was pounding a bass drum at the bottom of the lake and you could feel it in your chest through the kayak. It was almost like emptying a bottle, and we were about to come out of the spout. The second was before almost every rapid I have ever run, there were ripples above the drop. The ripples may have been from rocks or simply from water stacking before going over the drop itself, but the ripples were across the river. The ripples here were going toward the drop and following over it! There was so much volume of water going over this thing that the ripples were creating lines that headed over the dam. I knew that there was no particular way to run this drop other than just go over it in the center. But this phenomenon made me question myself for a moment.

As I approached the twenty-yard gap in the lake, I looked down the river and the only thing I could see was tree tops. I passed the buoys and started to paddle faster and harder. I was about to go over Laniel Dam. But now there was nothing more than a huge sluiceway with no obstruction to stop me from dropping off the end of the lake. I kicked into high gear as my fingers tightened around my paddle and my shoulders drove me forward. I leaned forward at the proverbial edge. The bottom dropped out, and I felt my boat leap forward as it changed its angle. I was falling as fast as I was moving forward. In front of me there were standing pulsing waves exploding into whitewater. I instinctively looked for a line through this chaos,

161

but with no immediate resolution, I drove myself into it. I went over the first smooth wave into the fast running smooth water! I was dumbfounded the river had gone flat, and I paddled out of the main flow and found a big eddy. I couldn't believe it, the river had given me free passage, it had simply parted and let me through. Perhaps this was a good omen of things to come!

I watched the guys run the drop one by one. They all had bigger water to go through than I did. At least it seemed that way to me. Bugsy, Clergy, Carpenter, and Si all gathered around me. This was our first time on this monstrosity, and we didn't have a clue. We only knew that downstream held the answers and we were going in with blindfolds on.

Rock and Roll to the next rapid. I have to remind you that this was a hundred year high. No one had ever seen the water this high before. Whatever line that may have been talked about the night before no longer existed.

As we rounded the corner to see the rapid for the first time, I was amazed at its beauty. It was as if a white and blue sheet had been draped over the deep green wilderness and had been sequined by granite boulders. The towering pine trees threw shadows into the river, looking like dark fingers that wanted to suck you to its depths. Make no mistake about it, this was a massive run.

The river took on a definite angle as we approached. A copious amount of pulsing water thrashed through the drop. Two holes at the top of the drop, left and right, exploded simultaneously throwing water eight to ten feet into the air. We never looked at the rapid. We dropped in on sheets of twisting water one after the other down the river between the two holes. At the pinnacle of every wave, we would peer intensely down river looking for the line. Sharply standing waves and small intense hydraulics drew our attention as we powered through looking for the silky water. I saw my friends scattered throughout the rapid, we were all making our own line on this one. We were not the follow the leader type of group. At a quick glance, we knew the real danger was behind us, there were no terminal holes in front of us. There were big holes, giant standing waves, but even if we swam it, the odds of dying were

162

low. But the first two holes, well they had a definite possibility of an introduction with another world.

We each picked our way down through independently as other kayakers walked the drop never having seen so much water in it. It was an advantage to never have been here before. We had no preconceived notion of what the river should look like. So, it must be perfect the way it was. We were all Taoist to a certain degree. If you were not grasping for breath and curling your toes trying to stay in the boat, then everything must have been mighty fine.

The next rapid was Tumbling the Dice which was a class III. This was a perfect name for this set of waves. They would build and build until they were about eight feet high then crashed down upon themselves and become almost a flat river before they started to build again. We had fun taking turns trying to catch the wave at its zenith. When we did catch a surf, it was fast, poppy, and barely controllable. We were tossed from one side of the wave to the other, cutting back and forth doing our best to keep from being flushed off the back of the supersonic wave. Then if you did not time it right, the wave simply dissolved beneath you. After several kayakers had passed and had given us strange looks, we started to get the timing down. Jump onto the wave just as it started building and ride it until it was passing or it kicked you off.

My last adventure of the day on this fluxing carnival ride would find me forever a capture in the mind of my friends, though that was not my intention. The river was nearly flat, my friends and I were on both sides of the now nonexistent wave in the eddies provided. I could see a spin of whitewater starting and a smooth scoop started to form before it. I worked my way out into the river with a hard-right lean, lifting my left knee toward my chest. I attained the wave just as it started growing exponentially. I shot across its face and changed my lean and cut back into it. It was a full-on surf now as the face became steeper. My shoulders were loose, and my torso became a shock absorber. The wave was building ever higher and I felt like I was ten feet in the air on two feet of the boat. My boat hydroplaned at the pinnacle of the wave, my elbows were up, and my paddle was low. Leaning forward, I anticipated cutting down the face of the wave. But all at once, the

163

top of the wave pulsed and broke losing its grip on me. Untethered by friction, I plummeted in a freefall to the trough with a downward angle. As I touched the careening water at the bottom of the wave, I was drawn in. My boat went three feet under water; I was up to my chest and still cutting left and right as fast as I could go. I held the position for five or six seconds then the friction of the water took over, and I started losing speed and moving backward. Eventually I was pushed into the face of the wave, and I was swallowed by the eight-foot wave behind me! I was taken into the great beyond where it became cold, dark, and quiet. I was careening downstream underwater in what seemed like a box of darkness. Then, with time to contemplate, I collected my thoughts. As I spun upside down and sideways, I came to the conclusion, "Yea, that's enough of that shit!" As my buoyancy kicked in, I ascended away from the mermaid's grasp back to the realm of ribbony light. I ascended past the fish and pierced the bubbles at the juncture between the water and the air. I gasped for breath, took a quick look around, and I realized I was passed the eddy. With no chance of recovery, I powered into the next eddy down and waited for the guys as I caught my breath.

Almost immediately they joined me. Carpenter was the first one to get to me. Usually extremely calm and Zen-like, he dropped into the eddy with a big smile on his face and started laughing out loud, setting his paddle on his boat in front of him. He attempted to show me what I had just done with his hands. Laughing and shaking his head as the other guys joined us. The move was called "Marty's Patented Subsurface Surf." We all got a great laugh out of it. Years later, I would hear the story told, but to this day, what impressed me the most was who was telling that story. One of the best whitewater kayakers I have ever known.

The next significant drop was Zipper. There were only a couple things I remembered about thinking about Zipper. The first was that it must have looked like a white bobsled track from space, and the second was to stay away from the hole on the right side of the river. The river went around a corner as it descended. Going into it we seemed to be taking our time, moving slow. We didn't know what was around the corner, hell we did not know the name of the drop. We just ran it! As we reached the corner of the point of no return, we saw huge waves and that big hole on the right. We worked our way down the river one by one, obviously working our way down left of the center. I saw a big wave on the left and I worked my way over to it planning on getting a look at it as I passed by. "Might be a good surf spot," I thought, but as I got closer I realize it extended farther into the river than I had anticipated. It did not seem to me that I was much closer to the wave than the Si was. But you know, I could have been wrong. I thought I had it beat, but the wave before this big kahuna kicked me sideways which made me struggle and lose speed. The big wave was rolling over on itself as I caught the tail end of it. It stopped me dead, I had a paddle blade in the water, I was leaning forward, and I was trying hard. Yea, that did not work. The wave towered above me and was angling to the left of the river. The only other place in the river you did not want to go was the left of the river. But not me, I was going there whether I wanted to or not and I was doing it backwards in a back surf picking up speed with no possibility of parole. The face of the wave looked like a moving wall of shattered glass, and I had no control as I tried to change my angle to get out of it. I was being typewritered across the river. Well, at least I could see where I was going as I looked to my left. In about fifteen yards I was going to slam into a boulder-strewn shoreline at an uncommonly attained speed of Mach 1. It was going to be great! All I had to do now was look like I meant to do that and not break anything!

I didn't know what happened really, with a quick jerk I flipped just before hitting the wall of rocks and was driven underwater into a violent surge of acrobatic movements, while mostly trying to stay in my boat. I rolled up in a calm eddy behind a boulder the size of a tiny house. I was not really sure that the violence from a moment ago was even real. I composed myself and looked to the other side of the river where I should be and thought, "Fuck! How the hell am I going to get over there?" I needed to be in the center of the river. Behind me was a battlefield of holes and bullshit I did not want to deal with. The center of the river looked friendly fun and inviting, like a beautiful woman with a nice dress and a smile on her face. Maybe I should just go through the mind field, but in order to get what you don't have, you must do what you haven't done, and I

165

haven't done this yet. Just then I saw another person in our group go by with what looked like a good line. It was not as far away as I thought, so I set my ferry angle and paddled. It had taken me about seven seconds to get from where I was to the center of the river. It took me over two minutes to get back paddling as fast as I could.

We gathered in an eddy below the rapid, and the Si said something to the effect of, "What the fuck was that? All I saw was you shooting left. You looked like a Frisbee on a windy day!" All the guys laughed, and I shrugged my shoulders with my palms up and out to my sides.

They let me catch my breath for a while. It was not a long run anyway, about ten miles or a little less. We knew it would not take all day.

The next drop was called Picnic. I ran into a friend of mine, George, in the small rapid above it. I had paddled with him on the Bottom Moose in the Adirondacks in NY and the Doe River in Tennessee. This was fairly common. I was always running into someone that either knew me or that I have paddled with before. We talked and he told me about this rapid. He said, "Start center and work your way right. I'll lead." The rest of my guys were fooling around surfing as we took off down the river. We started center, like George said. The waves were very steep, and at the apex of every wave I looked around at the wide expanse of this river. In the trough, however, the only thing I could see was water at the top of a wave of three waves and George was gone! At the peak of the next wave I saw him all the way over on the right of the river with his paddle in the air trying to get my attention. "Holy shit!" I thought that was quick. I pointed my boat to the right and used the waves to my advantage and blasted myself across the river. I barely made the eddy and my friend expressed some concern. I noted to myself that he had said "WORK my way right" not "GO right," this was a huge difference in my mind.

My guys came up right behind me. They had seen me make the run and Si, Carpenter, and Clergy all headed in my direction. But Bugsy was still in the middle of the river. George said in a stern voice, "Your buddy is in trouble!" Bugsy was heading directly into

166

a huge ledge hole, and he did not even know it yet. The ledge hole took over the entire left side of the river, and Bugsy wasn't going to make it. When Bugsy realized what was about to happen he paddled hard and fast, and hole heartedly dropped into the ledge hole with everything he had. It didn't work. We all took off down the river hoping to find his remains. The last we saw of him he was cartwheeling violently at about five revs per second. By the time we arrived below the hole he was out, he was upright in his boat, and breathing heavy. I didn't know how he did it, but he was able to stay in his boat, and more importantly, he was out of the hole.

He said that he had little choice in the matter. After spinning uncontrollably he went deep underwater into the bottom of the hole and he was spat out. With Bugsy's high voice and facial expressions, he told the story, he told the story of what it felt like to be completely fucked. I told him that if he was going to cartwheel like that he needed to turn his head to which he quickly replied, "I didn't have time!" Then he asked, "Where the hell did you guys go?"

We all told these stories, but the thing was I saw the hole he went into. There was a possibility of death. Fortitude mattered more than skill and skill meant nothing at this point. That's why my friend George was freaking out. We all made light of the situation, but the reality was the average person would never voluntarily expose themselves to that much danger and violence. But at the same time, the camaraderie and beauty were also unsurpassed. We let Bugsy recover before heading out.

George told us where to take out to walk the next rapid and made a point to say, "Everyone takes out at the Chute." Carpenter remarked that he had read about it and that yes everyone takes out. He was specifically looking at me when he made that comment. When we arrive at the Chute we took out and started walking, the moment we brushed the nearest bush we were inundated with mosquitoes. There were a hundred thousand mosquitoes on every bush. The morning was not bad, but it was cool in the morning so they had time to warm up by now and they were ready to eat. I did not even look at the river until we walked out onto the observation deck where there was a cool breeze coming off the falls.

167

Carpenter and I stared intently with delusions of grandeur. Rich brown granite walls glistening from the mist coming off the waterfall. This lead to a thirty-foot class VI falls with water being drawn back into the bottom of the falls from twenty yards away; then the water careened again off another drop. The second drop looked like a blender. The water was pulsing up and down, trying to get out of the narrow canyon. Its aerated boiling water vibrated the ground you stood on and the noise made all the adrenaline in your body run to your feet and adhered them to the observation deck. We snuck away quietly, reverently as if to say, maybe the rapid didn't see us. The noise of the waterfalls faded into the background as we slinked down the trail, it became white noise.

We simply followed the trail and put in at the bottom of it. "Ferry over to river center and run down the left side. All the water is pushing to the right, but if you go right, you will end up in Davey Jones's Locker." We all glanced at each other, "That's the name of the hole. A," some Canadian guy at the edge of the river told us. We worked our way through the mishmash of swirling water and there were waves that appear out of nowhere. We shot down the left of the river fooling around light-hearted, knowing that was the last rapid of the day. There were hundreds of people at the take out and several of them watching the hole known as Davey Jones's Locker. The carnage whore's sat around drinking beer and heckling. It was a fun pastime if you were a pussy. We had heard talk about Davey Jones's Locker, but really, we never looked at it. Apparently, it was a massive hole that would rip you from your boat and the clothes from your carcass before dismantling you one limb at a time. It was the stuff of legend.

Back at camp we ate dinner. It began to cool down and the mosquitoes receded back to hell to stay warm. We drank Canadian beer and walked around talking to the locals. Kayakers, rafters, open boaters, and I felt a sense of nervousness among the lot. I was accepted at every campfire I walked up to, but there were many more people tonight than the night before. I only told a few people that I had run the river blind that day with a small group of friends. Quickly they glanced around the fire as if to say he is full of shit. Then someone would ask me a question about some rapid. I would confirm what rapid they were talking about because I did not really know the names and gave them the breakdown of what I thought.

They seemed intrigued when I said things like, "Use the big wave on the left to surf across to river center that way you miss the big hole below it. Then turn back to river left and head back toward the hole, just miss the hole and catch the big wave behind it, it's a great surf!"

"You did not run it river right?" Someone asked.

My answer, "River right is boring."

After that, all guys in front of me lost their attitude, but no one wanted to paddle with our group. They were straight liners, shooting down the river avoiding the big stuff and never catching an eddy or a wave. They grew quiet after that and changed the subject. Until someone asked, "How much do you paddle?"

"I paddle around sixty or seventy days a year," I said. A look of disgust shot around the fire.

"Well, no wonder," was the only reply.

I moved on feeling that I had worn out my welcome. I wandered in and out of campfires until it was time to sleep. I worked my way back to the guys as everything was just breaking up.

The next morning after eating oatmeal, we dressed and put in on the lake and worked our way to the dam. Bugsy and Carpenter went first. I notated that the guru guy was sitting below the bridge on the abutment just before the edge of the drop. "Marty," he said "Have a good run!" I started back paddling yards above the drop and looked up at him with a smile. I didn't know what I had gotten myself into, "I'm not sure if I want to do this!" At that point, I was swept over the drop with no speed, but I did not care. The day before I barely splashed my face, so I was not concerned, plus my guess was that there were nearly a thousand people from hundreds of miles around here watching this drop. So, I should make the best of it!

169

As I was swept over the drop I started paddling, but I could not overtake the river speed. Looking down at the bottom of the drop, I saw a wave, a big wave. It was building and building, by the time I was in the trough it was eighteen feet high. I dug in with no choice but to go over it! My right paddle blade was deep in the river. I was leaning forward and picking up speed. My bow was pointed straight up and my legs were above my head. As I looked up I saw above me a curling white wave crashing five feet above my now vertical boat, and I calmly thought to myself, "Yup, I'm not going to make it!" The wave crashed onto me, and my boat did a complete backflip as the wave violently drove me under water. I gripped my paddle and held my breath; this could take a while. My boat and I spun in circles underwater. It was a combination of cartwheels, barrel rolls, and octagonal movements much too complicated to explain. The only thing I really knew was I needed some air. But my best guess was that I was still about eight feet underwater, upside down, and violently out of control. I felt my boat lift and when the lifting motion stopped, I set my paddle up and rifled it across the side of my boat and rolled. BAM!! I was up, and there was air here! One breath in and the next wave hit me. I was sideways, there was not a chance in hell. It picked me up, flipped me, and drove me back underwater dynamically. Knocking the wind out of me, now I really needed a breath! I flailed around underwater thinking, "No I'm not going to do it, I am not going to swim today!" I rolled up again getting a big breath only to be tossed over upside down again, but the waves were getting smaller. I was closer to the surface so I rolled again and was able to gain control and started to paddle my way out of the current. At that moment I heard a great sound rise above the rush of the river. The crowd was cheering, and I looked up at the drop to see what had happened. But the only person in the run was me. I took my hand off my paddle and waved slightly to hear another rush of cheers from the carnage hungry crowd.

I breathed deeply as I worked my way over to the big eddy that Bugsy and Carpenter were in. I looked up at them with a big smile like always. Bugsy waited until I was in earshot, "You should have seen it! I don't know how you stayed in your boat!" I smiled, still trying to catch my breath and did not say anything. The other two guys joined us. Clergy was upside down for a long time, but the waves weren't that big at the time. So, I didn't know what was going on there, but he rolled up fine and worked his way over to us. Si paddled over to me and said, "I don't know what happened we could not see it. All I know was that we were being told not to go; then we heard the crowd cheering like crazy! What in the hell happened?" He said it with a smile on his face and tight cheeks with his helmet tilted back on his head, leaning arrogantly back in his boat.

My reply was, "I really don't know I was underwater at the time." Bugsy filled him in.

We worked our way down the river for the second day. There were a lot more people that day. We did not have any problem because we were always on the side of the river that everyone else stayed away from. We had a great time all day. We knew the river much better today and shot back and forth playing as hordes of people shot by us like cars on a freeway.

When we reached Rock and Roll I was well behind the guys, and I was taking my time. I saw them disappear one by one over the drop. I was now alone and about to drop into the run. I had just started paddling hard to begin my line between the two raging holes. But something did not feel just right, the river was pulsing, I was paddling uphill, and the holes on either side of me were extremely loud! The water in front of me suddenly exploded. A huge mound of aerated water rose up in front of me three feet above my head, the only thing I could do was keep paddling. If I stopped I would be sucked left or right into one of the massive holes and be destroyed. I dug my paddle in and tried to paddle uphill, but the water was so aerated that my bow cut right through it. At the same time, the water was starting to dissipate and run down the river, and as it did it took my bow with it. I had paddled so hard that my bow ended up pointing at the bottom of the river. I was in a bow stall between two of the largest holes on the river. I couldn't flip! I worked my paddle furiously popping it off what little water was offered me. I slapped the water on both sides of my boat with my paddle blades just to stay upright. My boat was completely vertical, and my face was about a foot from the churning white aeration. I threw my body to the side and my boat followed me. Not wanting to flip, I quickly dug a paddle in. This caused my bow to pull up out of the churning

171

whitewater and my stern to slice through the water. I was now in the same position but facing up instead of down. I was in a full-on stern squirt with my bow pointing at the sky. I leaned forward as I bobbed up and down while I paddled like my life depended on it. The water finally subsided and I was able to get flat. Completely out of breath and putting distance between myself and the holes, I worked my way down the rest of the run one paddle stroke at a time. The guys were watching me the whole time. When I reached the safety of the eddy I heard one of the guys say, "Isn't that just like Marty doing cartwheels between two holes like that! Show off…" My reply was short, "Yea, that's what I was doing." They laughed, and we headed down the river.

We walked around the great chasm of boiling water with barely a glance. It was getting late in the day and I was hungry as we put in above Hollywood. I shot across the confused torrential waters to the center of the river and shot down the left side. Then I heard the crowd at Davey Jones's Locker starting to raise a ruckus. I looked over to see Bugsy on top of the BOTTOM of his boat. He had flipped in the mix mosh of water trying to ferry across the river and swam. He was now on top of his boat heading directly toward the flesh stripping hole! He disappeared as we worked our way across to the bottom of the hole. The crowd was going wild and were on their feet!

We met Bugsy below Davey Jones's Locker near the takeout as he floated down to us. He said that he had panicked after hearing all the stories about the hole and swam. But it really was not that bad. He was able to hold onto the boat and paddle and was mad at himself for swimming. We almost never picked on each other for swimming since it was just part of the journey of kayaking, everyone swam eventually. We shot back up to camp and quickly packed up our stuff. We wanted to get home and had a long drive.

We had a great time but being that was the one hundred years high, we would never see that water level again, so there was no point in going back. We had done it all already. We had done it with minimal input from our fellow kayakers and made our own lines. All of us were tested and pushed to our limits, and none of us would forget it.

19

The Gauley

Any American kayaker that had been around for more than a year or two had heard about the Gauley. The Gauley was the quintessential river and was a standard to be measured by. The Gauley was a good place to judge the character and skill of any kayaker. Crowds from all over would descend upon the river during the Gauley festival. It was the largest festival of its kind in the world. It had every boat manufacturer in the world, all the clothes and gear you needed, and thousands and thousands of spectators. I avoided it like the plague.

Bugsy, Shea, Carpenter, Cook, and myself wanted to do Upper Gauley and, like me, they did not want to go during the festival. We scheduled a trip around it but we needed a connection, someone to show us the way or at least tell us what to watch out for.

In came Saddle, he was a canoeist / open boater. He was far and away one of the best boaters I had seen, not just in a canoe but overall. He ran everything a kayaker could run, from steep creeks to big water. He was a great all-around paddler. He told us that he had a group of friends that lived not too far from the Gauley and they ran it all the time. His friend had a house that we could stay at for the night, and then his friends would lead us down the Upper Gauley. Saddle had it all arranged and we accepted that as fact. At that point, I had dozens of people that I could have called upon to take my group down. I paddled with a big group of people that not only ran the Gauley all the time but worked on it as raft guides and kayakers. But the arrangements sounded good to me so I went with the flow.

Bugsy and I went together in his truck together, with a couple other people driving their own vehicles we took off down south. Saddle led the way like a Roman Emperor with his canoe on the top of his van as a weapon of war leading a charge. It took about seven hours to get to Summersville West Virginia, so really you were killing a day just to get there. I expected we would arrive in Summersville then maybe buy some meat, fire up the grill, cook some barbeque, hang out, drink, and have a great time. That, however, was not what happened. When we arrived, it was late in the day and it was just getting dusk. The Gauley only released for six weeks in September so that was the amount of time you had to become famous in the whitewater realm. Only we weren't famous, but we did have kayaks on our trucks, so we definitely had the opportunity to be. However, in our haste we forgot a simple detail, we were kayakers not open boaters. Saddles friends were open boaters, we never gave this a thought until we arrived at the house. There, lined up on the well-groomed lawn were whitewater canoes. We were now at a house full of open boaters.

To the person not involved in the whitewater realm let me explain this to you, open boaters drank wine, red and white, kayakers drank beer and whiskey. Open boaters dressed in shirts with collars and kayakers dressed in tee-shirts that smelled. Open boaters paddled with a single bladed paddle while kayakers used a double-bladed paddle. Open boaters seemed to feel they were the upper echelon and looked at kayakers like the bastard red-headed stepchild that didn't deserve to eat at the table. With the exception of Saddle who was a great guy, most of the open boaters I had run into literally ran into me first! Needless to say, we didn't really like each other that much. Later in my years, I had met some new school open boaters with short play canoes that were really good to paddle with. But that was not this week…

At the house, several canoeists were milling around talking in there posh arrogant kind of way when we showed up. They all stopped and looked at us, glance at each other, then looked back at our group as if we were going to run into the house with a mad beehive or something. We quickly realized this was not the warm fun fuzzy place that we had anticipated. Saddle walked into the house and quickly spoke with the owner who greeted him with a handshake and a smile. He came back out and informed us that the house was full and we were camping for the night. That suited us fine. We cooked on the tailgate and ate outside with our group, until

175

it started to rain. We did not bring the usual tarps and tents since we were only going to stay for the night. Tomorrow after we ran the river, if any of us were left alive we were heading back to NY.

We quietly worked our way up onto the porch and hung out there for a while to get out of the rain. The guys in the house would walk to their cars and walk back past us without a word. Finally, a friend that came with us, Cook, just decided to walk into the house. Bugsy and I slowly followed suit. I tried to have some conversation with several people but I was given the cold shoulder as if I had leprosy, but I did not have leprosy I had a kayak. In their elite world of open boating we kayakers simply were not worth talking to. We walked through the house as if we were ghosts, unseen and unheard. Conversations were short and rude.

We slept in the back of Bugsy's truck that slowly leaked water one drip at a time onto my forehead like water torture. I diverted the water and went to sleep. The next morning, Saddle went into the house and asked about running the Upper Gauley. They informed him that they would be running it in the afternoon and that we were on our own. The guys had a primed discussion and came up with the fact that we had never collectively come across so many assholes in one place. We were surprised because we were all part of the whitewater community. I never looked at an open boater the same way again. "Fuck them guys, let's go paddle!"

We ran shuttle and just before getting dressed I wandered into the tall grass out of the line of sight to take a leak. I had long quick-drying pants on and when I returned back to the truck I started to take off my shoes. I noticed that I had four ticks crawling up my pant legs. I quickly informed the guys, and we all became paranoid of getting Lime Disease and checked every inch of ourselves. Being from Western New York at the time, the only time I had ever seen a tick was on deer that I was skinning and that was only occasionally. So, we were a little taken back! I even found a tick in Bugsy's truck on the ceiling weighting to pounce on me like a vampire.

I started getting dressed and it occurred to me that I was about to put on to one of the biggest class V rivers on the east coast. The only thing was, I didn't have a clue where I was going, how to run the rapids, or even how long this section was. I looked at the put in, about twenty minutes ago there were fifteen people at the put in. I even saw an old friend of mine and said hello. Now as I glanced over the put in it seemed desolate. The only thing I could hear was the roar of the release as I lifted my boat to my shoulder. I read about this river a few months ago, you know…so we should be ok. Bugsy, Cook, Saddle, Shae, and I lined up side by side at the edge of the river. We slid in one by one; Shae was the weakest paddler then Cook. Bugsy, Saddle, and I were about equal though we were all good at different types of water. We were all dependable. We worked our way across the river which was fast and pushy. I knew I needed to start my moves way ahead of time and I quickly needed to understand the timing of the river. The power of the water was all-encompassing. I understood why everyone made a big deal about it all the time.

It was ten miles to the take out and there were fifteen named drops. Nine of them were class IV or better. Every drop was littered with undercuts and sieves with holes that on a daily basis flipped fifteen-man rafts. We were winging it! Shae had hiked the river before so he knew where the big stuff was. But the reality of it was you could see crowds of people and hear the waters crashing sound upon arrival of the big drops. We were told by Shae not to surf AT ALL just stay with the program and keep on the main flow of water. Some of the best waves lead directly to the most dangerous sieves in the river. So, we shot down through the river looking for green water and big eddies. We had to read and run, hesitation made you question yourself. Strong paddle strokes through huge waves. We were using the edge of boulders as launch points and wanted to stay in the middle of the river, we were all jacked! Through the first rapid we found ourselves at the rapid known as Insignificant. We took turns and shot down through. It was a long rapid with a definite angle to it. High peaking waves and holes scattered through it. Now we were on our toes and needed to be sharp. I grew accustomed to looking for holes on the Hudson River at high water, so I was able to skirt a few holes that one of the other guys may have led us into. But getting near any rock was dangerous, the front was undercut, and the back of the rock probably had a bad whirlpool eddy behind it. We worked our way down looking for some big awesome gut-wrenching thing, but nope not really, there were a few holes here and there but not that big of a deal. We knew the real big stuff was coming up, so we were practicing our moves. Working our way back and forth in the river we were now feeling more comfortable and going through waves with confidence. I was starting to notice the day now. The coolness was starting to burn off and the water was no longer shocking cold. The nervousness had given way to a happy go lucky glow, and the realization that I was on the Upper Gauley and so far it was not kicking my ass.

I paddled past a boulder that stuck out from the wall and got sucked into a whirlpool behind it. REALLY sucked in! I was on my side sculling my paddle back and forth ferociously to keep from flipping. My eyes were bugging out of my head as I tried to keep my head above water, my breath was shallow, and I was at the edge of hyperventilating. "This is it," I thought, "I am about to become famous." I knew that flipping hear might be bad. If I got sucked out of my boat I would have to abandon it. No matter what happened, I could not get near a wall since everything was undercut. The water was being sucked into cracks and underwater ledges with a defined hollow sound until it filled to the top of the underwater cavern with a slap that sounded like a truck being dropped off a house. I would have no chance. My heart was pumping in my ears as I whirled in circles. I flipped my hips and took a few strong well-placed paddle strokes and shot out of the toilet bowl as fast as I went in. I was beside myself, I couldn't relax, I thought, that was stupid. I gripped my paddle and shook my head as I gritted my teeth looking at the deck of my boat. The canyon was taller now and people dotted its sides. Just a little farther down was an old man that sat on the side of the river and gave me thumbs up. He had seen what I did so I smiled and nodded my head.

I stayed tight with the guys when we went into the rapid called Iron Curtain. I saw a bunch of kayakers behind a hole near the wall. We worked our way over, and I pounded into the swirling eddy on a hard lean and stopped on a dime. Sitting straight up in my boat, my shoulders square, and my elbows high I surveyed the hole and the people around it. I was pointing upstream sitting in the eddy and there was a guy to my right looking at me with a puzzled look on his face. I turned to him and said, "Do you know the name of the next rapid?"

Not that it mattered really, I said, "I do not know what rapid I was in now."

He looked at me with shock on his face, "Is this your first time on the river."

"Yea," I said, "But I read about it once so I will probably be ok."

"I'll take you"! He exclaimed.

"I have guys with me." I stated matter-of-factly.

"Are they as good as you?"

"Yes." I said. He nodded his head, and I turned to the guys and told them what was going on.

Our new found friend yelled to his buddy and he came over to us. Pillow was the next rapid that they ran all the time. I looked over my shoulder at Shae, he had seen it from shore and knew what it looked like. I was sure he wanted to see it again. After talking with the group just to tell them what was going on, we all headed down the river with our new best friends. Pillow Rock was obvious. There were people all over the goddam place. As we paddled up to it Shae took out on the right of the river to watch us run it. I followed the two guys I just met at the rapid above. We stopped above Pillow to look at the run, but never got out of our boats. They explained to me where to go and what to do.

"Don't go too far left next to the wall or you will get swept into the Room of Doom. Don't go too far right or you will get sucked into that big trashy hole. Thread the needle, ok!" I smiled and nodded yes. As I saw it I realized that the thread the needle move was like thirty yards wide. I was used to threading the needle moves at four feet wide. Even on a bad day, I didn't see it being a problem,

179

but I thought, "There are like a thousand people watching so... something bad must happen here occasionally!"

I liked the way he gave me directions, simple and straightforward. He did not complicate his mind or mine. He was not trying to prove anything. He simply gave me directions. "Go down here and turn right, don't go where it looks bad. We will run it first," he said. I noticed that on the top of Pillow Rock there were about fifteen people just sitting there. Most of them had thrown ropes and were hovering over the Room of Doom. The Room of Doom was a small spot at the point where the river turned abruptly causing a whirlpool that was nearly impossible to get out of. People on top of the rock would occasionally get a chance to save the wayward soul stuck in Doom. This was not much comfort for me really.

After telling me where to go, our new friends took off. The talky one promptly got sucked into the big trashy hole wave thing and flipped and flushed. He went through the rest of the run upside down while trying to roll. The second guy went around the hole to the left. He hit a big wave, got shot up into the air, flipped, was swept into the Pillow which was caused by the massive vertical wall, and washed out around it upside down. So, there I was at the top of the run. Good thing I knew exactly where to go! Perhaps I had misinterpreted their mindset. Rather than the simplicity was the core of complexity idea I was thinking they represented, now I was thinking more along the lines that these guys suck! I felt eerily alone at the top of the run. I pushed myself out of the eddy and started my run, in theory, what they said held true. I floated sideways toward the line I wanted. My bow pointed to the right knowing that if I started my push too early I was hole bate. As I started to get drawn toward the wall, I went into all forward, I picked up speed then on the slope. My hands gripped the paddle and my breathing, well I'm not really sure if I was breathing. I looked at the hole and saw the gap I wanted. My speed carried me parallel to the hole and just past the hole the water on my left started to rise and tower above me. This was big, powerful, and pushy. I leaned forward and with strong shoulders pulled myself through the water. I was being tossed back and forth off staggered undulating waves. My paddle was popping off the water as fast as I could get a revolution in. I shot past the pillow rock heading toward the center of the river. Then I hit this big rock called Volkswagen Rock. Apparently, my guru guy forgot to mention this little detail. From above it was barely visible, but now by Jesus, I could see it plain as day. I was sideways on this rock in the middle of the river with no less than five hundred people watching me. I was riding a small pillow of water that formed on the top of it. I looked around for a second and gave people a smile and a wave, you know as if I meant to be there and worked my way off of it. I worked my way through the tumultuous water at the latter end of the run. I found my eddy, pulled my boat, and joined the spectators.

I never saw those guys again. I didn't know if they even really egested. No one in the group even remembered them! When Bugsy hit the top of the run he was in a hurry. His long arms reached almost past the front of his boat as he jetted himself forward. Around the big hole to the left he suddenly hit a reactionary wave that pushed him all the way left and almost into the wall. At least that is what it looked like. All the people sitting on top of Pillow rock stood up and ran over to see if he would get sucked into the Doom. He was riding the big pillow of water with his bow pointing to the right. He surfed past the Room of Doom and used the pillow from Pillow Rock to propel himself past the vertical Pillow Rock and past the Volkswagen Rock that I had gotten caught up on. By the reaction of the crowd, this must have not been the traditional line. But the crowd cheered and I was happy too! Saddle took a conservative line, but really nothing there was that conservative. We all watched for a while, for never having been here before I think we did really well. Particularly after watching several people completely screw up the lines, upside down, backward, and some out of their boat altogether.

After getting through Pillow Rock alive, I felt happy that we did not come down through the river with the group we met last night. I felt vindicated in some way when we all patted each other on the shoulder for making it through unscathed. The way the open boaters spoke last night when they spoke to us was that this run was the end of the world. This magnificent maelstrom was a one-way ticket to hell, and apparently, we deserved to go there for even

181

daring to be in the presence of their masculinity. I smiled and thought, "They would have probably looked at it before running it."

We bopped back and forth down the river fooling around. We came up to the next big rapid, Iron Ring. I had heard a lot about this run and Shae wanted me to look at it. It was the only time I was out of my boat to look at a rapid that day. I glanced at it quickly, and I noticed not to go too far right and not to get caught in the holes on the left. There seemed to be a lot of water, the tight sluiceways I had heard about were way underwater. Along with all the rocks on the left of the river side of the run. Apparently, the rain we had all night the night before had caught up with us. I jumped in my boat and ferried out into the river. I must admit it was much pushier than it looked and it was also very fast! I dug in and set my line to just miss the hole. The hole was aggressive, but I broke through the right of the river edge and zipped around the hole below without any issues. I grabbed an eddy and waited for the guys. One after the other they pounded down through. Shae ran this without a problem and floated by me with a big smile on his face. I knew he always wanted to run that. He had seen it several times from the shore. I knew this was a lifelong goal of his. I gave him thumbs up with a big smile. We were at ease as we worked our way down the rest of the river.

We arrived at Sweet's Falls and just ran it barely acknowledging it at all. The whole river was big but this drop did not seem any bigger than the rest. After that, Shae pointed out that it was Sweet's Falls. That was the Upper Gauley; the next move was the take out. I did not really understand what he meant until we arrived.

We opted to walk out with the boats on our shoulders. We went up the canyon. It was just like everywhere else we had ever been.

Bugsy and I had slept in water the night before, that's if we slept at all. We went forward with our plans like always, not letting someone dissuade us in any way. As I stood at the edge of the canyon looking down at the great white river I could still hear its gallant roar. We had not conquered anything. It would be there long after we were gone. Then I thought to myself character was built not bought.

20

Two Helping Hands- Watauga

We started the annual southern trip on the Nolichucky. An easy class IV with a fun surf hole called jaws. It was big and crunchy that day, and my good friend Walker ended up getting stuck. He was jumping up and down in there like he was on a rodeo bull. He started flipping over and over. I could see him gasping for breath as he finally gave up and swam. That was a hard way to start a trip, but the swim was not bad. We collected his stuff and headed down the river. We had fun on the rest of the river with a happy go lucky attitude and not taking things too seriously. We found our share of surf waves and took turns diving in and out of them. Walker was being very resilient and showed no fear heading toward the biggest waves. Or maybe he just wanted to redeem himself. He was already wet so either way you might as well have fun. At the end of the river we took out and me and my A-team sat around for a while talking about what river we wanted to do next. We weren't in a hurry since this was not a long river. It was also not hard and we had no place to be. The next river that we had decided to do was not that far away, so travel time was minimal. We definitely were not in a hurry.

I walked to the edge of the river to see a kayaker getting into his kayak. He looked to be in his forties. His gear, helmet, boat, and the paddle weren't completely old school, but I knew this guy had some time on the river. I walked up to him and he greeted me with a big hello and a smile. I just loved that, he seemed fun, happy, and unafraid. We talked for a minute and he then asked "Where are you going next?" When I mentioned The Watauga his head jutted out to the river. He no longer wanted to look at me. His eyes glazed over as he watched the water running by. He said one thing after that, "The Watauga is no fucking joke". He promptly slid himself into the river and shot downstream without as much as a glance toward me. I knew he had stories and he, by God, wasn't going to tell them to me. I never mentioned it to anyone, but it was in the back of my mind the rest of the day. Could be this guy was just like many that I had known before? A class IV boater that had no aspirations of running class V water? A great ambassador of kayaking and an instructor? It could have been he was a hardcore class V boater whose best friend died on the Watauga? I would never know and I never saw him again, but I had the feeling that his day had changed because of the words I had said.

The next day we arrived late at the Watauga put in. We had to run shuttle, so some of us waited while others set up the cars at the take out. As we waited two guys showed up, they were locals that were going to run the river today. We had a long conversation with them as we waited for the guys to get back. They questioned us extensively. What rivers had we run? How many days a year did we kayak? Have we done a lot of creaking? They seemed satisfied with our answers and then volunteered to take us down.

The Watauga dropped 103 fpm (foot per mile) with a max gradient of 140 fpm. It was the ultimate creek run with its share of dangers. Holes, strainers, undercuts, sieves, and pinning rocks all over the place. There was a labyrinth of lines, some of which ended in sieves where the water just disappeared in front of you. It was a technical run with fun moves all day. This section of the Watauga was about 5 miles long, but you would paddle more than 10 miles by the end of the day.

When the guys returned from the shuttle run they were happy to see we had company. We introduced our new friends to the guys and hit the river. We would be following the locals today.

The first guy was tall and skinny, and he wore old school black-rimmed glasses (definitely retro). He carried a nice digital camera, he was quiet, confident, and calm. He was not in a creek boat, but that did not seem to bother him so it didn't bother us. He was obviously the ringleader. But his friend was no slouch, he was quite a bit shorter and he was thin as well, with a pale complexion and light hair. He seemed excited to get on the river and in a bit of a hurry.

From the moment we hit the river, the locals dropped into every goddam eddy there was and there was a lot. I really thought

185

they were testing us for boat control and state of mind, or this was just their way of having fun. The one thing it did do for us was it established our timing for the day. In and out of these eddies were dropping in elevation more and more. We quickly found ourselves on a river that exceeded our expectations. It was aggressive and hard, with more water than we thought and more moves than we had dreamed of. We found ourselves ferrying from one side of the river to the other to make a boof, only to turn around and boogie to the other side to make another. Many of the drops were blind with no way to see what was on the other side or around the corner. Twenty minutes in and I already knew this was one of the best rivers I had ever been on. We dug our way out of every eddy just to get over the eddy fence. Using the water to help us get to where we needed to go, every eddy we caught was important at this point. We kept our heads up while we constantly looked downstream to see the person in front of us making the next line. We were always looking upstream to make sure the person behind us did not have any issues. This was teamwork, yet at the same time, every person was responsible for making the moves themselves. Boat control was paramount as we worked our way down this river. From time to time, there would be a big eddy that we would congregate in. The locals would say a few words, ask us if we were ready, and then we'd take off. We'd usually paddle directly away from where we thought we should go. We glanced at each other quickly and realize that they hadn't steered us wrong yet and set off back across the river. As the elevation of the drops increased, so did the speed of the water and the importance of making the line.

Each one of us had our own set of issues during the day. Sometimes it was timing. The person in front of you was too slow, or the person in back of you was too fast. We were all tripped up by fuck me rocks at some point during the day. Those rocks just below the surface that you couldn't see but would scrape the bottom of your boat which slowed you down or stopped you all together. This almost always made you blow your line, so you would have to struggle to get back to it. We were bobbing our line and slowing things down while we tried not to get pinned too bad. But really most of the time I could only see two people, the person in front of me and the person in back of me. The constant elevation changes

186

only allowed glimpses of anyone else on the river. From time to time we would hit a high vantage point. We were unable to see the rapid directly in front of us as we looked down upon a drop three rapids away from us. We saw one of the locals shoot the drop. However, three rapids later it was now unrecognizable. It was easy to second-guess yourself, but it was best not to. The dreaded second-guess caused panic, confusion, and in turn mistakes. We were trusting these gentlemen with our lives that day. We were there to have fun yet in the first half hour my body had pulsed through all the adrenaline it had. Every time the person in front of you dropped completely out of sight, you had no idea how high the drop was. You had no idea what direction you wanted to be pointing other than the angel of the person that just went over the drop. Is there a hole at the bottom of the drop that I should not get stuck in? Am I landing in a skinny shoot, or just missing a rock or boulder? All of this was an unknown until you were at the lip of the drop itself and that was where all of your decisions were made, within a two-paddle stroke time frame.

We went forward at a measured pace, and were not in a hurry but definitely weren't leisurely. I wasn't at the edge of my seat all day long, but I made every paddle stroke count. We all gathered in a big eddy, and the locals explained, "There is a ledge right in front of you. We call it the Kamikaze Boof!" That sounded fun, I thought. You had to hit this with speed, even though it looked like you were going to slam into an undercut knife -like ledge that looked like you were going to cut your head off. Then you had to turn in mid-air to your left, drop into the shoot, hit the water, and hang on. They would be down there waiting for us. They turned and took off and promptly disappeared off the drop and left us there to contemplate our fate.

At the time this sounded like a perfectly reasonable explanation, it reminded me of several books I had read about eastern philosophy. All of them generally reflected your face back to you as if in a mirror and whispered in your ear. The battle was not with the opponent, it was with yourself. The way you lived your life was an art, and you made it unique and beautiful. Anyone that made things complicated was telling you they were better than you and

187

you would never be as good as them. The greatest among us made it easy for us to succeed as if they had nothing to do with it.

The directions the locals gave us were sparse yet well thought out, they were definitely the greatest among us today.

I was not the first in line that day. Saddle was, and just like always he was in a great big canoe ahead of me. He took off, and at the edge of the drop he gave a mighty paddle thrust. He went off the ledge, wrenched his body sideways on a boof stroke, and dropped completely out of sight. We had no idea how high the drop was, but Saddle was a tall guy, and his head went completely out of sight in an instant. It was my turn and I did not hear any whistles or yelling, so off I went. I powered toward the drop with about five good power strokes and came up to the ledge. My fate became clear now. I was going to die. I was about to drop into a deep dark chasm that I could not see the bottom of. The undercut slab of rock in front of me seemed to have a razor-sharp edge, which was honed over millions of years of water shaping it. This, I thought, was not a good idea, but it was too late now. I gave a big boof stroke on my right side, turned my body to the left, and pulled my legs to the left at the same time. My boat followed as I dropped into the darkness. When I hit the water, it had the force of a fire hose and shot me toward the opening. Through the opening I could see the faces of the locals.

I shot through the gap in the rock like I was a potato out of a potato gun. After two or three paddle strokes to help my body catch up with my boat, I looked at the locals for approval. They sat in their boats in an eddy with big shit eating grins on their faces. I smiled back at them and at the same time was equally interested to see the next person's experience. I had never experienced anything like it; that was freaking awesome! I eddied out and watched the rest of the crew make the move. Each person had the same look of astonishment that I'm sure I did as they shot out of the chasm into the light. It was like being reborn again. Now we were invincible! No one spoke about our Kamikaze experience, we simply continued our run. Until the locals pulled to the side of the river and got out, I thought maybe lunch. But for whatever reason, if they were getting out, I was going to get out too. It had been aggressive water all day, and we could use a break. That break was called Stateline Falls.

We walked to look at the drop. It was 16ft falls with water pounding over it. The locals told us the line, and in my mind, it seemed easy. Catch the eddy directly above it and run the drop just right of the center of the river with the angle of right and boof. When I was asked what I thought I instantly fell back on to my personal rules of kayaking. Never run a big drop on the 2nd day of a weeklong trip. If you get hurt it would ruin the rest of the trip, and you would become the shuttle bunny for the rest of the week. On the 3rd day run only class IV unless you had a once in a lifetime run available, something that you may never get the chance to run again in your lifetime. Every day after that run you could run whatever you wanted. These were just my rules and over time they had proved beneficial to me. This was the 2nd day, and we had already pushed ourselves all day. I decided I was not going to run it. The taller of the two locals ran it flawlessly as we watched, and I nearly changed my mind. I had run stuff much harder and knew I would not have a problem, but I never broke my personal rules. Si and his son Lew decided to run it. The rest opted out, most of them knew my rules but also knew that I supported whatever decision they would make. But generally, the group had the same thought process I did.

On top of the falls, Lew lined up and powered toward the falls. He was nerved up and went straight over the falls with no angle, because of this he landed at the bottom of the falls in a pile of tumultuous whitewater.

Below the falls and just in front of it there was a rock ledge that with that amount of water was not visible. It was shooting water back toward the falls making a keeper hole. As Lew landed at the bottom of the falls, he had to struggle to get out of it. He was popping his paddle off what little surface area the water offered and was trying to stay upright by digging with his paddle. We could tell he was giving it all he had in order to get away from the frothy mess, fortunately he eventually made it. He had a shit line and paid the consequences. Even if he had angled to the right, he would have been in better shape, but he wouldn't even have been close.

Then Si started pulling out of the eddy. I really didn't know what happened, even though I saw the whole thing. My belief was this, he pulled out of the eddy too close to the edge of the falls. As

189

he arrived at the edge of the falls, he was leaning back in his kayak and pointed toward the left. By the time he was trying to correct himself it was way too late. At the precipice of the drop, he was way off his line. He went over the falls nearly sideways, pointing the wrong direction, and leaning back in his boat. It looked as if he were waving to the angels, it was like he was going to be hanging out with them soon. Over the falls he went. He fell over the falls, landed sideways, and hit hard. He went completely under water in the maelstrom of frothy white shit, and then the back of his boat shot up out of the water. The funny thing was that his waste came completely out of the water for a moment, but his head never did. The boat came over the top of him, and now he was in the frothy shit upside down while being thrown around like a colorful ping pong ball. We gasped collectively and knew we were powerless to do anything. Lew was trying to get to him, but getting out of his boat or going back upriver was impossible. He was helpless as well. Suddenly, Si just rolled up in the middle of all this chaos. At that point we really only knew two things, the first was he had not been knocked out, and the second thing was his life was not going to be getting any easier anytime soon. He struggled to stay upright and was closer to the falls than Lew was, and it was a violent place to be. He seemed motivated to liberate himself from the situation, so with a few hundred well-placed paddle strokes, he was out in no time. After we saw that we really did not want to run the falls! We carried our boats around and put in below the falls where the father and son sideshow was now waiting for us.

Si looked like he was in great pain. His breathing was labored and he was favoring his right side. When Si went over the falls he hit the water at the bottom of the falls almost sideways, changing the direction of his boat and slowing it down. Si was a shorter guy, the sides of a creek boat were higher on a short person, so as he hit the water his body kept going and slammed against the lip of his boat impacting his rib cage. We saw it happen and we suspected he had broken his ribs, and by the look of him, I would say we were right. His elbow was tight to his body with his other hand just past his sternum. Si was slumped over his boat rocking back and forth trying to breathe without pain. But that wasn't going to happen anytime soon. State Line Falls was four miles into a five-mile run.

Si was going to have to paddle a mile, go through three more class IV rapids, and boogie before he could get out of his boat. There was a possibility of walking out, but dragging a boat with possibly broken ribs was worse than just running the river. Also, if Si had a punctured lung, it would be better if he was around people. We checked him out as best we could but taking too much time and removing the life jacket and gear were not advisable. The best thing to do was get down through the river quickly just in case there were more complications.

We could tell he was in searing pain as we worked our way down the river. He was having difficulty breathing, much less working his way down a class IV river. There were only a few significant rapids and nothing really radical, but by the time we were done zig-zagging back and forth across the river to make the moves we needed to make we had easily gone three miles. We stayed close to Si and watched him through every move. He was missing paddle strokes and had no power left at the end of the river.

We were all tired, but Si really received an ass kicking. He needed help getting off his life jacket, dry top, loading his truck, and packing his gear. Luckily his son Lew took care of most of it. With at least two ribs broken he was down for the count and became shuttle bunny for the rest of the trip. We really needed to carry some bunny ears. Luckily his lungs were ok and not pierced by his broken ribs, and nothing else had been broken but his pride. We were all thankful for the help of the locals for showing us the time of our lives. The Kamikaze Boof would forever be a part of our vocabulary. So will the story that accompanied it. The rest of the trip went well for the rest of us. It obviously took several weeks for Si to get back into a boat. He said later that the only reason he ran the falls was that he did not want Lew to run it alone, but with his act of altruism came a price.

191

21

Pigeon Dries

Bugsy, Saddle, Joey, Cook, Carpenter, Si, and myself were on a southern trip looking for water, and we had a good crew with us. We were looking for something really fun, something to test our wherewithal. We heard a rumor that North Carolina had water. We heard another rumor that this river called the Pigeon Dries was releasing. The dam was offline or something, but none of us had ever been on it before and there was not much information about it. All that we knew was that it was supposed to be the shit! Continues class V for about seven miles. It sounded fun, so we took off and made a beeline for the river. A few hours later we stood at the edge of this little river.

The Pigeon that I had heard about was a class III and was a place that beginners went to hone their skills. The boys assured me that this was not that river. But from what I was seeing, it didn't look like much. We must have been in the wrong place. I expressed my concern and Saddle, the canoer on the trip said, "Well, take your play boat then." So, I did just that, I always carried two boats on my vehicle a Pyrannha Creek boat and a river running playboat by Wave Sport. I unhooked my playboat and got it ready. I did not take any particular notice, but no one else took Saddles advice. I simply grabbed all the stuff I needed for the day and tied it to the inside of the boat. I literally knew nothing about this river, I was just following the crowd. We put in and started to paddle when Bugsy told me that he only knew the names of two rapids. Chinese Arithmetic and Nowhere To Land! We slid into the river and started paddling, at this point, I sat up straight and sober to take a good look around. I was in the smallest boat on the river, and everyone looked very serious. This, of course, struck me as odd. This was a jovial group and usually we were pretty happy to get on the water, but today felt different.

We worked our way into the first drop one by one watching our timing so we would not run into one another. We gathered in two boat eddies as the river tightened up and became much faster. It occurred to me that I had overheard one of our guys talking to a kayaker from the area earlier and the last words I heard were, "If you run that at this level you are going to die." I wondered now if he was talking about this river? As we got further into the run it seemed kind of high. Saddle and I usually stayed in sight of each other on whatever river we were on. He was one of the best canoers I had ever seen. He was a technical boater and loved to catch the small eddies and run the hard lines. That was how I liked to run stuff, tight and fast pulling the boat up on edge to make the line or break into the eddy. But all at once every drop on this river was hard for me. Every eddy was heaving up and down four feet, the skinny back end of my boat was being handled, and I was having to lean forward to keep from being squirted. I had to put my elbow almost into the water with all the power I had just to get into an eddy. I definitely brought the wrong boat! Next to every eddy the rocks were undercut, and water was sliding underneath them like a drain. Drop after drop we boat scouted; the voraciousness of the water was becoming astounding. I was following Saddle and I saw him disappear over the next set and I followed his line. We ended up in a small cove of tumultuous water, that at that moment we were calling an eddy. We were way too close to each other. Saddle couldn't even get past me to get into the rivers main flow. I was in his way. "You will have to go," he yelled to me over the thunderous river. I nodded my head and took a look downstream. Just downstream of us was a wall that was about fifteen yards long. Past the wall I could see kayakers peeking around the corner. That wall undercut the whole length and water was being sucked into it from half of the river away. This was a bad spot, I thought, we should be on the other side of the river. But I couldn't get there from here. I was barely able to get here from the drop we just came from.

I looked at Saddle and he was trying to keep his boat from running into me. I knew I had to get the hell out of there. I tried to set an angle to leave the eddy and paddle hard forward, but things didn't go like I wanted them to. "Fuck I'm vertical!" I squirted coming out of the eddy. I was two feet from the undercut wall! If I touched that wall with my stern below me I would get sucked under it, and I was up to my chest in the water already. I threw a back paddle and leaned away from the wall. Normally that was a bad move and I should lean into the wall, but I couldn't because I was not on top of my boat. If I was on the top of my boat and lifted my knee, I could let the water slide underneath me. I was not even close to being in that position, so I pushed my legs downriver to bring the front of the boat down to water level. It worked, but now I was sideways and by sideways, I mean I was parallel to the wall. My chest was half in the water that was pushing me toward the wall. I worked my paddle back and forth feverishly, sculling the water. On the forward stroke of my scull, I tipped the paddle blade into the water to help pull me away from the wall. I was moving down the wall and knew if my head went under water I was a dead man. I kept it up. It seemed like it went on forever. At one point my lips were extended and sucking air inches above the water. I flipped my hips and it brought my head back up out of the river. The surface area of my boat was too much. The current was too strong. I hip snapped three more times just moments before my head disappeared. Every time I did, I would get a stroke or two. Every stroke of my paddle bought me a few more moments; "I will do ANYTHING to get past this wall!" I looked up and saw the end of the wall and I knew there was an eddy there. At the very edge of the wall I hip snapped, the river released me, and my chest came up out of the water. I slid into the eddy with my eyes as big as saucers, my heart couldn't pound any harder, and the adrenaline was oozing out of my skin. I was completely out of breath and my chest was expanding and collapsing not able to retrieve enough air. At least this eddy was not as bad as the last one. It was bigger with more room in it. A moment later, Saddle slid into it next to me. He said "That was a good move, not letting yourself go under water." I looked at him shaking my head, "I did not have any choice," I said.

We had been over ten or more drops, and I had no idea how far into this I was or how far I had to go to get to the end. All I knew was that I had to stay with it. I looked downstream for the next line and saw Bugsy on the river, and I peal out of the eddy. I made a conscious effort to control my speed and look where I was going without playing it safe. After a few more creaky drops, I was back into the swing of the river. Putting my boat on edge, keeping it down sliding through the edge of the holes and using the backwater of the holes to slow myself down and redirect my line. Then I was not too far from Bugsy, and he dove into an eddy so I could go past him and catch one myself. On this river I could only see one person ahead of me, Most of the time I could see him. I could also only see one person behind me. The elevation was too steep to see any further. I could see Bugsy and Saddle that was it I had no idea what the rest of the group was doing. If someone was in trouble, I would be hard pressed to even hear a whistle over the roaring river.

Bugsy and I swapped leads and worked our way down the river. We were boat scouting and never stopped to look at anything. We hopped from eddy to eddy like a hiker would jump from stone to stone to keep his feet from getting wet. As I lead, I came up to a skyline that I couldn't see over. I paddled into a micro eddy and turned my boat upstream. I looked over my shoulder and looked down into an abyss. I instantly grabbed the stone I was next to and wrapped my arms around it because I knew one thing, I was not fucking going down there. I was on the right of the river looking down into a column of water that fell off into a seem that stood about six feet high. On the other side of that seem was an actual whirlpool. Both sides were undercut. Just below that was a ledge with water spraying off it into the air that went almost all the way across the river. The only way to get around it was the extreme left side of the river. It was strewn with boulders and huge reactionary waves pushing you toward yet another undercut wall. Bugsy pulled in just above where I was and yelled, "Go ahead." I promptly yelled, "FUCK YOU! I'm not going down there." I tightened my grip and hoped the boulder didn't decide to let loose. Bugsy looked surprised and said, "Oh." Bugsy jockeyed himself into a spot that he could get out of his boat, stepped out, and placed his boat on the shore where it would not go anywhere. He then stepped down into the water, grabbed my bow loop, pulled me to him, and helped me out of the boat. I put my boat on my shoulder, stepped away from the river, and dropped my boat. The rest of the group followed suit, and we stood looking at the drop. "I think this is called Chinese Arithmetic," commented one of the guys.

195

Joey took out, I saw him talk with the other guys, and then he came over to me. Joey was a good paddler, he was pompous and cocky, but the chip on his shoulder wasn't so big that he wouldn't ask advice. He would also save your ass if you were in a bind. He stood next to me for a second then asked, "What do you think?"

"I see three lines," I said. "All of them are bad, go right and try to make the boof, if you get stuck in the hole… and you will get stuck, you are screwed. The second is hit the seam and ride it out letting it push you to the left side of the river toward the undercut wall past the water spraying straight up off what I can only assume is a massive rock or several of them, the trick is you cannot flip in that seam, or you will be washed into what is causing that water to go skyward. The third line goes in high, cut in just past the boulder in the center of the river and drive into the whirlpool, then work your way out and go to the left by the wall."

Joey thought about the options for a second and played them each out in his mind. Then he looked at me and leaned in, "What would you do?"

What I thought and what I was going to say were two different things. I think there were more ways of dying in that rapid than there were ways of running it. So, without turning my head I said, "If I was going to run it…whirlpool." If, was the operable word. I already knew I was not going to run it. I knew that the moment I glanced over my shoulder and caught a glimpse of this chaotic mess. Joey tilted his head and said, "Yea, the whirlpool is turning in the right direction, hitting the edge of it you can use it as a slingshot to propel you toward the left wall around all the shit in the middle of the river." Well, I thought, at least he could see the line…

Saddle immediately walked it, saying he would set safety downstream. Bugsy was thinking about running it and wanted to see Joey's line. The rest of us decided to walk it. I was hesitating of course, but we all stood on the side of the river watching Joey push himself into the river. But here was the thing, this was a class V water. If he ended up on the other side of the river and something happened he would be completely alone. Our throw ropes were not long enough, and we were not in a position to get him out from under that wall or unwrap him from a bad pin on all the boulders. He was alone on this river now. We could only get what washed downstream.

Joey slid across the river gracefully and lined up for the Whirlpool line. If he did it right he would miss the center boulder to the right, drop off the tongue before the seam started to get big, from there he would hit the edge of the whirlpool, and it would help him get out of it. As Joey headed past the boulder he looked good, strong, and fast. He split through the seam without a missed stroke, he went off the column of water and into the edge of the whirlpool. He looked good going in, but the whirlpool got him. It stopped him dead in his boat and pulled him backward into its depths. He was paddling for all he was worth, but ended up settled atop the spinning vortex with his boat going in circles. "Yup," I thought, "That's why I didn't run it." Joey and his boat were sucked underwater to his chest and was spinning in circles. He popped up and kind of squirted out of the whirlpool. In a moment of slack water, he turned toward me and vigorously shook his head "NO!" and he took his hand off his paddle and slid it in a slicing motion across his neck. The international sign for, "If you do this, you will die!" He was looking directly at me! Joey knew that my boat was three feet shorter than his, the whirlpool was too steep for me to be able to climb out of in my boat. He worked his way down the rest of the run, basically flushed down the river in the midst of the raging water with little control. He did make it to the left of the river, but Joey was in survival mode popping his paddle off the water and throwing his weight back and forth just to stay upright. He made it through the rapid without flipping, and now we had a safety guy downriver in a boat, which was always a plus. Saddle had put back into the river lower than where Joey stopped in an eddy.

Bugsy didn't say much next to a river, he was in the zone. I could see it, his body shifted slightly from side to side, and I knew that he was practicing the run in his mind. He flared his elbow on one side then the other. He was thinking about timing and paddle strokes. We all did it in some form or another. Bugsy was a strong paddler. I had paddled with him longer than anyone there, and if he thought he would be ok then I had to respect that just as he had for

197

me in the past. I knew there was nothing I could do for him if something happened.

He snapped his head toward me. I was already looking at him. He nodded his head, made a motion with his hand, straight then cut to the left, and I nodded. He was going to try to break through the seam. He turned and walked down to his boat. The next time I saw him he was in the middle of the river with the angel of left powering forward. Bugsy's head was steady and looking directly at the entrance of his line. He didn't look at me at all. I hadn't moved from my spot just in case he needed directions. I didn't want him to have to look for me. His boat rose onto the column of water and picked up speed. He drove his paddle into the river and lunged forward in the center of the flow. One, two, three, four, five paddle strokes, he changed his lean and lifted his right knee as he cut in toward the pulsing seam of water. The seam was much higher than it looked from above as he dove into it with his boat, and his head went under water with his full-size creek boat. For a moment, he was invisible, then he emerged from the other side. He had been slowed down and was caught by the water, which pushed him much further downstream than he anticipated. He should have been higher in the run. He was being blown toward the huge hole, but he was pointed in the right direction. He glanced downstream and in one paddle stroke he redirected his boat into a better angle and paddled with everything he had. He was now feet above the hole but making headway. At the outer edge of the hole he was blown into the big boulder field and caught a rock on the bottom of his boat. He flipped, and the raging current drove him directly toward the undercut wall. He was trying to do a role on the upstream side, like my attempt earlier, and he was not doing well. His arms were extended and his body was writhing with the knowledge that ultimate danger was moments away. The wall casted a shadow of darkness upon him, but he never gave up. He was hitting boulders, his boat and body were bucking, he was doing everything he could in the aerated water to just stay afloat with the wall now inches away. He was on the other side of the river and was now out of reach. With a long sweeping motion of his paddle he caught the solid surface of moving water, and his role was complete. He pulled himself away from the looming underwater ledges and was now able to use both paddle blades as he worked his way to the relative safety of the center of the river. He floated down to one kayaker and one canoer that were waiting for him. His chest was heaving from breathing heavy, we are all breathing heavy. I picked up my boat and worked my way down the river hopping from boulder to boulder until I was even with the rest of the crew. I gave Bugsy and Joey a thumbs up and a big smile. I had never seen a drop quite like this, and I stood looking upstream in contemplation of consequences, lines, and safety. I wanted to remember this rapid, it was complex and pushy, it was big and its power astounded me.

I was one of the last to put back into the river, so I was one of the last in the pack and picked my way once again down the river. It was like running through an obstacle course with a blindfold on. I was completely unaware of what was behind each piece of granite. I tried to not be too influenced by what I saw the guys in front of me do. I made my own lines. I would be lying if I said they were clean, but that day no one had clean lines. I was shot up in the air several times by my stern getting caught in the hole. I was pushed onto the rocks and spent half of the time up to my neck in raging water trying to keep my kayak on the surface. I shot back and forth across the river to run what I could see was clean. For every mile downstream, I paddled at least three. I was winded, tired, and mentally drained, but there was only one way out. I saw a couple of guys in our group standing on some rocks next to a skyline. Coming up from that skyline was something that sounded like a derailed train rolling down a hill. "Well," I thought, "This looks like a good place to get out and take a break for a while."

I joined the guys looking at this…this fucking monstrosity. There was so much water in the river that on the right of the river you could only see a spine of what looked like boulders. The river had split, and there were fingers of water working their way through the boulder field on the right of the river. We could see the main flow, and there literally was nowhere to land off the drop. But the volume of the river was outrageous. I had not seen Carpenter all day, he was in the very front of the group and had walked Chinese Arithmetic, and now he wanted retribution. We couldn't even really get close to the run to see what was going on. Carpenter wanted to get closer, so he got in his boat and jockeyed himself around and was able to find some dry land to stand on and surveyed the run. He turned back to us and gave us the customary thumbs up. We all jerked back wide-eyed and mouths gaped open. We glanced at each other in a panic, we did not think he was going to run it. We needed to set safety now! We had to go across a river to get to the section of the river he was going to run. Carpenter never waited long, once he had his mind made up, he ran it, just that fast. But he had to work his way back upstream, so we were able to get below the drop with ropes and boats. He could not get upstream in his boat, Carpenter had to work his way to the edge of the river get out and walk back upstream.

I could not see where he put in, I was below the drop. I could not even see the first section of the drop, but when he came over the horizon, he was moving at mock one! Paddling moving like a windmill in a hurricane, yet with perfect timing. His last blade entered at the edge of the last fall and propelled him into the air clearing the hole at the bottom. With perfect timing again, he landed with the other paddle blade at the ready to pull him out of the edge of the backwash of the hole, and he was clear. We all took a deep sigh of relief as we glanced at each other. That was an aggressive move, it was also the only move that was to be had. He floated past us with his hands resting on his paddle in front of him, looking back at the drop. Then Carpenter continued leading the way down the river without a second thought about what he had just done.

We worked our way down the rest of the river by hopscotching. There was still a lot going on, and from my own standpoint, I was running my own river. At that point the river was chilling out a little, the river was wider, and the holes were smaller. Our paddle strokes became more relaxed until we found ourselves in a quiet moving pool, it was then that we realized what we had just done. Some of the best paddlers I had ever kayaked with looked like they had just been through a war. We were exhausted. Our shoulders were no longer square, and we hunched in our boats drifting with the waning current. We had left some guys behind that did not want a class V adventure, and they stood at the take out eagerly awaiting our stories of the day. But when they saw our faces drawn, our eyes bulging, and our faces having little expression they didn't say much. We threw our boats on our shoulder one by one and walked past them without saying a word. Later that night, I heard my name mentioned a few times by the campfire, but I was too tired to inquire.

The next day we ran the New River, something easy, almost a day off. I saw a big hole with a big white backwash foam pile on it. I drove the same kayak I was in the day before at the edge of it. I turned my boat upstream surfed the length of the foam pile, dropped off it, and slid across the river into a big eddy. Joey was behind me and came into the same eddy that I was in. He looked at me for a long second, "That was a really good move, I did not realize how much of a hard time you must have had yesterday in that boat." He said.

"I was being pushed around out there in the play boat." I replied.

"You are a really good boater," he said humbly.

"Thanks," I said, "So are you." We both smiled and looked for the next surf wave.

Opinions on life and opinions on a river are two different things; that's why we have always gotten along.

The Pigeon had an average gradient of 85 fpm and a max of 148 fpm, it was a little over 7 miles long. From the information I could find from 600 to 1500cfs there were two class V rapids on the river. The day we ran it was estimated to be over 2000cfs. We had put in at the wrong place and did indeed paddle about two miles to get into the first drop. The conversation that I had overheard was with Bugsy talking to a kayaker about the Pigeon Dries who told him that under no circumstances should we run that river at that level. But we did it anyway, and I'm glad we did. It took us days to really understand what transpired on the river. Every person was only in sight of two people, as each one of us told the story of our experience on the river we realized that everyone in the group had several issues during the day. But for the most part, we never saw each other, so we really had no idea what had happened to the guys

201

behind and in front of us. Saddle talked about my move next to the undercut wall, while others talked about being stuck in holes and getting worked. A couple of people had gotten pinned but were able to free themselves without swimming. Paddles, boats, and people had been pushed to their limits, but the river itself probably didn't even know we were there.

22

The Phone call

Early one morning I was sleeping in the back of my truck and I got a phone call from my old buddy Jed.

I had met Jed years ago on some river somewhere. Probably the Moose, my friend Red knew him, and I had paddled with him a few times. Then I was on a trip on the Hawkinsville section of the Black River one cold day. I was with one of the outing clubs from a nearby college. At the end of the river where we take out, there was a bridge. On that bridge stood Jed, I hopped out of my boat and walked up the bank.

"Marty my good man, how are you doing today?" Jed greeted me.

"Jed what is going on" I said.

"Well, my house is just across the street and I have hot water on for coco and coffee going for your group. I recognized your van, if you guys want to change in the house feel free, it's pretty cold out. Come on over I will see you in a few minutes." He turned and walked across the street without another word. The folks from the outing club seemed amazed that not only did I know someone up here, but that he would freely invite us into his house. We took advantage of his hospitality and warm house. I would run into him sporadically through the years on rivers and roads. I helped him get a job at the Popular raft company that I worked for. He was a raft guide and also a kayaker. He ran the Black with me a few times in his kayak, and I showed him the tricks of this river. He had not spent much time on the Black, most northern kayakers would rather creek and stayed away from playboaters. That was what the Black in Watertown was known for, but when you got past the holes and the sharpness of the rocks it turned into a great fun river. I took Jed down a few times, and he felt comfortable and started training in a raft, more as a formality than anything. The rafting company just wanted to make sure he was not going to kill anyone. So, he worked as a raft guide a lot on big trips, and I knew that on this morning we had a big trip.

So, getting a phone call from Jed this early did not surprise me. He asked me to go to breakfast with him at a local diner. I said sure I would be right there. Jed worked a full-time job and could only work with the raft companies on the weekends, that was the busiest time of the week anyway. So, I shot down to the diner where he was already inside. We promptly ordered and talked about the trip that was going down the river that morning. We talked about local kayaker gossip. Who had been trashed on the Moose, what boyfriends and girlfriends had broken up, the usual stuff.

Jed was quiet for a moment, and he looked at me. "So, Marty, I have to ask you a question. The rafting company wants to run two trips next week on the same day, and they asked me to Safety Kayak for them on the second one. Do you think I could borrow one of your kayaks?"

"I said sure, But why?" I knew Jed had a quiver of kayaks, he was an instructor and always kept extra boats around. I had seen him in at least five different boats. So, I was amazed when he asked me about borrowing a boat.

Jed took a deep breath contemplating my question, "I had to sell them," he said. "My daughter Sammy needs a new kidney, hers are dying. I sold all of my boats to pay for the genetic testing to make sure we are a match so I can save her life with one of my kidneys. Insurance wouldn't cover the genetic testing."

I was speechless, I had no idea about Sammy's issues. Jed had never bothered anyone with the details of his life. He told me about all the bad doctors they had been to, all of the money spent on traveling halfway across the country for consults, all the drugs she was on, she was even having dialysis at home, and she was only twelve years old. Her childhood had been spent in hospitals on sterile gurneys in white rooms. I sat motionless for a half hour as he talked and I listened.

Jed did not know it, but that was how I spent much of my childhood as well. I knew what that pain was like, and the indifference of the doctors and nurses that had three appointments after yours. The needles and tests, being placed in a small room and told the doctor will be with you in a little while as you heard the buzzing of fluorescent lights that were sucking the life out of you. Having your adrenaline jump when the door opened, every time a door opened shortly thereafter, there was always some sort of pain. Being told you were brave because you no longer had the energy to flinch when they pushed a needle through your skin. The smell of the revealing hospital grounds and the embarrassment of being a kid walking down a long hallway in one. Yea I knew what that was like.

"Jed," I said, "I'm going to do something for you. I don't know what or when, but I am going to help you out." I felt like the godfather "Everything I say by definition is a promise."

I started doing research before becoming too boisterous. I wanted to put on some sort of fundraiser but quickly learned I needed the help of a non-profit organization. Jed told me about Community Alive. Their purpose was to promote their little town, build up tourism, and bring in new people. It turned out that every kayaker passed through this town. It was the gateway to a myriad of rivers. The town also had a park, camping grounds, pavilions and more. It was the perfect location for a fundraising event.

Jed gave me the name of a man he knew was active in the Community Alive group, so I gave him a call.

I was living below Rochester, NY at the time. It was a four-hour drive from my house, but I had friends in Syracuse so I started making phone calls. Ben and I were going to meet on Saturday at a small bar for lunch, but I wanted to shorten the distance by staying in Syracuse the night before. I called my good friend Beamer.

Beamer and I had a long history. He said no problem come on up. But I had alternative motives, Beamer was one of those crazy people that would try anything once. He was also one of the foremost flamethrower experts in the world, and yes, it was nice to have really fucking cool friends. When I got there we went out for

205

dinner and drinks, and I told him my plan with Jed and Sammy. Then I asked him if he thought he could bring a flamethrower and fire it at the festival. He smiled, held up his beer, and said "You just tell me when and where I will be there." Awesome, tomorrow I could tell Ben I had a guy with a flamethrower coming!

I met Ben the next day for lunch. He told me that he was the mayor of the town and that he knew Jed. I explained that I had talked with several people about the event, I even had a guy with a flamethrower coming and not to worry he was licensed for that sort of thing. (He also had a license to kill in his wallet that he didn't carry.)

We talked about a lot of possibility's, a band would be nice, a big fire so everyone could gather around. After all, that was what I really needed the Community Alive group for.

I told Ben that I was going to have a silent auction and that I was looking for donations for that auction. Any local artists or store owners that wanted to donate something were more than welcome to give something. Everyone in town knew Jed and Sammy, and I thought this would be a great way to get local people to the fundraiser as well as let the kayaking community know that this town has something to offer them. We both agreed on what would take place, and Ben was happy to help out and thought that getting the Community Alive group involved would not be a problem.

We just needed a date. We decided on the weekend of May 13th. This would ensure our fundraiser did not interfere with any other kayaking festivals. All the festivities would take place on Saturday night, at $10 a head. The Moose/Black Spring Fling was now a reality. May was the month when both the Black River and the Moose River rivers were releasing, so Ben and I thought May was a good time. May 13,14,15 was decided on, people could check in on Friday night or Saturday anytime, with all the festivity's taking place on Saturday night. A $10 fee from each person was to be collected for the weekend. The event was to be called The Moose/Black Spring Fling.

I felt that my meeting with Ben was very productive, he was a really nice guy. He gave me great insight into the community's thoughts, and we both were looking forward to working together. Now that we had a date, it was my job to get the word out and put everything together, I had about six months.

The first thing I did was call my crew and told them to put the date on the calendar. Bugsy, Carpenter, Sail, Pops, Si, and Shae were all in along with a few others. I knew that they would bring a big good group of people. Many people I had paddled with for twenty years were gone, and the whitewater kayaking community was shrinking. But we still had enough to make a dent. I reached all the raft company's in Watertown; not a great response from a couple even though Jed had also worked for all of them, but the others responded favorably. I also reached out to the local paddling club in Rochester, most of them did not know Jed. The infighting among the members had them split on the idea. I called paddling shops looking for donations for the silent auction. The donations that I received were surprising, and the donations that I did not receive were just as surprising. I called an old school friend of both mine and Jed's, Mr. Clean. Mr. Clean was a mountain of a man strong and outspoken. He had saved my ass a few times. When I told him what I was doing he simply said, "When you get a chance to come to the house, I have some stuff for your auction." He gave me more stuff than any company or individual had ever thought of giving me. Paddles, life jackets, throw ropes, and multiples of each.

I, as you can tell by now, loved to talk. So, I was in Old Forge one day sitting at a small bar talking to a patron and suddenly he gave me twenty dollars. He said he did not know the man, but it made him feel good to give. Then I ended up talking to the barkeep, and she told me that she made jewelry. I asked her if she could make a one of a kind kayaking peace for the auction. A month later I received it in the mail. I hit up different stores of people I had kayaked with years before. They gave me helmets and other accessories. I called the boys in Lake Placid, the videographer who had traveled the world put together a crash and burn CD and sent me a bunch of copies. The manager of one of the raft companies who also ran a ski shop in Placid in the winter told me that he did not have any kayaking gear, but he did have a coat that was on his rack for over a year. This coat was a very high-end skiing coat with internal sleeves and places for hand warmers. But it was a child's coat. It was too much money to give to a kid that was still growing so he could not sell it. He asked me if I could use it for the auction? ""Yes, of course, I could." I told him. I received it in the mail a week or so later, and that thing was beautiful!

I called a major boat company and the biggest paddle company in America and told them what I had going on. The boat company said, "Wow let me make you a deal. I will sell you a boat at a pro deal cost of $500, you can auction it off and any amount of money you can make past the $500 you can keep and donate to your friend in need Jed. But here is the best part, the person that buys the boat can pick ANY boat that we offer, and I will ship it at no cost to the kayaking shop closest to him or her." I was speechless, typically their creek boats ran around $1300, so I knew I would not have a problem selling the idea and we did not need to have the boat there. It could be ordered later in any color the person wanted! He was going to make a special certificate out for me, and I could use that as a proof of purchase and as a representation so people would have something to look at and bid on.

A big paddling company told me that they had filled their quota for the year in donations, but he could send me small stuff such as spray skirts, key changes, bumper stickers, and a multitude of other small items I could do anything I wanted with.

Now the biggest obstacle was that I needed more people, I needed awareness. I called AW (American Whitewater) and they put out a monthly magazine to every one of their members across the world. I talked to someone there who sat quietly as I told him the story of Jed and Sammy. Jed was in the kayaking hall of fame in NY, and a kayak instructor who had helped hundreds of kayakers in the community. His daughter Sammy was a beautiful, bubbly, happy little girl that didn't deserve this kind of pain and I wanted to help them. Over the phone, I heard him sniff then take a deep breath. "Well," he said, "If we can't help someone like that then we don't have any business being part of the whitewater community. You write me an article and I will get it in." So, I did just that. I showed the article to my good buddy Sail just to make sure that it made sense and had everything I needed in it. I watched his face as he read it, at the end of the peace he pursed his lips, squinted his eyes, lifted his head, and looked out the window. "It's perfect," he said, "Don't change a thing." I was happy with his response.

I sent the article to AW with my contacts name on it, and he called me with a request. He was really happy about the way I had written the article, but he also wanted a photo to go with it. I called Jed and had him send me a photo of him and Sammy. It also ended up in the article.

About two weeks after, the article came out as a full page in AW magazine. I received a phone call from Jed. One of his friends had brought over the magazine and showed it to him. He had started receiving personal checks in the mail from kayakers that he had paddled with years before and could not understand why. I did not tell him my plans or what was going on. Honestly, I did not want his input He was such a humble guy that he would have downplayed the situation and I did not want that to happen. I wanted a ruthless self-promotion. He had no idea that I had put this all together, he just knew that I kept asking him questions about stuff.

On January 3rd, 2011 the article was printed on the AW web site. Jed was surprised, to say the least. My only downfall was at the time I was not into Facebook and really had little interest in being a computer geek. In retrospect, I should have put more effort into computer promotion. I had traveled all over collecting goods for the auction and lining up people. I had a volunteer band coming and Beamer with his flamethrower. Ben had called me and told me that he had a one-man band and that the guy was highly respected in the community. He also had a construction company that was going to come in with a huge tire ring. They were going to put down a rug and cover it with sand and put the ring on top of it so we could have a community fire. Someone else was going to give us the wood for free. He had breakfast lined up with a local woman's auxiliary club for Saturday and Sunday morning.

It was all coming together, and the closer the date came, the more confident I became with the whole idea. It was really going to happen. I had always considered myself a very lucky guy, but luck was where opportunity met talent. It seemed, in this case, the talent I had was knowing the people that got things done. But luck was like river levels, and everything in life waxes and wanes.

Years before I had a conversation with a guy after bungee jumping out of a hot air balloon. He told me that he would talk to me about it because I had done it. He said that he did not do it for anyone other than himself, and he did not want people living their lives through him. He had a point, and now I understood that point. Yet at the same time, sometimes all it takes is a small introduction to something to change someone's life.

Many of the things that people feared were an everyday occurrence for me. I was once told that I may never walk again and five years later I was throwing myself off twenty-foot waterfalls into class V rapids every day and sleeping in hammocks next to a river for six months at a time. I had thousands of hours on the water, but now that had all faded away because it didn't matter. For the weekend I would be the me that everyone expected. I would drink a little too much, tell a lot of stories that people wouldn't believe, and hit on all the ladies. I would look at the river as if it was the only thing that really mattered in the world. But that too was fading. I did know that Jed needed help and for whatever reason, he was going to get it.

When I woke up Friday morning it was raining, in fact, it had been raining on and off for the weeks in the ADK. The rain was bringing the water levels up, and the rivers were becoming treacherous. I always liked high water; my motto was always that my boat floated on top of the water. That meant my head was farther from the rocks on the bottom of the river. People sometimes bought it for a moment, but then realized that drowning became a greater possibility. I was concerned that the rain would affect the festivals patronage, but time would tell. I took a drive around and looked at some rivers. I knew no one would be pulling in until Friday night after everyone finished with work. Also, it was a long drive for many, I did not really expect people until late. It was still raining a little, but that was what the ADK was like in the spring.

Friday afternoon, some people from the Community Alive group set up a check-in tent. My only contact people were Ben, the Mayor, and my original contact, Cole. I had not met anyone else, so the people setting up the tent were surprised that I was already there. They seemed to think that I should have been older, but they were happy that I was there to bounce ideas off of from about checking in and where to put people. The place was not really set up for a campground, and they seemed to be fretting about that. I expressed to them that kayakers, in general, were a clean self-sufficient lot of people. The people who would be camping would most likely seek the shelter of the trees. No one was going to camp out in the middle of the baseball diamond, and if they did, I would ask them to move. They seemed happy with that, and people started trickling in about six o'clock.

The construction company came in and we all decided where to put the fire, although I had my doubts about the fire itself. But when I saw how they set it up I was amazed and pleased. They had definitely done this before. A nice pile of wood was placed next to the giant rim that would contain the fire and then a tarp was thrown over it.

Bugsy, Carpenter, and Si showed up and quickly took up a camping sight next to me and strung lines for tarps. I did have a problem with the people at the check-in tent directing everyone to me. I went to the tent and told them that anyone can camp anywhere, they don't have to check with me, and that I did not know everyone showing up. They seemed confused until I told them that I had people coming in from three states away! They glanced at each other in amazement. Then I explained to them that I put an article in a national magazine and many people had seen it. I really had no idea how many, then they understood.

I understood that most people would come in on Saturday after running the river of their choice. I did get a few phone calls about the rivers being too high, it being too cold, and people were canceling, but they promised to send a donation check. I ran into Ben and Cole who were driving around in a golf cart. I was happy to see them both and we talked about events, the fire, band, breakfast, and the things I had going on. I told them about the boat

211

I had procured and the article. They had no idea and were very happy about it, but the weather might be an issue.

Pops showed up, "Mart I have an idea, I brought my computer, photo printer and a bunch of CD's to burn. I will take my camera to Agers Falls on the Bottom Moose and take photos of everyone going over the falls and ask them for a donation for the photo at the end of the day what do you think?"

"Great Idea Pops! Are you sure you want to do that all day?" I asked. I

"'ve kayaked with Jed, yea I want to do this." he replied.

Pops was there with the camera and a little after I arrived at Agers Bugsy, Carpenter, and Si came flying over the falls. I asked Bugsy how the river was, his reply was that it was a little pushy but fun.

I went down to Crystal Falls and watched some people run that for a while. I started cheering for everyone going by and the guys joined in. People responded by cheering back and throwing their arms up in the air. Some other people were there and started cheering people on too. It turned into a great atmosphere, but I had to go. I wanted to shoot to Watertown, so I took the guys back to the campsite to drop them off and took off. I walked into the Popular Raft company that Jed and I worked in and saw every one and talked briefly about their day. They were bitching about something or other just like always. I reminded them about the party tonight and told them to bring some beer. They always had lots of beer. They all nodded their heads in agreement. I took a tour around and talked to some people at other raft companies and sped back to Lyons Falls.

I had to set up for the silent auction. My good friend Norse showed up and helped me out tremendously! He had also brought with him several people from the rafting company that he worked with down by Letchworth. I unloaded my truck, and he took over labeling and cataloged everything. The fire was being made. Beamer was there dressed in fatigues for full effect with his flamethrower. The violin player showed up with her own small band that where was also kayakers, and the one-man band was just pulling in to set up. Everything was looking good.

I walked around after it became a little later and had the opportunity to talk to everyone. There were people from Ohio, Pennsylvania, and all over New York. What did surprise me was the lack of people, I had about seventy-five people there. No one from the rafting company showed up. No one from the Rochester paddle club showed up, and several people that I considered good friends never showed up. People that I would have traveled through hellish weather for to anywhere within a thousand miles. But they never showed up! The amount of money that we raised for the number of people we had was great! But nowhere near my projection.

The bands were a hit, Beamer with the Flamethrower was awesome! The auction went well, my friends kept putting bids in to drive up the price on the things that people wanted. Of course, the Boat was the main attraction, and it went for a nice price for both the buyer and the charity. The guy that bought the boat called me later in the month and told me that the trucker called him and delivered the boat directly to his house!

We did have a few locals come over and hang out with us under the big pavilion. Jed showed up with Sammy, and I introduce them around. The moment everyone saw Sammy, another wave of money came flowing in.

I had noticed that no one had bid on that kid's ski jacket, so I walked over to the table and grabbed it. Without Jed looking I said to Sammy, "Hey try this on." She put it on and it fit her perfectly. I knelt down beside her and said, "Go show your Dad your new jacket." She turned to me with a smile, zipped up the coat, and she ran off to her dad as I blended into the background.

We all had fun, my disappointment however, overshadowed my thoughts. I knew the weather and big water were factors, and I knew that I did everything I could do at the time to bring people in.

I hadn't kayaked at all during the festival, somehow, and I ended up going back to the Black River. I guess I went to ask the

213

Popular Raft company why the fuck they didn't show up. The River Master came over to me as soon as I pulled in and apologized to me and said that he had forgotten about it, and the rest of the crew talked about it. They had decided not to go because of the weather. I kept my cool even though I did not work there anymore. I wanted to distance myself from these kinds of people, so I made my appearance and left. Just to let everyone know how the festival went. Before I walked out of the office I surrounded myself by people and I stated, "Well, I hope Sammy lives during her kidney transplant, see you guys." They all looked shocked. Apparently, the life or death of their friend's daughter never actually occurred to them.

It rained on the way home, and when I pulled in the driveway, I had a sense of peace. I unloaded the boats and put my gear away. I did not have to worry about drying or washing my stuff since I hadn't used it. I went into the house and slept a quiet dreamless sleep.

Three days later the rain had stopped, the sun was out, and the weather was warm. I threw my playboat in the truck and headed to Letchworth early that morning. I sat in my boat at the edge of the river and slid into the silty water that was older than the time of man. I worked my way past the layers of rock that for thousands of years had been wearing away and changed by waters. I glanced up and down the river, I was all alone. I looked upstream and beneath the great wall was my wave. I worked my way up until I was even with it and started back across the old river to the wave. With a few paddle strokes, I was next to the wave that was once my goal in life but now was small in comparison to the places I had been and the waves I had surfed. I slid smoothly onto its bowled shaped and took my paddle out of the water. I used my hips and knees to glide back and forth on its face without the use of my paddle. I spent the rest of the day like that, about four hours moving in and out of the waves that I liked so much.

At the end of my paddling day, I stepped out of my boat onto a cobblestone beach. I picked my boat up with my right hand, put it on my right shoulder, and held my paddle in my left. I looked up river and then down and I realized once again that I was all alone in the canyon. I turned up the trail toward the hill that I once dreaded

214

so much. The sun was shining, and I thought, "The trees will steal the water for their leaves soon. The river will drop and if I am going to kayak, I will need to go north." as I approached the base of the hill through the thick foliage, from time to time, a ray of light would cross my face. I could feel its line of warmth pass over me, and I closed my eyes until I receded into the shadows again. With every step, it happened time and time again. The air became warmer as I ascended from the canyon. I was walking out the same trail as I walked in, but it was not the same. I was light on my feet and I felt strong, stronger than before. I was the best now that I had ever been. I considered for a moment what I had done. Not only a weekend but a life, a life of rivers, a life of overcoming. As these thoughts flickered through my mind, the anger melted from my skin and ran back to the silty waters of the cold canyon.

Almost at the trail head I realized that the ground was dry, as I raised my head a brilliant light shined upon me. At the edge of that light was a vignette of fresh light green leaves atop a platform of young grass and I thought to myself with a smile, "The new life is already here."

Epilogue

The New Life

When I walked up out of Letchworth that day, I felt the umbilical cord fall to the ground; the river never drew me back again. A few years later, I sold all of my equipment and boats in a yard sale. I had paddled whitewater for twenty-two years, at my peak, I was kayaking around one hundred days a year. I did this for years at a time logging nine hundred downriver miles a year. I changed a few rules, I changed a few minds, and I changed a few lives, but most of all I changed me. As a kid whenever I walked into a room people always knew me, I was the clumsy kid with the back brace and bifocals on. I couldn't read or wright well and people spoke to me as if I were slow. But how I was thought of and the way I truly was at the time were incomprehensibly different. As a kayaker in the middle of my career every time I walked into a room people always knew me. I was steadfastly loved or hated, even by strangers. Preconceived notions somehow had quarantined my life. I needed more anonymity perhaps. There were things I needed to learn, like not to be so hard all the time and to truly love myself and the people around me. Leaving kayaking behind was liberating for me, though I seldom cross a river without looking at the line, I have no desire to run it. I still smile and wave when I see whitewater kayaks going by on vehicles. I know they are headed north to the blue line where the great rivers make legends of men.

I took a walk back to the old world that I played in as a kid. I had spent much of my life in the wilderness, but as I walked through the woods that I knew so well as a child it certainly felt different. I worked my way through the tall wispy ferns that once brushed my face as a kid, I smelled the moss beds as my feet sank into them softly, and from there I quietly slipped into the open hardwoods trail. I cleared my mind as the crisp breeze reminded me that fall was here. I sauntered up to the hill where I see the skyline that beckons me. Past the old barbed wire now absorbed by a tree that still stands strong. I stand at the top of the knoll next to the old oak that offers

216

every color that fall can provide. Above me is the forever blue sky, and below me are the rolling hay fields of my youth. A calmness overtakes me as my eyes meander down the valley. Beyond here, there are other worlds and great adventures to be had, and I smile with anticipation.

What is the best river you have ever been on?

That is the question people eventually ask me. That is a complicated question for me. My mind flips back through over twenty years of rivers and I simply cannot explain it. The first time I slid myself into the local creek, flooding and brown with silt knowing that I was going to swim. Being on the Fish on a big day makes my face ache from smiling so much. The hundred-year high that brings me to a river with the drops that make you hold your breath as you are looking at them. In my mind I can still see myself standing at the edge of the jungle canopy at the head of a canyon next to a river that disappears into lush green earth. From time to time I still do see my friends face moments before jumping off that cliff in the ADK, with a voice in the background telling me that I'm going to kill him. I'm glad he made it! I think about never having a flawless run on the Bottom Moose even though I tried so hard for so many years. I still feel the camaraderie of a bunch of kayakers working their way down a river just having fun on the Salmon.

After taking into account all the rivers and people I have paddled with I have come to this conclusion. Once you get past the idea that class V is better than class IV, that big drops are better than small drops, then you realize that it is the experience of life that matters. When our fears have faded away and we can breathe without hesitation. Our bodies move fluidly as we are connected to the water, the earth, and each other.

People may want to hear about the crash and burn or the privations of living next to a river in a hammock as I often did. But if I am honest with myself, I end up thinking about the wave. The best experience I have ever had in a kayak was not on a river at all.

217

About ten years into my kayaking career I thought I had seen it all when My friend Cliff called me and explained that the tide would come in about one o'clock in the morning. It would be dark, but the wave would be there. Pencil and I looked at each other and shrugged our shoulders, "Yea why not."

We arrived at the bridge at twelve o'clock midnight and immediately looked at the water. It was flat, but we could see starfish and other aquatic life on the bottom of the salt marsh, and we stood looking into the water. But Cliff seemed to be in a hurry. So, we got dressed and I was ready for whatever hell I was about to deal with. When my helmet was on I became strong and independent. I made the decisions and lived life my way. But on this night, I was melancholy. Yet I stood adorned in the armor of my choosing with my blade, my boat, and my muscle memory to guide me into the darkness. The water was still flat as we walked out onto the bridge one more time. Cliff explained that there was a rock just under the water that caused the wave. There was a lead in wave that went right to it. The only problem was that it was a dark night and we couldn't see shit. The moon was in and out of the clouds and seemed to be far from the earth that night. The only street light was too far to be effective but close enough to screw up our night vision if you looked at it. That one light seemed to glint off of every little shiny thing because it was so dark. As I turned to go back to the van something changed, the air was electric and fresh, and the tide had started moving. I felt what I could only describe as a richness, as if the land itself had awoken and had taken a deep breath in. I suddenly realized that this land was very old. My hearing seemed to be enhanced, and even though I was still on land I could feel the movement of the water. I could taste the ocean in the breeze that had traveled so far to get there. We sat in our boats and prepared. Stretching our spray skirts we snapped them on, we tightened our helmets, and slid into the quiet darkness. With the first pull of my paddle through the water I noticed the water was glowing. There were bioluminescent plankton in the water by the billions. With every movement of my paddle and boat came a glowing blue-green waft of light through the water. It was as if I was on a cushion of light that was guiding my way. This was unbelievable.

The wave was in, but it took us a little while to get to it. The lead in wave was small and hard to see. The wave was not big yet, but it was there. When I finally found myself on the wave, I was mesmerized as I carved back and forth across the face. There were streaks of light coming over the bow of my boat in all directions. I could see the rock below me outlined by the green luminescence. Turning my head to the side I could see swirling whirlpools of light coming off my paddle, only to disappear into the deep once again. We took turns surfing and hardly said a word to each other, and when we did, we whispered. It was like we did not want to disturb whatever presences were there. This place felt old and comfortable, like I had been there all of my life. It seemed as if old friends were watching us from the shores, and wishing all the best for us. Something about this place was special.

The wave was big now and the surf became more aggressive, so I did a flat spin into a back surf. As I surfed backward, I saw a stream of light in the water as wide as my boat follow me like a ribbon on a soft wind trying to catch up. It seemed effortless as I left the wave moving toward shore to work my way back up to the eddy again. Next to me I heard bloop, I looked and saw nothing, then bloop. Looking to my left, I saw a half ring of luminescent light in the water pulsing, bigger, smaller, bigger, smaller. Above that blue-green light ring, I saw two black eyes looking at me from out of the darkness. They were highlighted by the streetlight in the distance with a pinprick of light in the center of each eye. We acknowledged each other's presence before the seal only a few feet away, and then the eyes slipped back into the darkness. I smiled and shook my head. I turned to watch my friends surf the incoming tide on a cushion of light in the middle of the night at the mouth of a salt marsh next to shores that had been there since before the time of man. I realized then that humility does give it it's power.

This was greater than me; it was greater than all of us.

219

Thank you for reading, ***One More Breath: The Memoir of a Whitewater Kayaker*** by Martin Murphy. We do hope you enjoyed this journey and will let the author know by leaving him a review.

About the author

Martin Murphy was raised in a small town in central New York State, where he still resides. Martin struggled with learning disabilities all throughout school, but he would not let those disabilities determine his future.

Upon graduation from high school he had the twelve thoracic vertebrae in his back fused together, spending many days and nights in a horizontal position while he healed. Determined to enjoy the most out what life has to offer after this, he spent an adventurous twenty-two years in a whitewater kayak becoming a professional safety kayaker, securing sponsorship from boat companies.

Every step Martin has taken has been to live life to its fullest and explore excitement at every bend and turn —in any river he could conquer while enjoying the extreme sport of whitewater kayaking.

Martin is a Certified Life Coach and the author of, *One More Breath: The Memoir of a Whitewater Kayaker.*

You can contact Martin Murphy via email:
hourglasslc@gmail.com

Made in the USA
Monee, IL
14 July 2020

35815135R00125